When approaching the Revelation, readers typically make one of three errors—they can hyper-sensationalize the text, they can turn the material into a series of newspaper headlines joined together by red string, or they can render John's pastoral letter into a science fiction novel with little to no real-world application. *Vengeance Has Come* is a much-needed correction of those three errors. By grounding the Apocalypse squarely in the first century, approaching the prophecies through Old Testament lenses, and focusing heavily on application for the follower of Christ, Dave's commentary is a welcomed breath of fresh air for any student of the Scriptures, whether it be a layperson or a pastor.

Andrew DeBartolo
Teaching Elder, Encounter Church, Kingston, Ontario
Director of Operations, Liberty Coalition Canada

David Forsythe's commentary on Revelation is an excellent bridge between the academic and the pastoral. The commentary is obviously aware of current scholarship on the Apocalypse but is aimed at the reader who wishes to see through the popular hype regarding the end times. As he makes clear, Revelation must be understood on its first century terms before it is to be applied to the present. His very helpful introduction clearly lays out the various approaches to both eschatology and the Book of Revelation. Its relative brevity makes it extremely helpful as a preaching and teaching guide within the local church or to recommend to any serious reader.

Scott Jacobsen
Pastor, Mountain View Christian Church
Hamilton, Ontario, Canada

Finally, an honest approach to the importance of scriptural context in understanding the book of Revelation. The oracle of judgment from Jesus in Matthew 23 is given its place of importance as the last prophecy concerning Israel and for which the early church waited and anticipated to be fulfilled in a generation of time. Most Christians do not know the significance of the destruction of the temple and Jerusalem in AD 70 let alone its place in biblical prophecy. *Vengeance Has Come* clearly portrays God's judgment on the covenant unfaithful Jews as key to interpreting the book of Revelation.

Vengeance Has Come is a verse-by-verse analysis of the book of Revelation following the footsteps of the Reformed and Puritan forefathers while seeking to remain true to the inspiration of Scriptures as a unified message that ties the text to the first century recipients. *Vengeance Has Come* helps us to focus rightly on Jesus as the true revelation and builds trust in the sovereign rulership of King Jesus over the kingdom of man. The Messianic mission of Jesus will not fail. This message encourages us in our hope of eternal life, gives strength to our faith to live daily in perseverance, and ignites our love for God and others even as the circumstances that surround our lives get hectic similar to the days surrounding Jerusalem in the 1st century. We can draw great comfort and courage knowing that God is in absolute control of all things throughout history.

David does something which most authors of commentaries do not do, and that is he identifies his theological presupposition up front so that the reader does not have to guess where he is coming from. I for one appreciate this. Whether or not you agree with his position, David gives an honest presentation that is consistent with his beliefs. This is a view that deserves the attention of serious students of the Bible. If nothing else, this commentary will force you to think critically about the different schools regarding the interpretation of the Revelation. I highly recommend this commentary on Revelation as a must have book for every pastor and serious Christian who wants to know and understand God's word.

C. S. Linnard
Pastor, Sovereign Grace Family Church
Belleville, Ontario, Canada

I want to thank my good friend David Forsythe for taking the time to write this commentary on Revelation. While I do not agree with all that he has written in this book, I have found it to be of benefit to read an exegesis of Revelation through a Preterist-Postmillennial lens. He has helped me to understand Revelation and challenged my own Idealist-Amillennial perspective. David goes through the book of Revelation verse by verse providing insights into the text for the contemporary reader. I recommend this book to those who are leaning toward Postmillennialism or for any others who are not afraid to have their own views challenged.

John Greenidge
Pastor, Harmony Road Baptist Church
Oshawa, Ontario, Canada

VENGEANCE
HAS
COME

DAVID A. FORSYTHE

VENGEANCE HAS COME

*A Puritan-Minded Exposition of the Apocalypse
for the Modern Church*

Vengeance Has Come

Copyright © 2022 David A. Forsythe

Published by Founders Press
P.O. Box 150931 ♦ Cape Coral, FL ♦ 33915
Phone: (888) 525-1689
Electronic Mail: officeadmin@founders.org
Website: www.founders.org

Printed in the United States of America

ISBN: 978-1-943539-38-3

Library of Congress Control Number: 2023946637

Book Editor: Travis McSherley

Cover Design by: Trinity Rael Art

All rights reserved. No part of this publication may be reproduced, stored in a retrieval system, or transmitted in any form by any means, electronic, mechanical, photocopy, recording or otherwise, without the prior permission of the author, except as provided by U.S. copyright law.

Scripture quotations are from the ESV® Bible (The Holy Bible, English Standard ersion®), copyright © 2001 by Crossway, a publishing ministry of Good News Publishers. Used by permission. All rights reserved. The ESV text may not be quoted in any publication made available to the public by a Creative Commons license. The ESV may not be translated in whole or in part into any other language. The Holy Bible, English Standard Version®, is adapted from the Revised Standard Version of the Bible, copyright Division of Christian Education of the National Council of the Churches of Christ in the U.S.A.

Dedications

*To my five wonderful children, whom the Lord has given me—
Judah, Malachi, Evangeline, Ezra, and Hosanna.
May you passionately build culture around the gospel
and teach your children to do the same!*

~ & ~

*To my beautiful wife, Alyssa, the treasure of my heart, second
only to the Lord Jesus. May we continue to be a united gospel
force in the lives of our children to this most noble end!*

Acknowledgments

I would like to give my heartfelt thanks and appreciation to several valuable voices in my life who have helped me greatly in producing this work of penmanship. First, I must express my gratitude to my beloved wife, Alyssa, for all her hard work in proofreading my manuscript. This has helped greatly in readability. Second, I would like to extend deep appreciation to my adopted uncle, Dr. Geoffrey Hale, for his close examination of internal and external consistency in my argumentation. This has resulted in resolving several contradictions that were unapparent to me in the beginning. In addition, I'd like to extend my thanks to my brother-in-arms, Cpl. Philippe Loyer, for his recommendations for readability and overall encouragement throughout the process of bringing this work to publication. Furthermore, I would like to sincerely thank Fred Boekee for his necessary insights in consistency of application flowing from my exegesis. Lastly, I must extend heartfelt gratitude to my dear friend, Pastor John Greenidge, for his many insights, both technical and practical. These have aided me greatly in presenting my thoughts well for an audience who likely is unfamiliar with the convictions to which I hold. May the Lord bounteously bless each of these His servants for their contributions to this work! More importantly, may His name be lifted up and more greatly honored as a result of their efforts! Soli Deo Gloria. Amen.

David A. Forsythe
Oshawa, Ontario, Canada

Contents

Dedications XII

Acknowledgments IX

Preface XV

John's Prologue (1:1–20) 1
    Introduction 1
    Salutation 3
    The First Vision 13

The Letters to the Congregations (2:1–3:22) 21
    To the Congregation at Ephesus 21
    To the Congregation at Smyrna 25
    To the Congregation at Pergamum 27
    To the Congregation at Thyatira 31
    To the Congregation at Philadelphia 37
    To the Congregation at Laodicea 40

The Second Vision (4:1–5:14) 45
    The Lord Enthroned On High 45
    The Unopened Scroll 50
    The Lion Who Is the Lamb 52

The Third Vision (6:1–8:5) 61
    The First Seal 61
    The Second Seal 63
    The Third Seal 63
    The Fourth Seal 64
    The Fifth Seal 65
    The Sixth Seal 67
    An Interlude 68
    The Seventh Seal 75

THE FOURTH VISION (8:6–11:19) 77
    The First Trumpet 77
    The Second Trumpet 78
    The Third Trumpet 78
    The Fourth Trumpet 78
    The Eagle 80
    The Fifth Trumpet 81
    The Sixth Trumpet 85
    An Interlude 87
    The Seventh Trumpet 100

THE FIFTH VISION (12:1–14:20) 105
    The Woman and the Child 105
    The Dragon Cast Down 108
    The Beast out of the Land 120
    The Lamb on Mount Zion 125
    Babylon's Fall Predicted 127

THE SIXTH VISION (15:1–16:21) 133
    A Prelude 133
    The First Bowl 136
    The Second and Third Bowls 137
    The Fourth Bowl 138
    The Fifth Bowl 139
    The Sixth Bowl 140
    The Seventh Bowl 144

THE SEVENTH VISION (17:1–19:10) 149
    Babylon Rides the Beast 149
    The Judgment of Babylon 158
    The Marriage Supper of the Lamb 170

THE EIGHTH VISION (19:11–21) 175
    The King's Conquest 175
    The Overthrow of the Beast and the False Prophet 180

THE NINTH VISION (20:1–15) 183
    Christ Reigns Triumphant 183
    Christ Judges the World 195

The Tenth Vision (21:1–22:5) **199**
    The New Heavens and New Earth 199
    The New Jerusalem 209
    The New Creation 218

John's Epilogue (22:6–21) **221**

Outline of the Entire Book **232**

Preface

I can hear it now. "Why would someone take it upon himself to write an exposition of the biblical book that has been the center of so much controversy?" Indeed, why would such a historically minded Christian as myself find it necessary to enter the fray, as it were, even to bring a view into the heart of it that is considered irrelevant, at best, by many today? There is one overriding answer to this question, an answer requiring an explanation.

The response is, in fact, one word: *worldview*. Working to form a consistent, biblically derived foundation on which to live before God, not only in the private sphere but also in every nook and cranny of the public sphere, has become an intense passion of mine. In seeking to be consistent in pushing my theological convictions into the public square—whether it be in terms of art or music, banking or economics, education or public discourse—I've been challenged to reconsider some deeply held convictions in light of Scripture and the theological views of those who have come before. Through the process of re-examination, I've come to largely embrace both the theology and the systematic, big-picture mindset expressed in the Second London Baptist Confession (1689). This puts me squarely in the seventeenth-century English Puritan tradition, along with confessional Presbyterians and Congregationalists. Furthermore, in building on this robust, consistent reading of Scripture, I've been led to examine every issue of life from a foundational, worldview perspective. The more I have engaged with other believers from this angle, the more I have come to realize how much we, as the body of Christ in the West, assume a biblical world-and-life-view under the surface and thus focus primarily, if not exclusively, on teaching and reinforcing broadly accepted doctrine and tradition. The problem with assuming, rather than actively building, a consistent worldview as arising from the Word of God is that unbelieving worldviews are allowed to creep in unchallenged and unaddressed and leave the local church unable to adequately respond with the law and the gospel, not only in the home and the congregation but also in the public square. Indeed, when the prevailing world-and-life-view of the masses has successfully reshaped culture on *its* faith principles, and that culture becomes totalitarian about enforcing conformity to its faith commitments from the top down, followers of Christ end up with three problems: we haven't the categories by which to make sense of what we're up against, nor do we have the ability to offer a consistent response, nor do we have a consistent faith to pass on the next generations. Since the book of Revelation brings up many of these foundational issues and it seems clear that the Lord is moving the church in the West into a period of suffering and persecution, now seems to be a fitting time for a fresh commentary with application to the present time.

This work is not the first attempt in church history to present an in-depth, consistent reading of Christ's revelation to John, the apostle, nor will it be the last. For this reason, wherever shared interpretations exist, within the scope of being faithful to the text itself, I have sought to highlight those commonalities among orthodox commentators. To this end, in my studies, I have consulted commentators from historic and modern viewpoints. Although I find myself in largest agreement with Douglas Wilson, as a fellow preterist postmillennial, I also sought insights from others such as John Gill (historicist premillennial, eighteenth century), G. K. Beale (idealist amillennial, twentieth century), Steve Wilmshurst (idealist premillennial, twentieth and twenty-first centuries), Matthew Henry (historicist postmillennial, seventeenth and eighteenth centuries) and Daniel Akin (futurist premillennial, twentieth and twenty-first centuries).

With regard to the interpretation of the Apocalypse, there are four main schools: preterist, historicist, idealist, and futurist. These interpretative approaches tend to have a far greater impact on the interpreter's exegetical conclusions than his millennial position. The only exception to this generality is a futurist premillennial approach, which absolutely depends on their millennial view. In terms of approach and conclusions, preterism and idealism head off in a similar direction, while historicism and futurism have much in common. Preterism comes from the Latin word *praeteritus*, which means "past." In this understanding, the majority of New Testament prophecy was future from the biblical authors' perspective but has already been fulfilled in our past. Therefore, the preterist reads the Apocalypse in this light. This is the view of which I have become convinced from the text of Scripture since it is the only reading that allows consistency of interpretation while keeping John's original audience in view. The historicist interprets the Revelation as progressively rolling out throughout history from Christ's first advent straight through to His second. The idealist views this final book of the New Testament as symbolically portraying the time period from Christ's first coming to His second from various and sundry vantage points. Finally, the futurist understands the Revelation, sometimes save the first three chapters, as wholly in our future and outlining the last events of human history. Those of a dispensational premillennial persuasion not only interpret the Apocalypse through a futurist lens but also through their own hermeneutical grid. Through seeking a consistent, exegetically faithful understanding of the book as a whole, I have found the most unanimity outside my own view with the idealist interpretation, especially that of both Hendriksen and Beale.

Before getting into general structural issues concerning the Apocalypse, I would like to address two common misconceptions. These are important for properly understanding the angle from which I approach the book of Revelation. The first concerns the actual beliefs of postmillennialism. Postmillennialism does indeed teach that, through the Christianization of the nations, the world is getting better and better until, one day, there will be a "golden age" on earth. However, this is most often misunderstood to mean an imposition of Christianity on the world by believers and a kind of social betterment, as if sin and trials *will not* continue until Christ's second coming. The charge is usually summarized as an "over-realized eschatology." While it is beyond the scope of this work to fully defend the postmillennial hope, I would like to offer a brief explanation of what we, as evangelical postmillennialists, actually believe.[1]

Simply put, postmillennialism teaches that the Great Commission (see Matt. 28:18–20) will be entirely fulfilled within human history; that is, all the nations will actually be discipled, baptized, and taught to obey all

---

1   For a full-length treatise on the subject, see Kenneth L. Gentry Jr., *He Shall Have Dominion: A Postmillennial Eschatology*, 3rd ed., (Draper: Apologetics Group Media, 2009).

that Jesus commands prior to the Last Day when He returns to judge all the living and the dead. As Jesus Himself promised, He will be with us to the very end to ensure our success, lest His universal authority be blasphemed among the nations. This necessarily means that Christ's kingdom will be victorious within history; that is, He will actually rule over all the nations as His own possession, as was promised to Him in Psalm 2. On this point, postmillennialism may rightly be thought of as a highly optimistic amillennialism.

The real difference between amillennialism and postmillennialism is on the point of societal transformation as a result of the Great Commission being successful in the hearts and lives of the nations. While amillennialists insist that Messiah's kingdom-rule was inaugurated at His first advent, but will not be consummated until His second advent, they want to take all the passages concerning the *effects* of His rule in the world and place them in the eternal state, thereby interpreting those passages in solely spiritual terms. Postmillennialists would heartily agreeing on the first premise but would part ways on the second, insisting that the effects of Messiah's rule in the earth cannot be separated from His kingdom-rule and that those effects must be interpreted in equally earthy terms as the prophets present them. This means that the effects of His kingdom-rule are equally as "now but not yet" as the kingdom itself. Thus, postmillennialists hold that the success of Christ's pre-ascension mission given to His church necessarily means that the cultural (dominion) mandate of Genesis 1:26–30, later repeated in Genesis 9:1–7, will likewise be fulfilled before the return of our Lord. All of this will be accomplished by the Lord Jesus working through His people because it is *He*, not us, who has been given "all authority in heaven *and* on earth" in His exaltation. *He* is the one who is reconciling "to himself all things, whether on earth or in heaven, making peace by the blood of his cross" (Col. 1:19–20). Paul summarized these truths well when he taught, quoting Psalm 110:1, "For He must reign until He has put all His enemies under His feet. The last enemy to be destroyed is death" (1 Cor. 15:25–26). In this context, death will be destroyed on the Last Day when Jesus bodily resurrects all the living and the dead. As Jesus taught, the sure transformation of the whole world through the power of the gospel takes place gradually, not all at once (see Matt. 13:31–33). This is the primary means by which He is putting all His enemies under His feet. This will result in a lengthy period of global righteousness, peace, and prosperity until our Lord's second advent (see Isa. 65:17–25). It should be noted that, after taking into consideration the whole counsel of Scripture, *none* of these things mean that sin and death, or trials and temptations, will be erased prior to the end. Nor do these things mean there will not be a consummate new heavens and new earth brought in as part of the final resurrection. Postmillennialism insists that all these elements are true and ought to be taken seriously in harmony with one another, since they are a part of divine revelation.

The result of holding all this together—that is, Scripture's consistent witness to the gradual realization of Messiah's kingdom victory within human history—is the hope-filled pursuit of "cultivating a uniquely Christian society . . . 'a city on a hill.'"[2] This is the mindset with which the New England Puritans sought to colonize the New World, and which they had inherited from the vast majority of English Puritans, which they in turn had inherited from Knox and Calvin before them. "The Puritans did not conceive of the end times only in abstract theological terms but saw themselves moving through history toward its final consummation."[3] Those, like myself, who hold to this view of history and the future are following hard in the footsteps of our Reformed and Puritan forefathers, the theological shoulders on whom we stand. As has been well put, our mindset can accurately be summarized as "all of Christ for all of life for all the world!"[4]

Secondly, there's a common misunderstanding concerning the issue of the preterist view of New Testament prophecy. Just as many synergists mistakenly hear hyper-Calvinism when an orthodox Calvinist begins discussing God's sovereignty in salvation, the same problem exists with preterism. This is to say that, when preterists begin explaining their views, many non-preterists mistake them for hyper-preterists. Hyper-preterism, or full preterism, teaches that *all* biblical prophecies, including the Messiah's second coming and the resurrection of the dead, were fulfilled by the end of AD 70. The reason this doctrine has historically been rejected as heretical is that it necessitates turning both the second advent and the general

---

2   Joel R. Beeke and Mark Jones, *A Puritan Theology: Doctrine for Life*, (Grand Rapids: Reformation Heritage Books, 2012), 773.
3   Beeke and Jones, *A Puritan Theology*.
4   This is the pithy slogan of Christ Church, Moscow, ID, and its printing press, Canon Press. This slogan succinctly encapsulates the teaching of the New Testament. See https://www.christkirk.com and https://canonpress.com.

resurrection into solely spiritual events. It also involves accepting the time period since AD 70 as the eternal state, though it continues to be ravaged by the effects of the fall. This all is contrary to the plain witness of God's Word, which teaches us that the effects in the world of Christ's bodily resurrection are far greater and more powerful than the effects of the fall, such that even death itself will finally be destroyed on the Last Day!

On the other hand, orthodox preterists (partial preterists) wholeheartedly reject hyper-preterism as heretical, affirm the Apostles', Athanasian, and Nicene creeds, and seek to be faithful to Scripture as a whole, rather than selectively reading certain portions and then ignoring others. This breed of preterism has long been accepted as being within the "pale of orthodoxy" amongst Bible-believing, gospel-preaching theologians and commentators. For example, along with many preterist theologians, I would maintain that Matthew 24:1–44, Mark 13:1–37, and Luke 21:5–36 are parallel passages and should be interpreted in light of one another. In addition, Matthew 24:1–44 is the final part of a whole section in Matthew's gospel concerning God's coming judgment on apostate Israel—namely, 21:12 through to 24:44. Therefore, the Olivet Discourse in Matthew 24 must be interpreted within that context. With these two hermeneutical principles in mind, the natural reading of the Olivet Discourse points to an AD 70 fulfillment of Jesus' predictions therein, since it deals exclusively with the events surrounding the destruction of the Jewish temple.

Now that I've dealt with these two points of concern, I will turn to the general structure of the book of Revelation. This includes the letter's author, recipients, dating, purpose, occasion, and main theme, among other overarching issues.

AUTHORSHIP:

There is debate among scholars as to which John is properly the author of the Apocalypse (Rev. 1:1). The apostle John seems to be the best fit for two main reasons. First, the entire tenor of the book is very Jewish, being saturated with Old Testament allusions, references, and imagery. Secondly, the parallels in language to both John's gospel and his epistles are obvious. This is particularly true in the way the Revelation frequently presents the Messiah as the "Lamb of God, who takes away the sin of the world!" (John 1:29).

RECIPIENTS:

It is clear from chapter 1 to whom John writes. Verse 4 says that John is writing "to the seven churches that are in Asia," and then in verse 11, Jesus provides the identity of these seven congregations: Ephesus, Smyrna, Pergamum, Thyatira, Sardis, Philadelphia, and Laodicea. These were contemporary believers to John in his day, all of whom lived in Asia Minor.

DATING:

Many theologians have dated the Revelation after AD 70, perhaps as late as 96 during the reign of Domitian. The basis for this is a passing comment in one of Irenaeus's letters. Because Irenaeus was a church father during the second century, as well as a disciple of Polycarp, who in turn was a disciple of John the apostle, his comment concerning the dating of Revelation is considered to be a strong piece of external evidence. "Undoubtedly, Irenaeus's observation is the strongest weapon in the late-date arsenal."[5] However, even if this interpretation of his words is correct, which is itself legitimately debatable, the internal evidence to the contrary far outweighs the external evidence presented. Internal evidence for an early dating can be found in passages such as 1:1–3, 11:1–2, 17:10, etc. Thus, a date shortly before AD 70, likely 65 or 66, seems to fit much better.[6] This would place the writing of Revelation during the reign of Caesar Nero.

Conservative textual scholars agree that proper textual analysis ought to weigh the relevant internal evidence much heavier than any external evidence. This approach presupposes that Scripture is entirely God-breathed, inerrant, and unified in all that it is.[7] Scholarship that favors the opposite is normally scholarship that devalues the divine origin and inerrancy of Scripture, which results in methods that massacre the unity of the text and, consequently, its validity. Such methods include the documentary hypothesis (JEPD), Markan priority among the synoptic gospels, and the Jesus Seminar's colored-bead approach in search of the

---

5   Kenneth L. Gentry Jr., *Before Jerusalem Fell: Dating the Book of Revelation* (Chesnee: Victorious Hope, 2010), Kindle Location 1883.
6   See Gentry, *Before Jerusalem Fell*, Kindle Location 482.
7   See *1689 London Baptist Confession*, Chapter 1, https://www.arbca.com/1689-chapter1; *The Savoy Declaration [1658]*, Chapter 1, https://www.the-highway.com/savoy_declaration.html#1; *The 1647 Westminster Confession of Faith*, Chapter 1, https://www.apuritansmind.com/westminster-standards/chapter-1.

"historical Jesus." As one fully committed to the inspiration, inerrancy, and unity of the Word of God, I have come to my conclusions regarding the dating of Revelation by following the methodology of textual scholars who presuppose the same. Indeed, "the internal witness must be given the highest priority."[8]

Nature of the Letter:

We are explicitly told at the outset of the book about its nature. It's a revelation *from* God the Father given *to* Jesus the Messiah who made it known *to* John the apostle *via* an angel (1:1–2). An *apokalupsis* (unveiling, revelation) is a highly symbolic visionary message that is *intended* to be understood by its recipients. We're explicitly told who these first-century recipients were in Revelation 1:11.

Purpose:

The purpose of the Apocalypse is clearly presented at the outset "to show [God's bondservants] the things that must soon take place" (Rev. 1:1). His "bondservants" are those who truly belong to God in Christ. "The things that must . . . take place" are certain acts of the Messiah in history that are sure to take place. Finally, those events "must soon take place," meaning the imminency of those events in relation to the apostle receiving this revelation, scribing it, and then sending it to the seven congregations in Asia Minor.

Occasion:

John writes as a prisoner for the gospel on the Isle of Patmos, a Greek island in the Aegean Sea just off the coast from the port city of Miletus. The apostle describes himself as a fellow "brother and partner in the tribulation and the kingdom and the patient endurance that are in Jesus" (Rev. 1:9).

The "tribulation" they mutually faced was that all peoples of the Roman Empire, both citizens and those conquered, were required by law to confess, "*Kaisar Kurios*" ("Caesar is Lord"). Usually this was done through offering a pinch of incense on a small altar to signify loyalty to Caesar as the chief deity among all others represented in the Empire. As devout Trinitarian monotheists, first-century believers refused to become disloyal

---

8   Gentry, *Before Jerusalem Fell*, Kindle Location 1463.

to the only true Lord and Savior, and so confessed *"Yesus Kurios"* ("Jesus is Lord") instead.

This resulted in persecutions that were relational, economic, and eventually physical. Roman persecution only served to compound the severe abuse Christians were already experiencing at the hands of their foremost antagonist, the Jewish community. This was due to their loyalty to Jesus as the long-expected Messiah.

Concerning the "kingdom," John explains in chapter 1, verses 5–6, that Jesus the faithful Witness has "made us a kingdom, priests to his God and Father, to him be glory and dominion forever and ever. Amen." All true believers comprise a kingdom of priests by virtue of belonging to Jesus's dominion over all things. The only way into this Messianic kingdom is through being united to Him by the Holy Spirit's work of regeneration (see John 3:1–8).

John also counts himself as a brother with those to whom he writes in the "patient endurance." This means they must persevere through these tribulations with long-suffering, knowing that they were united to the one who is the Ruler of the ends of the earth, and that "he must reign *until* he has put all his enemies under his feet" (1 Cor. 15:25, emphasis mine).

Main Theme:

The primary theme, which undergirds all others in this letter, is clearly expressed in John's prologue: "Behold, he is coming with the clouds, and every eye will see him, even those who pierced him, and all tribes of the earth will wail on account of him" (Rev. 1:7). The living, exalted Lord Jesus would come in judgment on the covenant-breakers of Israel, those of that generation who lived while He was on earth. This would come about exactly as He had promised them at the temple in Jerusalem and then at the Mount of Olives (cf. Matt. 23:34ff.)

Main Message:

Believers must look to King Jesus through their tribulation since He comes to conquer old Jerusalem and bring in new Jerusalem. Old Jerusalem stands for both that ancient city and the nation of Israel to which she belonged, being plagued with all her hypocrisy and spiritual adultery. New Jerusalem represents the church, the true Israel of God with the same faith as Abraham, who are clothed in the perfect, seamless obedience of her Husband, Savior, and Lord.

Beloved student of the Word of God, as you now enter into this wonderful and fantastic biblical book with me, I pray that your love for the Messiah and His most holy rule in the world will increase significantly and that you will find Him to be the greatest treasure that He truly is! I also pray that your confidence in the Lord Jesus will grow greatly as we see in this book that He really is accomplishing all of His Messianic purposes in His world. May studying the Revelation through this commentary aid you in approaching all of life from a foundational, worldview perspective. Finally, I pray that the lessons learned in studying this God-breathed book would cause you to find greater comfort in our Good Shepherd through various and sundry trials that we all must face in faithfully following Him. To God alone be all the glory! Amen and amen.

John's Prologue (1:1–20)

INTRODUCTION

Chapter 1, verses 1–3 form a short introduction leading into the letter's prologue. Verse 1, "The revelation of Jesus Christ, which God gave him to show his servants the things that must soon take place." John tells his readers that the *apokalupsis* is "of Jesus Christ," the sense being that it is "concerning Jesus Christ." The letter itself *is* the revelation—that is, that which has been unveiled. The focus of the letter is Jesus, *not* the Evil One or the tribulations. When many twenty-first-century folk, both believers and unbelievers, speak of the Revelation, the primary topic on their lips is great and catastrophic evils befalling the world sometime in our future. Yet our attention must align itself with these opening words of John. *He* says that the entire focus of his letter is the rule of King Jesus, and therefore, it must be ours also.

Verses 1b–2: "He made it known by sending his angel to his servant John, who bore witness to the word of God and to the testimony of Jesus Christ, even to all that he saw." Through the agency of an angel, God gave this highly symbolic visionary message to John, who had a certain quality; namely, he "bore witness to the word of God and to the testimony of Jesus Christ." This is to say that he was faithful to preach the gospel of the Messiah's kingdom. The Lord did this for a specific purpose—"to show to his [bondservants] the things that must soon take place" (verse 1).

He must "show" these things since its message is intended to be understood by its recipients. Many in the last hundred years have treated the Apocalypse as a book full of complicated riddles and hidden messages that are nearly impossible to decipher. The takeaway is that since there are so many differing and contradictory interpretations (several being quite fanciful at that), what's the point of trying to understand this portion of Scripture? However, contrary to this popular view, we must not be afraid of this God-breathed letter. Why? Because *apokalupsis* means "a revelation," "a manifestation," or "a revealing"[1]—it was meant to be understood by its original recipients in its very Jewish context.

Those who are being shown these things are His "bondservants," those who truly belong to God in Christ. They are being shown the "things that must ... take place," which are those certain acts of the Messiah in history that are sure to take place. This is cause to celebrate with greater confidence in our Messianic King, rather than to fear! Why? Because He sovereignly orchestrates all events in history so that He keeps His promises right on schedule. Therefore, He can be trusted at every point along the way!

These are the things that "must soon take place." In relation to the apostle receiving the revelation, scribing it, and then sending it to the seven churches, these events are truly imminent, even right at the door, as it were.[2] Futurist theologians have interpreted the majority of Revelation as taking place in our future, and have thus created the doctrine of the imminent second advent of Christ. The problem with this view is that it has been more than two thousand years since John penned his letter in the first century, a time period that cannot possibly fit within the semantic domain of "imminent," "soon," or "near." We must understand the events written in this letter as being close at hand from the standpoint of John and the seven congregations in Asia Minor to whom he writes in order to properly respect what "soon" means.

Verse 3: "Blessed is the one who reads aloud the words of this prophecy, and blessed are those who hear, and who keep what is written in it, for the time is near." The original recipients are promised to be blessed if they both read the whole letter out loud and hear what is written therein and then live by it. Why? The text answers, "for the time is near"; that is, the events referred to in verse 1 are close at hand for them. Even though many of these events are in our past today, the divinely given blessing still remains for the

---

1   The NAS New Testament Greek Lexicon, *Apokalupsis*, https://www.biblestudytools.com/lexicons/greek/nas/apokalupsis.html.

2   See Kenneth L. Gentry Jr., *He Shall Have Dominion: A Postmillennial Eschatology* (Chesnee, SC: Victorious Hope, 2021) 437–438.

Christian who hears what is written in the Apocalypse and then lives in light of the truths revealed therein.

These introductory remarks must be kept in mind throughout this study of the book of Revelation. To continue without taking strict heed to these words will inevitably lead to forcing the apostle to mean things he never intended to communicate to his original audience.

SALUTATION

Verses 4–8 present John's prologue to the rest of his letter to the seven local churches. It is within this prologue that he indicates the main theme to his readers in verse 7, a theme that runs straight through the various and sundry visions he is shown and binds them all together.

Verse 4a: "John to the seven churches that are in Asia: Grace to you and peace." First, the apostle John identifies himself as the writer and "the seven churches that are in Asia" as those to whom he writes. He greets them in a way similar to how Paul begins many of his letters—with the words, "Grace to you and peace."[3] At this point, John begins to answer the question, "From whom does this grace and peace come?" He does this by mentioning all three persons of the Godhead—it is from these three divine persons that grace and peace come.

Verse 4b: "from him who is and who was and who is to come." Firstly, this grace and peace come from the God who is from everlasting to everlasting. This is another way of saying what was said to Moses in Exodus 3:13–15 when God revealed His name as *YHWH* (Yahweh)—He is the Self-Existent One, who is covenantal by nature.[4] This is the same God who now gives this revelation to John via an angel.

Verse 4c: "from the seven spirits who are before his throne." Secondly, this grace and peace come from the Spirit of God, who is perfect and complete in every way, as represented here by the number seven.[5] The third person of the Godhead is just as equally and completely Yahweh as the Father with regard to being, yet He remains truly distinct from the Father

---

3   See Rom. 1:7; 1 Cor. 1:3; 2 Cor. 1:2; Gal. 1:3; Eph. 1:2; Phil. 1:2, Col. 1:2; etc.
4   See G. K. Beale and Sean M. McDonough, "Revelation," in *Commentary on the New Testament Use of the Old Testament*, eds. G. K. Beale and D. A. Carson, (Grand Rapids Baker Academic, 2007), 1089.
5   Beale and McDonough, "Revelation," 1089.

with regard to personhood. The trinitarian formulation of this greeting ought to cause us to see how the unified work of the Father, Son, and Spirit is not only central to properly understanding redemptive history, but without it there would be no eternal *pactum salutis* (covenant of redemption),[6] nor its gradual historical outworking in the *foedus gratis* (covenant of grace).[7] Put another way, no one in all of history would be saved from their sins through the one Redeemer and King without this perfect unity in the Godhead.

Verse 5a: "from Jesus Christ the faithful witness, the firstborn of the dead, and the ruler of kings on earth." Jesus is God's Anointed One, first named in Hebrew as *Meshiakh* (Messiah), and then translated into Greek as *Khristos* (Christ). But who is He really? Here John draws from Psalm 89:27 and 37, which psalm as a whole emphasizes the "anointed" king.[8]

Jesus is the "faithful witness." He is the "true light" who has come into the world, the Word who "became flesh and [tabernacled] among us, and we have seen his glory," the Way, the Truth, and the Life, the one who shows us the Father (John 1:9, 14; 14:6–9). He is the "eternal life, which was with the Father and was made manifest to us" so that we may have fellowship "with the Father and with his Son Jesus Christ" (1 John 1:2–3). We can trust in the Lord our God because, instead of giving up on us when we became His enemies in Adam, He has entered into our midst in the person of Jesus of Nazareth. He has done this to faithfully show us the Father's glory and make a way for us to permanently experience His presence!

The Messiah is also the "firstborn of the dead." He is "the resurrection and the life" who is the "firstfruits of those who have fallen asleep" so that "in Christ shall all be made alive … at his coming. … He is the beginning, the firstborn from the dead, that in everything he might be preeminent" (John 11:25; 1 Cor. 15:20–23; Col. 1:18). Without the Lord Jesus's resurrection, nothing would ever be rescued from sin's corruption, neither rebel-sinners nor creation itself, first progressively in the inter-adventual

---

6 The Reformed doctrine of *the covenant of redemption* is not meant to suggest that each Person of the Godhead somehow has His own center of decision-making—for the Being of Yahweh has eternally existed in the three divine Persons, which Being is simple, not composite. Rather, it's meant to defend the eternally unified and covenantal nature of Yahweh in those three divine Persons, specifically as it relates to the salvation of the elect.

7 *Pactum* and *foedus* can be used as synonyms in Latin, as they are in this context.

8 See Beale and McDonough, "Revelation," 1089.

period and then in glorified, consummate form on the Last Day. Why? As the firstfruits of the final resurrection, Jesus's resurrection guaranteed that everything He fully accomplished in His humiliation would surely come to pass in His exaltation. His resurrection guaranteed all other resurrections in the universe! For this reason, we can fully trust that Jesus will indeed eternally rescue all for whom He died because His resurrection guarantees success!

Finally, John declares that God's Anointed One is the "ruler of kings on earth." While the word *ge* usually refers to "a tract of land" or "a country," it can occasionally be used to mean "the inhabited earth as a whole."[9] The latter usage is intended here as Jesus is described as the ultimate Ruler over all earthy authorities everywhere. Indeed, He is the greater Son of David whose "kingdom has been made sure forever before Yahweh, and his throne has been established forever" (2 Sam. 7:16)[10]; He is Yahweh's Anointed King, who has asked and "the nations have been made his heritage, and the ends of the earth his possession in order to break them with a rod of iron and dash them in pieces like a potter's vessel" (Ps. 2:7–9); He has "sat down at his Father's right hand, until he makes his enemies his footstool" (Ps. 110:1); His "government and peace will increase without end, who sits on the throne of David and over his kingdom to establish it and uphold it with justice and with righteousness from this time forth and forevermore" (Isa. 9:7); He "will not grow faint or be discouraged till he has established justice in the earth; and the coastlands wait for his law" (Isa. 42:4); His dominion is like a "stone that . . . becomes a great mountain that fills the whole earth" (Dan. 2:35); He taught us to pray "your kingdom come, your will be done, on earth as it is in heaven" (Matt. 6:10); He said, "But if it is by the Spirit of God that I cast out demons, then the kingdom of God has come upon you" (Matt. 12:28); He sent us out to make disciples of all the nations since He has "all authority in heaven and on earth" (Matt. 28:18); He is "destroying every rule and every authority and power because he must reign until he has put all his enemies under his feet, and the last enemy to be destroyed will be death" (1 Cor. 15:24–26). This means we can fully trust our Messianic King through our trials and suffering in this life because He is progressively dealing with all the evil

---

9   The NAS New Testament Greek Lexicon, *Genesis*, https://www.biblestudytools.com/lexicons/greek/nas/genesis-5.html.

10 Passages in this paragraph are paraphrased, based on the ESV.

in the world as we speak and, on the Last Day, He will judge all the living and the dead once and for all. This also means we can be actively engaged in obeying Jesus as His salt and light in the earth with confidence since our King is actually being victorious in history and will indeed get all the nations as He's been promised!

Verses 5b–6: "To him who loves us and has freed us from our sins by his blood and made us a kingdom, priests to his God and Father, to him be glory and dominion forever and ever. Amen." In response to these incredible truths about the Godhead, John breaks out in joy-filled worship. He directs his praise to the Son, the one of whom he's just finished speaking, by using active, participial forms of the verbs *agapaʼo* and *eleutheroʼo*[11]—giving the sense of "the one loving" and "the one freeing." Just as John has described the Lord Jesus with three attributes, he now exalts Him for three ways in which He has blessed His people.

The Lord "loves us" with a peculiar love. He came to do the Father's will for our benefit—the Father gave us to Him, those who come to Him as the Bread of Life, so that He would be sure to lose none of us who were given to Him, but that all of us would be raised up on the Last Day (cf. John 6:35–44). He gave us the example *par excellence* of abiding in His love by He Himself abiding in His Father's love through keeping His Father's commandments. In imitating His perfect example, our joy in Him will be made full (cf. John 15:9–11). He prayed that we would be united together in Him, just as He and His Father have enjoyed everlasting perfect unity (cf. John 17:20–23). He always intercedes for us as our High Priest, which is to say that He now effectually prays into the reality of our day-to-day lives everything that He fully accomplished for us in His death on the cross (cf. Hebrews 7:25)—this is an aspect of how "his enemies [are being] made a footstool for his feet" (Hebrews 10:12–13). For this reason the Heidelberg Catechism begins with this question and answer: "Q. What is your only comfort in life and death? A. That I am not my own, but belong with body and soul, both in life and in death, to my faithful Saviour Jesus Christ. He has fully paid for all my sins with His precious blood, and has set me free from all the power of the devil. He also preserves me in such a way that without the will of my heavenly Father not a hair can fall from my

---

11   The NAS New Testament Greek Lexicon, *Agapao* and *Eleutheroo*, https://www.biblestudytools.com/lexicons/greek/nas/agapao.html, https://www.biblestudytools.com/lexicons/greek/nas/eleutheroo.html.

head; indeed, all things must work together for my salvation. Therefore, by His Holy Spirit He also assures me of eternal life and makes me heartily willing and ready from now on to live for Him."[12]

He who loves us "has freed us from our sins by his blood." This is the ultimate way that God has loved us in His Son. This sentiment is expressed elsewhere: "For God loved the world by giving his only Son, so that all those believing in him will not perish but will have eternal life," which is to say, "God shows his love for us in that while we were still sinners, Christ died for us" (John 3:16, personal translation; Rom. 5:8). By the power of His shed blood, we have been set free from slavery to sin to become the sons of Abraham and disciples of the one in whom Abraham was ultimately trusting, and so was counted as righteous by God (see John 8:31–41; Rom. 4:13–25). Because of having "redemption through his blood, [we have] the forgiveness of our trespasses, according to the riches of his grace" (Eph. 1:7). This is fantastic news, for without the Almighty's mercy toward particular rebel-sinners, we all would remain under His wrath and be eternally without hope!

He who loves us has "made us a kingdom, priests to his God and Father." These words echo 1 Peter 2:9–10, which in turn echo Yahweh's words at Mount Sinai right after He had rescued Israel out of Egypt (see Ex. 19:5–6).[13] Both Peter's and John's words show that the physical nation of Israel under the old covenant was really a shadow pointing forward to spiritual Israel in Christ under His new covenant. This means that we have been made to enter into His holy rule and live thereunder. This also means that each and every one of us in Christ has been given the indwelling presence of His Spirit, and thus are permanently in the presence of Yahweh and permanently have the Anointing who "teaches you about everything, and is true, and is no lie" (1 John 2:27)—it is the Holy Spirit who guides us into all truth. This is what the Lord Jesus has done for all those for whom He died in making the new covenant with them in His blood. There is no reason in and of ourselves that we deserve this—it is simply God's free grace toward poor, wretched sinners such as us!

Unto *this* Lord Jesus, "to him be glory and dominion forever and ever. Amen." This echoes Paul's words of praise in concluding his teaching to the

---

12   Zacharias Ursinus, *The Heidelberg Catechism* [1563, 1619], Q. 1, https://www.apuritansmind.com/creeds-and-confessions/the-heidelberg-catechism-by-zacharias-ursinus.

13   See Beale and McDonough, "Revelation," 1090.

Roman church about the grace of God in the gospel (see Rom. 11:33–36). This also echoes Paul's teaching to the congregation in Colossae concerning the excellencies of Christ (see Col. 1:15–20). Truly, this is the only proper response to having received such amazing grace—heartfelt gratitude and praise unto Yahweh! Reflecting deeply on the truths of the gospel of the kingdom ought to result in worship unto the triune God of Holy Scripture. Theology must lead to doxology because the purpose for which we've been created is "to glorify God and to enjoy Him forever."[14]

Verse 7: "Behold, he is coming with the clouds, and every eye will see him, even those who pierced him, and all tribes of the earth will wail on account of him. Even so. Amen." At this juncture in his prologue, John announces the baseline theme undergirding the rest of his letter. Thus, it is crucial for the student of God's Word to pay close attention to what is precisely said in this verse.

The theme verse begins, "Behold, he is coming with the clouds." This is almost identical language to that found in Matthew 24:30, which appears in the context of judging national Israel through the destruction of the temple. Jesus prophesied, "Then will appear in heaven the sign of the Son of Man, and then all the tribes of the earth will mourn, and they will see *the Son of Man coming on the clouds of heaven* with power and great glory" (Matt. 24:30, emphasis mine). Luke 21:27 is parallel to this verse and has similar wording. At this point in the Olivet Discourse, Jesus picks up the prophecy of Daniel 7:13–14 and applies it to Himself—the prophecy concerns the Messiah's inter-advental rule from the heavenly Davidic throne, *not* His consummate reign in the eternal state. This is given as an encouragement to His disciples that, even though the situation around Jerusalem would soon become hectic, this judgment would be a part of His rule over all the nations. This means His Messianic mission would not fail. John intends for his audience to understand these words here in verse 7 with the same background in mind.

Verse 7 continues, "every eye will see him, even those who pierced him." This is a quotation from Zechariah 12:10, which Jesus picks up in Matthew 24:30 in speaking about the coming destruction of the temple and its beloved city, Jerusalem.[15] This necessitates that there be at least some

---

14 Benjamin Keach, *The Baptist Catechism* [1677], Q. 2, http://baptiststudiesonline.com/wp-content/uploads/2007/02/keachs-catechism-of-1677.pdf.
15 See Beale and McDonough, "Revelation," 1090.

individuals still alive out of those who crucified Him to witness "the Son of Man coming on the clouds." This is in keeping with what the apostle has already twice said—namely, that the Apocalypse was given to show "the things that must *soon* take place" and that those who keep what is written therein are blessed, "for the time is *near*" (verses 1 and 3, author's emphasis).[16] "And all tribes of the earth will wail on account of Him." This is the response of all those who see Him at His coming. These "tribes of the earth" are better understood as "tribes of the land." As mentioned earlier, the Greek term *ge* most naturally denotes "a tract of land" or "a country,"[17] which is how it is predominantly used throughout the Apocalypse. It is the Greek equivalent to the Hebrew *eretz*. Thus, the land spoken of here is the Promised Land, first-century Palestine.[18] In addition, this phrase does not distinguish between those who may be mourning out of fear of Him as their Judge and those who may be mourning out of repentance over their transgressions against Him. The latter is the Psalm 51 kind of mourning to which all men must come in order to be saved, which can only come about by the powerful work of the Holy Spirit in a sinner's heart (see Acts 5:31; 8:22).

The theme verse ends with these words: "Even so. Amen." With this forceful affirmation, John concludes this kind of prophetic doxology.

Since the Olivet Discourse is so central to understanding the Apocalypse, it is vital we deal with the main concerns of that most important sermon. Firstly, we must recognize that the sermon does not stand alone and isolated, but its context begins back in Matthew 23, where Jesus brings seven woes against the Jewish religious leaders for their hypocrisy. As a conclusion to this massive indictment, He says, "Therefore I send you prophets and wise men and scribes, some of whom you will kill and crucify, and some you will flog in your synagogues and persecute from town to town, so that on you may come all the righteous blood shed on earth, from the blood of righteous Abel to the blood of Zechariah the son of Barachiah, whom you murdered between the sanctuary and the altar. Truly, I say to you, all these things will come upon this generation" (23:34–36). As He leaves the temple mount and the city of Jerusalem, Jesus turns around and

---

16 See Gentry Jr., *He Shall Have Dominion*, 440.
17 The NAS New Testament Greek Lexicon, *Genesis*, https://www.biblestudytools.com/lexicons/greek/nas/genesis-5.html.
18 The NAS New Testament Greek Lexicon, *Genesis*, 440–441.

weeps over the city and its apostate leadership, saying, "See, your house is left to you desolate" (23:38). Not only does the Messiah assure the scribes and Pharisees that divine retribution would befall *their* generation, but He likewise promises the destruction of the temple, meaning the end of the old covenant economy as a whole. In fact, He explicitly prophesies to His disciples, "You see all these, do you not? Truly, I say to you, there will not be left here one stone upon another that will not be thrown down" (24:2).

The disciples understood this and were immediately shocked. So, while the buildings of the temple were still in their line of vision, they asked their Lord, "Tell us, when will these things be, and what will be the sign of your coming and of the end of the age?" (24:3). What were the "these things" they inquired about? The destruction of the temple. Likewise, which "age" was about to come to an abrupt end? The old covenant age. Again, for which "coming" of the Messiah did they request to know the signs? His coming in judgment against Jerusalem and her apostate leadership in order to avenge all the righteous blood of the prophets throughout history up until their day. This "coming" was already promised "upon this generation"—that is, the first-century generation to whom Jesus was speaking. This is repeated for emphasis toward the conclusion of the sermon at 24:34. It was to these specific concerns that our Lord was responding.

For many Christians, what has been explained above will immediately raise questions on three points: (1) the great tribulation in 24:15ff, (2) the cosmic deconstruction language in 24:29, and (3) the coming of the Son of Man in 24:30. On the first, Jesus interprets Daniel's prophecy for His disciples. He instructs, "So when you see the abomination of desolation spoken of by the prophet Daniel, standing in the holy place (let the reader understand), then let those who are in Judea flee to the mountains." In writing to a Jewish audience, Matthew expects his readers to understand to what Jesus here refers. However, for us, removed by time and Jewish training in the *Tanakh* (the Jewish Old Testament), it is difficult for us to surmise. Yet the Holy Spirit has not left us empty-handed, for Luke records the same sermon, except in writing to Gentiles rather than Jews. At this precise point in the Olivet Discourse, he records Jesus as saying, "But when you see Jerusalem surrounded by armies, then know that its desolation has come near. Then let those who are in Judea flee to the mountains . . ." (Luke 21:20ff). The "abomination that brings desolation" spoken of in Daniel 9:27 is interpreted by Jesus Himself as the Roman armies surrounding the holy city to destroy it and its temple. The ones instructed to flee when they begin witnessing this very thing are first-century Christians living within the city. Therefore, the great tribulation predicted here is the period in *that* generation wherein these historic events took place, specifically AD 70, just as Jesus predicted. This means the great tribulation was in the disciples' future at the time of the Olivet Discourse, but was fulfilled long ago in our past.

Secondly, in Matthew 24:29 Jesus says, "Immediately after the tribulation of those days the sun will be darkened, and the moon will not give its light, and the stars will fall from heaven, and the powers of the heavens will be shaken." Here our Lord is quoting this language of cosmic deconstruction from Isaiah 13:10. In that context, the prophet spoke of Yahweh's coming judgment on Babylon through the armies of the Medes and Persians. Did Yahweh come in judgment on the Babylonian Empire? Most definitely. Did He literally deconstruct the universe in order to do so? Obviously not! Thus, just as Isaiah used this kind of prophetic hyperbole to describe how dramatic God's judgment would be, so also Jesus picks up the exact same language to describe His coming in judgment on apostate Israel and her temple. This means there is nothing here indicating the end of the world, as many have supposed.

Finally, in the following verse Messiah promises, "Then will appear in heaven the sign of the Son of Man, and then all the tribes of the earth will mourn, and they will see the Son of Man coming on the clouds of heaven with power and great glory" (24:30). As noted above, this is another quotation, one directly out of Daniel 7:13–14. There, Messiah ascends to the Ancient of Days on the clouds of heaven in order to be seated at His right hand and be given "dominion and glory and a kingdom, that all peoples, nations, and languages should serve him." Which direction is He coming on the clouds? Up! This is describing Jesus's bodily ascension forty days after being raised from the dead as part of His exaltation to glory. Thus, the dominion and kingdom rule given Him is current, not merely when human history comes to an end. Thus, in quoting from Daniel 7, Jesus is indicating that His coming in judgment against Jerusalem, her leaders, and her temple is "Exhibit A," as it were, of His Messianic rule from His Father's right hand over all the nations. This means His coming in judgment here is metaphorical in nature rather than physical, just as was the case with Egypt, Babylon, Assyria, and many others.

This most famous yet oft misinterpreted sermon not only stands behind Revelation 1:7, but also much of the judgments coming forth from Messiah's scroll. Thus, getting this piece interpreted correctly is key to unlocking the rest.

Verse 8: "'I am the Alpha and the Omega,' says the Lord God, 'who is and who was and who is to come, the Almighty.'" *Alpha* (α) and *omega* (ω) are the first and last letters of the Greek alphabet. By ascribing to Himself these opposite extremes, the Lord is saying that He came before all things and will continue after all things. Therefore, He is in absolute control of all things in between the beginning and the end of time. This understanding is confirmed by how the Lord God follows this up: "who is and who was and who is to come, the Almighty." This agrees with the entire testimony of Scripture, especially the Old Testament. God's self-disclosed name ,*YHWH* (Yahweh), means "I AM WHO I AM" (Ex. 3:14), which can be understood as the "Self-Existent One," while *Adonai* means "Lord, Sovereign." Taken together, this relates directly to the doctrine of omnipresence, as well as omnipotence, since the emphasis here is on God's absolute control of all things throughout history. Many a well-intentioned person has misunderstood this definitional teaching to mean that God is everywhere all at the same time, as if God were bound by time just as we are as His creatures. This understanding is one step away from pantheism, the Eastern concept that the divine is integrated into all elements of creation (e.g., hugging a tree equals hugging the divine). Yet the biblical, historical understanding of omnipresence is that God, as the sole eternal Being, not bound by time and space as we are, is actively involved in carrying out His wise purposes in each and every circumstance at each and every point of history simultaneously. This should be a great comfort to God's people through various and sundry trials experienced in faithfully following Him. Why? Because their suffering is entirely within the counsel of His eternal will! This means it has an intended purpose, even if they cannot see or understand it in the moment. God really is working all things together for the good of His saints and, ultimately, for the glorification of His own name! What a wonderful encouragement this is to the Lord's people!

The apostle concludes his prologue by repeating the description of the Father given in verse 4: "who is and who was and who is to come." This repetition serves to once again emphasize the eternality of God the Father. As was noted at verse 4, whatever is true of the Father as to His essence is also true of the Son and the Spirit since the three persons of the Godhead have fully and eternally shared the same Being.

THE FIRST VISION

Verses 9–20 bring to us John's first visionary encounter with the Son of Man. This takes place within the context of Christ's lordship over and amongst the seven churches to which he writes.

Verse 9: "I, John, your brother and partner in the tribulation and the kingdom and the patient endurance that are in Jesus, was on the island called Patmos on account of the word of God and the testimony of Jesus." John identifies himself with those seven congregations to whom he writes as their "brother and partner" in three things.

Firstly, the apostle is a brother and partner with them "in the tribulation." John was exiled "on the island called Patmos on account of the word of God and the testimony of Jesus." He was suffering persecution within the Roman Empire. In his day, the emperor required that everyone in the Empire give honor to him as the highest god by burning incense to him and declaring, *"Kaisar Kurios"* ("Caesar is Lord"). Nero was emperor at the time, and he hated Christians because they refused to do this. In response, he did terrible things to them, such as using them as torches to light up his garden parties, as well as tying them to poles in the Coliseum, dressing up as a wild beast, and then attacking their genitals to their utter agony. In addition, Messiah-rejecting Jews passionately hated first-century followers of Jesus and tried to eliminate them in any way they could, even collaborating with the Roman government to do so. These Jews had apostatized from their national covenant with Yahweh in three main ways. First of all, they treated the *Mishnah* (oral at this point in history) as more authoritative than the *Tanakh* (what Jesus calls "the Law and the Prophets"—see Matt. 15:1–9). Next, they strove for external obedience to the neglect of internal obedience (see Matt. 5:17–48; 15:10–20; 23:1–36). Lastly, and most importantly, they rejected Messiah's release in favor of Barabbas the Zealot's. Not only this, but they traded in Yahweh's Anointed King for Caesar as their ultimate authority (see Matt. 27:15–23; John 19:12–16).

Secondly, John and the seven congregations in Asia were brothers together in "the kingdom." They were brothers and partners together because they had seen and entered into Christ's kingdom, not because of their own ability, but rather due to the Spirit seeing fit to grant them the new birth (see John 3:1–8). Thus, they had equal access to the same Father through the same Holy Spirit, who was building them up together as the temple of God (see Eph. 2:18–22).

Finally, they were partners together in "the patient endurance that [is] in Jesus." They were encouraged to keep on persevering through their hardships, "[laying] aside every weight, and sin which clings so closely, [running] with endurance the race that [was] set before [them], looking to Jesus, the founder and perfecter of [their] faith" (Heb. 12:1–2). They must wait just a little longer until Jesus would come to vindicate the blood of the saints who had been killed on account of Him.[19] In contrast to Christ's judgment on Jerusalem, we are not guaranteed any specific time frame concerning Jesus's physical second coming. Yet believers today can have utmost confidence that Jesus is firmly seated on David's throne right now. He is actively working to right wrongs done everywhere, even driving out the darkness of sin's corruption throughout the whole world with His glorious light (Isa. 9:1–7)! On the Last Day, He will sit in judgment over each and every one, exacting perfect cosmic justice across the board.[20]

Verse 10: "I was in the Spirit on the Lord's day, and I heard behind me a loud voice like a trumpet." It was the Lord's Day when John received this revelation concerning Jesus Christ. This was the day of rest set apart unto worship since the creation of the world, recapitulated in light of Christ's resurrection under His new covenant.[21] For this reason, John was busy keeping the Sabbath on the Lord's Day, not using his exile as an excuse to do otherwise.

As he was enthralled with the beauty and majesty of his Lord and Savior, the Spirit somehow transported him to a realm where he would receive these visions. This is akin to how the Spirit transported David into the

---

19 See 6:10–11; 18:20; 18:24; 19:1–2.
20 See notes at 20:12.
21 See Gen. 2:1–3; Ex. 20:8–11; Deut. 5:12–15; Heb. 4:9–10. For an excellent treatment of the perpetuity of the Sabbath, see Richard C. Barcellos, *Getting the Garden Right: Adam's Work and God's Rest in Light of Christ* (Cape Coral: Founders Press, 2017).

heavenly realm to overhear the divine counsel in session (the content of both Psalm 22 and Psalm 110), as well as how He transported the apostle Paul into the third heaven, which he mentions in 2 Corinthians 12:1–6. As with David's and Paul's experiences, John didn't know if he was in his body or out of his body. It could be that he was experiencing what today would be called an "out-of-body experience" (OBE).

If so, there are three radical differences between the OBEs of these regenerate men of God and those of modern new-age practitioners. To begin with, the experience of the apostle John was Spirit-induced rather than being created through the use of means to open a channel to the other side. John clearly was not seeking after these experiences since the text indicates he was about the business of keeping the Sabbath holy to the Lord. In addition, the heavenly messengers with whom he met directed his attention to the triune God, in full agreement with what He had already revealed, rather than being directed to the secret knowledge of others on the other side, whether they be living or deceased humans or spiritual beings. These heavenly messengers were holy, truthful, and faithful to their Creator rather than being malevolent, deceptive, and abusive in various and sundry ways. We can see that throughout this lengthy letter to the seven congregations. Lastly, upon entrance into that spiritual realm, he "heard behind [him] a loud voice like a trumpet." Trumpets were used in ancient Israel for two purposes: for the making of official announcements and for public worship in the congregation. Since what John received was an unveiling concerning Jesus the Messiah, this indicates that the "loud voice like a trumpet" was a messenger given to prelude an official announcement from heaven. This is very much unlike the type of messages people have reported receiving from their contacts on the other side while astral projecting.[22] Thus, John's experiences in receiving these visions "in the Spirit," whether in or out of his body, stand in stark contrast to those of modern-day new-age practitioners.

Verse 11: "saying, 'Write what you see in a book and send it to the seven churches, to Ephesus and to Smyrna and to Pergamum and to Thyatira and to Sardis and to Philadelphia and to Laodicea." The plain reading of the text indicates that upon completing this epistle, John was meant to literally and temporally send a copy of it to each of these literal, temporal

---

22 Steven Bancarz and Josh Peck, *The Second Coming of the New Age: The Hidden Dangers of Alternative Spirituality in Contemporary America and Its Churches* (Crane, MO: Defender Publishing, 2018). Steven was saved out of the new age, having been one of the world's leading new-age experts and practitioners.

congregations in his day. All seven of these congregations were located in Asia Minor, which is present-day Turkey. This is what the heavenly messenger told him to write. The number seven here is used, as in other places in Revelation, to symbolize completion. Each of these churches, though very flawed, confessed true and complete union to Christ in His death and resurrection. Five of the seven were confirmed as being true visible, local expressions of the universal, invisible body of Christ, while two were on the verge of being rejected as impostors. Those true congregations were indeed in the process of becoming what they already were as new creations in Him.[23]

Verse 12a: "Then I turned to see the voice that was speaking to me." This is the first occurrence of this particular form that continues throughout the book—John *hears* the angel describe one thing, but when he turns to look at what has been described, he *sees* something completely different (e.g., 5:5–6; 7:4–10). That which he heard from the messenger a moment ago and what he now sees are starkly different vantage points describing the very same thing. Having been caught up in the Spirit, the apostle now begins beholding the visions.

Verse 12b: "on turning I saw seven golden lampstands." The Son of Man later tells John that these "seven golden lampstands" are, in fact, symbolic representations of the seven congregations mentioned in verse 11 (see v. 20).

Verse 13: "and in the midst of the lampstands one like a son of man, clothed with a long robe and with a golden sash around his chest." The title "Son of Man" refers back to Daniel 7:13–14, which it specifically describes the Messiah's enthronement at His Father's right hand and everlasting dominion over all the nations.[24] The image presented here of the Son of Man "clothed with a long robe and with a golden sash around his chest" also speaks to His rule as King. Thus, the enthroned Messiah is shown here as actively ruling in the midst of His congregations.

Verse 14: "The hairs of his head were white, like white wool, like snow. His eyes were like a flame of fire." The Son of Man's pure white hair symbolizes His absolute purity in all He does as the Messianic King. His eyes like fire refers to His nature as the "consuming fire" (Ex. 24:17; Deut. 4:24; Heb. 12:29). He is absolute purity and consumes all that is impure.

---

23 See Rom. 6:1–14; 2 Cor. 5:16–19; Eph. 2:1–10; Col. 3:1–17.
24 See Beale and McDonough, "Revelation," 1092.

Verse 15: "his feet were like burnished bronze, refined in a furnace, and his voice was like the roar of many waters." In Daniel 2, Daniel interpreted Nebuchadnezzar's vision of a multi-sectional statue. Its middle and thighs were of bronze and represented the third kingdom to come, progressing from the then-Babylonian kingdom until the coming of the Messiah and His kingdom (Dan. 2:32, 39). Unlike this third kingdom, the foundations of the Messiah's kingdom are sure, such that it will never be destroyed! The actual image here is drawn from Ezekiel 1:24–25,[25] in tandem with Daniel 7:13–14, where the Son of Man is coronated to sit at His Father's right hand to rule over all the nations. Taken together, the message is that when the Son of Man speaks, His word is completely overpowering and nothing can resist it. To those united to the Lord Jesus by faith, this is a great comfort since, by His most powerful word, He has raised us from death in sin unto new life in Him! Yet to those still living under His wrath, this truth ought to incite great fear and trembling at the impending judgment about to befall them, which they rightly deserve.

Verse 16: "In his right hand he held seven stars, from his mouth came a sharp two-edged sword, and his face was like the sun shining in full strength." The Son of Man is holding secure in His ruling hand the seven stars (cf. John 10:25–30). He explains later that they are the seven angels of the seven congregations—that is, messengers or elder-pastors (see v. 20). His right hand is the hand with which He holds His royal scepter. This means that, as believers, we have no reason to fear God's wrath because He keeps us securely as His beloved children. Thus, when the Father disciplines us, He does so as our Father, not as our Judge, and when the Son rebukes us, He does so as our elder Brother.

Not only this, but when Jesus speaks, His words are penetrating and effect exactly what they are intended to—none of His purposes can be thwarted (see Job 42:1–2; Dan. 4:34–35)! As for His face shining like the sun in full strength, this portrays His radiant glory and majesty, that He dwells in unapproachable light, which compares to none, into which no man can enter in his naturally impure and sinful state (1 Tim. 6:16). Entering in is only possible if a man comes unto the Lord with an empty hand of faith to receive His full acceptance only on the basis of the Son's perfect, meritorious obedience freely imputed unto him. Only through this justification can a man be joined to the Messiah and enter into

---

25   See Beale and McDonough, "Revelation," 1092.

Yahweh's most glorious presence safely and there fellowship with Him (Rom. 5:18–19; 1 John 1:1–4).

Verse 17a: "When I saw him, I fell at his feet as though dead. But he laid his right hand on me." This is the same reaction Isaiah had when seeing the majesty of Yahweh as He sat on His throne—the prophet was completely undone (Isa. 6:1–7; see also Ezek. 1:28). Nevertheless, unlike the angel who came unto Isaiah with a fiery coal, here it is the Messianic King coming to John to touch him with His right hand—this hand holds His royal scepter with which He rules over the nations (cf. Gen. 49:10). Falling prostrate in worship before the Lord is appropriate since we have been commanded to worship Yahweh "with reverence and awe, for our God is a consuming fire" (Heb. 12:28–29). In imitation of Isaiah and Ezekiel, under the influence of the Holy Spirit, this prostration is an expression of being undone, as it were, when coming face to face with the immense majesty and holiness of the Lord. This practice must never be confused with mere emotionalism or euphoria, as is sometimes the case in charismatic circles.

Verses 17b–18: "saying, 'Fear not, I am the first and the last, and the living one. I died, and behold I am alive forevermore, and I have the keys of Death and Hades.'" The Son of Man encourages John to not be afraid. This is the same as what happened to Peter, James, and John upon seeing His glory and hearing the voice of His Father from heaven—the disciples were afraid and so Jesus reassured them (Matt. 17:1–8, esp. verses 7–8). Jesus here gives John His own character as the rationale for following this exhortation.

Jesus first identifies Himself as the "first and the last." He is eternal, just as His Father is eternal, which is expressed in verse 18. He is indeed the "living one."

Secondly, He declares Himself to be the one who "died, and behold [is] alive forevermore." Truly, He is the one who has accomplished the complete defeat of all His enemies in His death, and now, in His resurrection, He is making those things a reality in space and time. Due to a strong emphasis upon the work of Jesus in His death, over against His work in His resurrected glory, many Bible-believing Christians view our Lord as being on a kind of extended hiatus until He ushers in His kingdom at His second advent. Yet the message conveyed here is that our Messiah is just as active in bringing His redemptive purposes to pass in His current exaltation in heaven as He was in accomplishing them in His humiliation on earth. Such is the gospel of the *kingdom*.

Lastly, the Lord describes Himself as having "the keys of Death and Hades." He alone controls how long Death and Hades will continue since, on the Last Day, He will throw them into the lake of fire (cf. 20:14). Just as there is an intermediate state for the regenerate upon death, that is, Abraham's Bosom, so also there is an intermediate state for those who die unrepentant, namely, Hades (cf. Luke 16:19–31; even if this is a parable, it must be based in reality, just the same as every other parable). The difference between Hades and hell (referred to as the "lake of fire" in Rev. 20:14–15) is not one of permanency of judgment for the wicked, but rather one of nature. The former is a metaphysical prison for the ungodly upon death in this life. The latter is the permanent, eternal, and physical place where all God's wrath will be poured out in judgment on the same. Both of these are compartments within Sheol, which is the place of the dead mentioned in the Old Testament. The reason Death and Hades will not be cast into Gehenna (hell) prior to the Last Day is that it doesn't yet exist, in the same way the consummate new heavens and new earth won't exist until the Lord resurrects this physical universe on the day of His return. Knowing these things ought to help set our expectations for the course of history, as well as for when those around us die.

Verse 19: "Write therefore the things that you have seen, those that are and those that are to take place after this." The reason for the writing of this unveiling of the "things that must soon take place" (1:1) is the person and work of the risen Lord Jesus, the Messiah ruling in the midst of His congregations. Again, He says, "those that are to take place after this," denoting immediacy to John's readers in his day.

Verse 20: "As for the mystery of the seven stars that you saw in my right hand, and the seven golden lampstands, the seven stars are the angels of the seven churches, and the seven lampstands are the seven churches." It is clear from Jesus's own interpretation that since the seven lampstands represent the seven local congregations mentioned in verse 11, the seven stars likewise represent the elder-pastors of those congregations. The Lord Jesus is the head of each and every one of His local assemblies and the true Shepherd over them all. This should radically impact the way we think about how Jesus wants us to organize ourselves under Him as His visible body. For example, this means that elder-pastors, while truly a set-apart office of the local congregation, are *a part* of the membership, *not* a separate class above it. Thus, they are equally subject to loving correction back to glad submission under our one true Master.

The Letters to the Congregations (2:1–3:22)

Revelation 2:1–7 opens a section devoted to particular letters addressed to each of the seven churches. Within these verses are Jesus's words to the congregation at Ephesus.

To the Congregation at Ephesus

Chapter 2, verse 1: "To the angel of the church in Ephesus write: 'The words of him who holds the seven stars in his right hand, who walks among the seven golden lampstands." The letter is addressed to the leaders of the Ephesian congregation, and John is scribing the direct words of Jesus Himself. The opening refers back to 1:12 and 16 with the purpose of encouraging the Ephesian believers that He is with them. Not only this, but He is in full control of all their circumstances, including the persecutions they now face. This reference back to chapter 1 shows that the whole of the Revelation is meant for the Ephesian believers, not only this short letter. The same can be said for the other six congregations.

Verse 2: "I know your works, your toil and your patient endurance." The Ephesians have been faithful to their Lord and Savior, even through these great trials they have been facing. It's worth noting that the wording here is similar to that back in 1:9, which shows continuity. In considering this, when we face trials of various kinds, do we become cynical and bitter toward the world, or is our response like that of the church in Ephesus? During such tribulations, are we keeping our eyes fixed on our Messiah and pursuing His kingdom and His righteousness in the world?

Verse 2b: "and how you cannot bear with those who are evil, but have tested those who call themselves apostles and are not, and found them to be false." They have tested those supposed apostles against God's revealed will. Are they doing signs and wonders, but leading others away from the truth (cf. Deut. 13)? Are they claiming things on behalf of God, but those things fail to come to pass (cf. Deut. 18)? Are these even qualified apostles, in that they have personally seen the risen Lord Jesus and follow Him as the true Messiah prophesied of old? According to such tests, the believers at Ephesus found these false apostles greatly wanting and put them out from amongst them, refusing to tolerate their deceptions and heresies. This harkens back to John's first epistle, where he speaks of those who were put out of the assembly of Christ because they were antichrists—that is, those denying Jesus as the promised Messiah (1 John 2:18ff). Most likely these antichrists were Jews trying to pull believers back into the old covenant through denying Jesus's divinity and Messiahship.

If we are elder-pastors in our local congregations, are we being careful to do likewise? Many don't mind freely quoting Matthew 7:1–5 but find it difficult to remember that Jesus followed it up with verse 6: "Do not give dogs what is holy, and do not throw pearls before pigs, lest they trample them underfoot and turn to attack you." Godly discernment is crucial for godly leadership.

Verse 3: "I know you are enduring patiently and bearing up for my name's sake, and you have not grown weary." The wording here is similar to that in the first half of verse 2. Jesus commends the Ephesian believers for standing firm in the truth and for defending His name through many difficult times. If we could listen in on what is being discussed amongst the three persons of the Godhead, would They be commending us for this kind of steadfastness in the truth, both personally and corporately, as one of His local assemblies? One hundred years from now, will history look back on us as men who were always "hedging our bets," as it were, or as men who were willing to risk everything for the sake of Messiah's fame, rule, and glory in the earth?

Verse 4: "But I have this against you, that you have abandoned the love you had at first." While commentators debate the exact meaning of "have abandoned the love you had at first," it would seem that since these believers are fiercely committed to the truth, the objects of their failure to love as they once did are Messiah and their fellow man. Indeed, their affections for their Messiah have now waned. The issue is not doctrinal commitment, but rather heart affections that ought to be stirred up by a close attention to the truth. In the next verse, Jesus commands them to "repent, and do the works you did at first." This shows there's a lack of love-driven action toward others as unto the Lord. This falls in line with John's epistle: "By this it is evident who are the children of God, and who are the children of the devil: whoever does not practice righteousness is not of God, nor is the one who does not love his brother" (1 John 3:10). This also falls in line with James's epistle where he says that "religion that is pure and undefiled before God the Father is this: to visit orphans and widows in their affliction, and to keep oneself unstained from the world" (James 1:27). He then goes on to explain, "For as the body apart from the spirit is dead, so also faith apart from works is dead" (2:26). Love for God and love for neighbor, and a desire to grow therein, is the natural result of the new birth. Believers are commanded to fervently pursue these things according to God's law. When this love is lacking in a person's life over an extended period of time, either toward the Lord or toward neighbor, this is cause for great concern. Thus, Jesus rebukes the Ephesian congregation and calls them to repentance.

It is important for every believer of every age to personally examine himself to identify areas that need repentance and special attention for growth in holiness. It is always a temptation to slip off into the ditch of legalism on one side, or that of antinomianism on the other. Legalism tries to pursue the new life in Christ without seeing any real need for a prior giving of the new heart. Antinomianism does the opposite—it tries to maintain that a person can experience the new birth without this necessarily resulting in a new life lived under Jesus's lordship. Yet Jesus teaches that it is impossible to have one without the other! Such is the power of His gospel!

Verse 5a: "Remember therefore from where you have fallen; repent, and do the works you did at first." Jesus reminds them that at the beginning of their walk with Him, they were faithful to love their neighbors as fellow image bearers of God. Because they have fallen from where they began, He commands them to turn from their unloving neglect of neighbor, come to their Lord with a broken and contrite heart to find forgiveness and cleansing, and then strive to love others with the help of the Spirit who is at work in them. He calls them to repent before Almighty God in the same way King David did after committing adultery and murder, as recorded in

Psalm 51. When we fail to love our neighbors as those also made in the image of God, the Lord likewise calls us to respond in repentance.

Verse 5b: "If not, I will come to you and remove your lampstand from its place, unless you repent." It is important to recognize that Jesus is here speaking to the congregation at Ephesus *as a whole*, not to any one individual therein—this is also true of the other six churches to whom John writes. He warns them that they are in danger of losing the Spirit's presence among them, and thus will cease to be a true congregation of Christ in God's eyes. If they fail to repent, just as "Ichabod" was said of others, so it will also be said of them (cf. 1 Sam. 4:21–22). The Messiah cares deeply about the spiritual state of each and every one of His local assemblies, that they all should be presented unto Him on the Last Day pure, just as He is pure (1 John 3:2–3).

Verse 6: "Yet this you have: you hate the works of the Nicolaitans, which I also hate." The Nicolaitans were a "heretical group, probably holding views similar to the teaching of Balaam and Jezebel (vv. 14, 20 notes). . . . Balaam (Num. 22:5) gave Balak advice leading to Israel's harlotry in Moab (Num. 25:1–4). Jezebel (v. 20) and other professing Christians in the seven churches were indulging in pleasures offered by their pagan environment."[1] "Though these Christians had left their first love, yet they bore an hatred to the filthy and impure practices of some men, who were called 'Nicolaitans'; who committed fornication, adultery, and all uncleanness, and had their wives in common, and also ate things offered to idols."[2] The Lord commends the Ephesian believers for hating this group, just as He Himself does.

Verse 7a: "He who has an ear, let him hear what the Spirit says to the churches." This is very similar to what Jesus taught His disciples in describing the sons of the kingdom: "But blessed are your eyes, for they see, and your ears, for they hear. . . . As for what was sown on good soil, this is the one who hears the word and understands it. He indeed bears fruit and yields, in one case a hundredfold, in another sixty, and in another thirty" (Matt. 13:16, 23). Even in Matthew 13, the Lord makes the connection back to Isaiah 6:9–10, which He again utilizes in these personalized

---

[1] Reformation Study Bible notes, Revelation 2:6, 14.

[2] John Gill, *Exposition of the Old & New Testaments*, (Washington, DC: OSNOVA, 2012), Kindle Location 354168.

epistles.[3] Thus, Jesus encourages those who have been given spiritual ears through regeneration to not only listen carefully to the words of the Holy Spirit throughout this letter, but also throughout the Revelation as a whole.

Verse 7b: "To the one who conquers I will grant to eat of the tree of life, which is in the paradise of God." The apostle James writes, "Count it all joy, my brothers, when you meet trials of various kinds, for you know that the testing of your faith produces steadfastness. And let steadfastness have its full effect, that you may be perfect and complete, lacking in nothing" (James 1:2–4). The only way any of these Ephesian brothers will conquer through their trials is by listening to the words of the Spirit throughout the Revelation, as well as by following the teaching of James chapter 1. This conquering leads to gaining access to the tree of life, which represents all the eternal blessings Adam and Eve would have enjoyed if they had kept the terms of the covenant of works (see 22:1–2). These blessings have been barred for all humanity since the fall, but in Christ they are guaranteed to all in the consummate new creation. The elect experience them more and more until the Last Day, yet somehow still in a limited way but then, at Christ's return, they will experience the fullness thereof. What a glorious blessing is the new creation for all those in Him!

TO THE CONGREGATION AT SMYRNA

The second church to whom John writes is the one at Smyrna. Verses 8–11 bring to us the words of Jesus unto the Smyrnan saints.

Verse 8: "And to the angel of the church in Smyrna write: 'The words of the first and the last, who died and came to life.'" This letter is addressed to the leaders of the congregation at Smyrna. Jesus refers to Himself according to how He described Himself to the apostle back in 1:17–18. This is to remind the Smyrnan believers that He is eternal and in full control of all details throughout history. It is also to remind them that He Himself has accomplished the full defeat of evil in the world in His death, and now, in His resurrection, He is making it a reality in each and every area of life. Do we actually believe these things, such that they are deeply impacting the way we live out our lives? Do we live like Jesus is actually winning in history? Are we walking by faith or by sight?

---

3   See Beale and McDonough, "Revelation," 1093.

Verse 9: "I know your tribulation and your poverty (but you are rich) and the slander of those who say they are Jews and are not, but are a synagogue of Satan." Jesus comes to comfort the Smyrnan believers in their affliction experienced on account of Him. It seems that a part of the suffering these believers were going through was economic loss, as He reminds them that their true treasures are found in heaven. This is a reference back to Matthew 6:19–34, especially verses 19–21 and verses 31–34. It also seems that the Jews, especially their leaders, were intentionally spreading lies about them in order to bring them to ruin. He says, "They are Jews and are not, but are a synagogue of Satan," which is a repetition of the teaching found in John 8:39–47 and Romans 2:28–29.[4]

Verse 10a: "Do not fear what you are about to suffer. Behold, the devil is about to throw some of you into prison, that you may be tested, and for ten days you will have tribulation." The Lord exhorts the Smyrnan believers to not be afraid. This requires them to put their trust in Him, who has given them "a spirit not of fear but of power and love and self-control" (2 Tim. 1:7). These ten days of persecution are to be instigated by Satan, but most likely temporally carried out by apostate Jews[5] in the form of beatings, imprisonment, seizure of property, executions, mobbings, etc.

Verse 10b: "Be faithful unto death, and I will give you the crown of life." In addition to the Jewish persecution, "the city of Smyrna prided itself on faithfulness to Rome."[6] Just like in Acts 4:12, Jesus here sets Himself up as the one true Lord of all over against the imperial cult being initiated by Caesar Augustus, which demanded worship of all in the Roman Empire unto the falsely deified emperor. Instead of receiving some kind of temporary reward for faithfulness to the emperor, the church is promised a true and everlasting reward to those who are faithful to Jesus to the end of their lives, no matter the suffering they must endure along the way.

Verse 11a: "He who has an ear, let him hear what the Spirit says to the churches." Just as to the other six congregations, Jesus exhorts the regenerate to pay close attention to the words of the Holy Spirit, not only in this letter, but also throughout the whole Revelation.

---

4   See Gentry, *Before Jerusalem Fell*, Kindle Location 506.
5   See Douglas Wilson, *When the Man Comes Around: A Commentary on the Book of Revelation* (Moscow, ID: Canon Press, 2019), Kindle Location 283.
6   Reformation Study Bible notes, Revelation 2:10.

Verse 11b: "The one who conquers will not be hurt by the second death." Just as to the other six assemblies, Jesus makes a promise at the close of His letter to them. To the Smyrnan believers who conquer amidst their trials, He promises they will not receive eternal punishment in hell, which is reserved for those who live their lives in rebellion against Him (see 20:6, 14–15).

Twenty-first-century evangelicalism in the West has succumbed in large part to a breed of antinomianism that says it is possible to live one's entire Christian life in spiritual apathy and yet still be saved. Why? The claim made is that only faith, apart from any repentance, is required for justification, and thus the decision to "accept Jesus as one's personal Savior" becomes the grounds of assurance, one's "holy fire insurance," as it were.[7] It is clear from Jesus's words here to the Smyrnans that how we come to Jesus, and then follow Him, matters greatly in the final analysis of our lives on judgment day. As those who confess allegiance to the Lord Jesus, are we striving to live under His kingdom-rule in every area of our lives since we have been transformed into new creations by His powerful grace? Are passages like Romans 6:1–14 and Colossians 3:1–17 guiding the way we are thinking about life in His kingdom? Such passages are extremely important to our mindset as Christ followers since they specifically address how we ought to live as new creatures in Christ Jesus in light of our union with Him.

TO THE CONGREGATION AT PERGAMUM

At this point, the apostle turns his attention to the believers at Pergamum. Verses 12–17 record his epistle to them.

Verse 12: "And to the angel of the church in Pergamum write: 'The words of him who has the sharp two-edged sword.'" Jesus now turns to address the congregational leaders at Pergamum. He refers to Himself with the words of 1:16 in order to remind them that when He speaks, His words are precise and effect exactly that for which they are intended.

Verse 13: "I know where you dwell, where Satan's throne is. Yet you hold fast my name, and you did not deny my faith even in the days of Antipas

---

[7] For a clear, biblical refutation of this error, see John MacArthur, *The Gospel According to Jesus: What Is Authentic Faith?* (Grand Rapids: Zondervan, 2008). See also Paul Washer's message at the 2002 Youth Evangelism Conference in Mongomery, AL, https://www.youtube.com/watch?v=uuabITeO4l8.

my faithful witness, who was killed among you, where Satan dwells." "Pergamum possessed the oldest temple in Asia Minor devoted to emperor worship."[8] Because of this, the believers in that city suffered greatly for remaining loyal to King Jesus and refusing to give false worship to the emperor. Jesus specifically makes reference to a martyr amongst them, Antipas, and greatly commends them for their faithfulness, even under such tremendously difficult circumstances.

It is often a temptation for believers of every generation to justify their unfaithfulness to Yahweh by appealing to their suffering. Yet there is no room for self-pity here. Jesus calls us to faithfully follow Him, even when our circumstances are anything but convenient! He commends the believers at Pergamum as godly examples for us to follow.

Verse 14: "But I have a few things against you: you have some there who hold the teaching of Balaam, who taught Balak to put a stumbling block before the sons of Israel, so that they might eat food sacrificed to idols and practice sexual immorality." At this point in the letter, the Lord begins to bring charges against this congregation. The first is that they tolerate some amongst them "who hold the teaching of Balaam"—that is, to "eat food sacrificed to idols and practice sexual immorality." These things Balaam taught Balak to lead astray the congregation of Israel in the wilderness (Num. 22:5–25:3).[9] The continued condemnation of these practices was confirmed at the Jerusalem Council, specifically by the apostle James (Acts 15:13–21). James noted this was nothing new, but was, in fact, the teaching of Moses in Leviticus 17:10–16 amidst the holiness code—that israel ought not become like the pagans dwelling around them.[10] Paul also brings up the spiritual nature of food in contrasting partaking of food sacrificed to idols with partaking of the Lord's Supper.[11] It should also be noticed that this teaching of Balaam is very similar to that of the Nicolaitans.

Verse 15: "So also you have some who hold the teaching of the Nicolaitans." The Pergamum believers were tolerating those among them who held to this heresy. This is the exact opposite situation to that of the Ephesian congregation—they were commended for hating the Nicolaitans,

---

8   Reformation Study Bible notes, Revelation 2:13.
9   See Beale and McDonough, "Revelation," 1094.
10 See Reformation Study Bible notes, Revelation 2:14.
11 See 1 Cor. 10:18–22.

while Pergamum here is rebuked for accepting them (see v. 6). As is always the case, there is a great need to guard against false teaching since it has a tendency to spread much faster than the truth. It must be noticed that there is an intimate connection between right doctrine and right practice, or the lack thereof, as is evidently the case with some members of this congregation. This is precisely the reason Paul taught Timothy, "Keep a close watch on yourself and on the teaching. Persist in this, for by so doing you will save both yourself and your hearers" (1 Tim. 4:16).

We must never allow ourselves to be deceived into thinking that we can behave in a way pleasing to God apart from the objective truth of His Word transforming the categories in which we think (see Rom. 12:1–2). Despite what many well-meaning Christians have tried to maintain, it is simply impossible to rightly relate to our Lord and Savior, and grow in intimacy in that relationship, without paying close attention to what He has revealed in His most holy Word. Not only must we closely listen to what He has revealed concerning Himself, but also to His revelation concerning us as fallen image bearers, the world in which we live, spiritual entities and how they relate to physical beings, the details of salvation, the goal of history, and many other foundational, worldview-shaping issues.

Verse 16: "Therefore repent. If not, I will come to you soon and war against them with the sword of my mouth." The Messiah first commands them to repent before God with broken hearts for tolerating these teachings and practices in their midst. They must grow up to be a pure and spotless bride to their King. He then warns them that if they fail to repent, He will war against those who tolerate these heresies and will decisively destroy them when He speaks judgment against them with the word of His mouth.

This ought to be a great warning for us today in our assemblies. Are we tolerating dangerous errors in our midst, or are we corporately repenting of them when they rear their oft attractive, yet terribly venomous heads? Do we take it seriously that if we as local churches are willing to tolerate these things, we are inviting the Lord Jesus to war against us, to bring judgment on us?

Verse 17a: "He who has an ear, let him hear what the Spirit says to the churches." Like with the other six congregations, Jesus exhorts the regenerate among them to pay close attention to the words of the Spirit, not only in this letter, but throughout the Apocalypse as a whole.

Verse 17b: "To the one who conquers I will give some of the hidden manna, and I will give him a white stone, with a new name written on the stone that no one knows except the one who receives it." He promises that those who conquer through their providentially given sufferings will receive two things: hidden manna and a white stone.

First, the Lord promises hidden manna. Considering the discussion about Balaam in verse 14, this seems to be a reference back to God's provision in the wilderness.[12] Yet just like Jesus Himself is the true bread of life that comes down out of heaven, so also the food He promises here is unending spiritual food, found only in Him (see John 6:22–59).[13]

Secondly, He promises a white stone with a name inscribed thereon, which is known only to the recipient. White often represents pure righteousness in the Apocalypse. For example, in 7:13 the saints are clothed in white robes, symbolizing the pure and perfect obedience of the Lord Jesus given unto them. In addition, stones often represent something solid and immovable, like the foundation of the house built on the rock in Matthew 7:24–27. Thus, Jesus promises that those who conquer will be an immovable and pure dwelling place for God.[14] They are also a people fully acquitted of the guilt of sin by the tender mercies of God. The white stone here seems to be an allusion back to the stones of acquittal and condemnation used by the high priest in ancient Israel.[15] Furthermore, the name known only to the recipient seems to be "Mount Zion ... the city of the living God, the heavenly Jerusalem" (Heb. 12:18–27, esp. v. 22; cf. 21:9–27).[16] The reason only the elect know its name is that they alone will finally become what their Bridegroom has purchased them to be. It is for this reason alone they will conquer throughout their trials. What a tremendous privilege it is to belong to the King of kings! Truly, the only proper response to receiving this entirely undeserved privilege is heartfelt gratitude!

---

12 See Beale and McDonough, "Revelation," 1094.
13 See Reformation Study Bible notes, Revelation 2:17.
14 See William Hendriksen, *More Than Conquerors: An Interpretation of the Book of Revelation* (Ada, MI: Baker, 1998), Kindle Location 1172.
15 See Matthew Henry, *Commentary on the Whole Bible*, Revelation 2:12–17.
16 See notes at 3:12 for a further discussion on the usage of names in the Revelation.

To the Congregation at Thyatira

Now we come to the fourth assembly to which John the apostle writes. He records for our benefit the words of Jesus to them in verses 18–28.

Verse 18: "And to the angel of the church in Thyatira write: 'The words of the Son of God, who has eyes like a flame of fire, and whose feet are like burnished bronze.'" Again, Christ comes to these congregational leaders describing Himself with the words of 1:14–15 to remind them that He is a pure, consuming fire and that the foundations of His throne will never be moved. What a great comfort!

Verse 19: "I know your works, your love and faith and service and patient endurance, and that your latter works exceed the first." These are works of the Spirit rather than works of the flesh. Indeed, all of these appear as part of the fruit of the Spirit in Galatians 5:22–23, since "those who belong to Christ Jesus have crucified the flesh with its passions and desires" (5:24). Jesus commends these believers for their spiritual fruit. The words "patient endurance" are specifically a repetition of Revelation 1:9, and the concept of "conquering" has concluded the last three letters. He also says that as time has gone on, they have grown in these works, which have become more and more excellent.

This most certainly is given to us as an example of godly living to follow, just as Paul exhorted the Corinthian church, "Be imitators of me, as I am of Christ" (1 Cor. 11:1). Are we personally and corporately growing in these aspects of the fruit of the Spirit: love, faith, service, and patient endurance?

Verse 20: "But I have this against you, that you tolerate that woman Jezebel, who calls herself a prophetess and is teaching and seducing my servants to practice sexual immorality and to eat food sacrificed to idols." It seems that this false teacher was either a part of the Balaam cult or the Nicolaitans, both of whom were teaching these abominable practices. Like Jezebel in 1 Kings, this lady was seducing others into idolatry and immorality—Baal worship and the pagan temple worship of Thyatira both featured prostitution and sexual debauchery.[17] Although some commentators want to render *porneia* (immorality) at this point metaphorically, there is no reason from this text to do so, especially considering the parallel to the time of Queen Jezebel. Jesus therefore rebukes the Thyatiran congregation for

---

17 See Beale and McDonough, "Revelation," 1095.

tolerating this teacher and her teaching in their midst, just as He rebuked the believers at Ephesus and Pergamum.

Verse 21: "I gave her time to repent, but she refuses to repent of her sexual immorality." Here shows the patience of the Lord in giving Jezebel time to repent. But instead of listening, she has grown even harder of heart! How often pride insidiously manifests itself in just such a manner!

Verses 22–23: "Behold, I will throw her onto a sickbed, and those who commit adultery with her I will throw into great tribulation, unless they repent of her works, and I will strike her children dead. And all the churches will know that I am he who searches mind and heart, and I will give to each of you according to your works." In order to show all believers everywhere that He is, in fact, the infallible Judge of all the earth, Jesus promises to bring low all those who participate with Jezebel in these practices and follow her heretical teachings. The way He will do this is through repaying them with great physical travail, even death. We have clear examples of this type of judgment elsewhere in the New Testament. For example, Ananias and his wife Sapphira were struck dead for lying to the Holy Spirit (Acts 5:1–11), and some of the brethren at Corinth had become violently sick, even some dying, due to improperly participating in the Lord's Supper (1 Cor. 11:27–32).

We must never think that just because we live in the twenty-first century instead of the first, we are somehow allowed to presume upon the mercies of God as if Jesus would not afflict us in like fashion for ongoing rebellion against Him. Do we take it seriously that He very well could bring such judgment upon us in response to unrepentant false worship—either personally, corporately, or societally—in order to incite true repentance (cf. Ps. 2; Ps. 90; Luke 13:1–5)? Could this be the Lord's design in bringing about the present cultural revolution, giving many of us over to a blindness and willingness to be deceived, whereby we can neither recognize how deeply entrenched leftist (cultural-Marxist/postmodern) ideology has become in the consciousness of Western societies nor how very insidious it truly is? It certainly seems that Almighty God is in the process of cleansing His church in the West and destroying the foundations of those nations that would vehemently shake their fists at Him in open rebellion.

Verses 24–25: "But to the rest of you in Thyatira, who do not hold this teaching, who have not learned what some call the deep things of Satan, to you I say, I do not lay on you any other burden. Only hold fast what you have until I come." Just like in Pergamum, Jezebel's heretical teaching was directly linked to the imperial cult. Evidently there was a significant portion of the congregation that had rejected her teaching, and Messiah here exhorts them to hold fast to the true faith, which they have received from His apostles. They must do this until He comes. This "coming" was brought up already in 1:7 and refers to His visitation in judgment in AD 70 upon the breakers of the old covenant—that is, the nation of Israel. Through decisively bringing low one of their persecutors—namely, the Jews, and so vindicating them, He shows Himself to be the Lord over all. He is the one who likewise will eventually bring low the rest of His enemies, even death itself, when He bodily returns on the Last Day (see 1 Cor. 15:25–26). For all those faithfully holding fast to the true faith once for all delivered to the saints, we can continue to confidently trust in the very same Son of Man. Even today, He is continuing to faithfully fulfill His Messianic role in putting all His enemies under His feet. This truly is good news!

Verses 26–27: "The one who conquers and who keeps my works until the end, to him I will give authority over the nations, and he will rule them with a rod of iron, as when earthen pots are broken in pieces, even as I myself have received authority from my Father." This is a clear reference back to Psalm 2:7–9, where the Father promised to give His Anointed King authority to rule over all the nations with a rod of iron.[18] This also shows the intimate union that Christ has with His people. We died with Him in His death, were raised with Him in His resurrection (Rom. 6:5ff), were seated with Him in the heavenly places (Eph. 2:6), and will finally be glorified with Him on the Last Day (Col. 3:4). Just as 2 Corinthians 2:14–17 testifies, the Messianic King is gradually conquering the whole world through the faithful gospel preaching of those united to Him. Indeed, our Christ-imitating gospel preaching is *not* in vain!

Verse 28: "And I will give him the morning star." In 22:16, Jesus calls Himself "the root and descendant of David, the bright morning star." Jesus is the Morning Star because He is "the light of the world. Whoever follows me will not walk in darkness, but will have the light of life" (John 8:12). This is in direct contrast to the Roman emperors Julius and Augustus, who claimed to be descendants of Venus (the morning star of Rome) through

---

18 See Beale and McDonough, "Revelation," 1095.

her son Aeneas.[19] To those who persevere through their trials by faith in the true Morning Star, our Lord promises more of Himself as the light who conquers all darkness in the world. What a great comfort this promise is to those suffering for His name's sake!

Verse 29: "He who has an ear, let him hear what the Spirit says to the churches." As to the previous three congregations, Messiah exhorts the regenerate Thyatirans to pay close attention to the voice of His Spirit, both in this letter and throughout the rest of the Revelation.

The opening verses of chapter 3 give us the Son of Man's words unto the Sardisian congregation. As he was carried along by the Holy Spirit, the apostle penned them here in verses 1–6.

Chapter 3, verse 1a: "And to the angel of the church in Sardis write: 'The words of him who has the seven spirits of God and the seven stars.'" Through a reference back to 1:4 and 1:20, Christ reminds this congregation that the Holy Spirit is the Spirit of Christ, since the Godhead is completely unified in purpose, and that He is Lord over the shepherds of His congregations. It is a great temptation for church leaders to begin thinking of themselves too highly, as if they are the top authority in the assembly. In reality, though, elders are under-shepherds beneath the Good Shepherd and are simultaneously just as much sheep as the rest of the membership. This is most necessary for every saint to remember.

Verse 1b: "I know your works. You have the reputation of being alive, but you are dead." Even though everyone around them is under the impression that they are faithful followers of the Lord Jesus, their faith is, in fact, not bearing spiritual fruit in keeping with repentance. James chapter 2 is applicable to them, at least to a great degree. This local church is in grave danger!

Verse 2: "Wake up, and strengthen what remains and is about to die, for I have not found your works complete in the sight of my God." They are commanded to come to their senses—that is, to recognize the severity of their spiritual condition. They must strive to strengthen what little spiritual life remains so as to please God.

Verse 3: "Remember, then, what you received and heard. Keep it, and repent." They are given an explanation as to how they ought to strengthen

---

19   The J. Paul Getty Museum, Roman Venus, https://www.getty.edu/art/exhibitions/aphrodite/venus.html.

their spiritual lives. First, they need to remember, and pay close attention to, the instruction they received from the apostles. In addition, they must repent before God of their neglect of these things and return to carefully keeping them, motivated by love for God and neighbor alike. How many of us today, both personally and corporately, need to receive this same admonition? In which area have we become spiritually apathetic in our hearts toward the Lord, and thus need to repent lest He war against us?

Verse 3b: "If you will not wake up, I will come like a thief, and you will not know at what hour I will come against you." Jesus warns the Sardisian congregation that if they don't take this rebuke seriously, He will bring judgment on them at a time when they least expect.

There is a popular Neo-Marcionite view today in major Christian circles that claims that the God of the Old Testament was a God of wrath and justice, but the God of the New Testament is a God of love and grace. Thus, they surmise that Jesus expressing divine anger against sin and delivering real threats of judgment against those who persist therein cannot be. This view can be traced back to Marcion, a second-century heretic, who was originally from Asia Minor and was excommunicated from the church at Rome in AD 144. "Marcion's theological errors (and there were many) came from one main root: he refused to believe that the God of the Old Testament was the same as the Father of the Lord Jesus Christ. Marcion simply could not believe in a God full of wrath and justice."[20] Yet this is contrary to even a cursory read through the Scriptures. For example, a demonstration of Yahweh's redemptive mercy in the Old Testament is the exodus from Egypt (Ex. 3:1–15:21). As well, the pinnacle of God's just wrath against sin is demonstrated in the death of His own dear Son (see Rom. 3:21–26; 5:6–10). Jesus's warning here serves as yet another scriptural example that cuts the legs from underneath this heretical teaching. We must take this warning just as seriously for ourselves and our congregations today.

Verse 4: "Yet you have still a few names in Sardis, people who have not soiled their garments, and they will walk with me in white, for they are worthy." Here and elsewhere in the Revelation, white garments represent the pure righteousness of Christ with which all true believers are clothed.[21]

---

20 Kevin DeYoung, "Marcion and Getting Unhitched from the Old Testament," The Gospel Coalition, May 11, 2018, https://www.thegospelcoalition.org/blogs/kevin-deyoung/marcion-getting-unhitched-old-testament.

21 See notes at 2:17 pertaining to white stones.

The Lord is happy to find at least a few remaining members of the Sardisian congregation who have persisted in faithfulness to Him in their hearts. The obedience imputed to them in their justification is showing up in their lives during both persecution from without and large-scale spiritual apathy from within.

In reflection, are those in our congregations bearing fruit in keeping with repentance, or are they slipping into a kind of apostasy of the heart? For those of us serving as elder-pastors, how are we helping the situation, either in the way of encouraging spiritual fruit to grow or speeding up the internal apostasy of the assembly? May we look to the Lord for much help to do the former and to return to Him in deep contrition over the latter.

Verse 5: "The one who conquers will be clothed thus in white garments, and I will never blot his name out of the book of life. I will confess his name before my Father and before his angels." In chapter 7, those with white garments are the ones who cry out, "Salvation belongs to our God who sits on the throne, and to the Lamb!" (7:10). They have been faithful in going through the great tribulation and "have washed their robes and made them white in the blood of the Lamb" (7:14). In chapter 13, "all who dwell on earth will worship [the beast], everyone whose name has not been written before the foundation of the world in the book of life of the Lamb who was slain" (13:8). Thus, those who conquer do so because they are clothed with the pure righteousness of the Messiah, looking only to Him for the ability to do so. They remain faithful to Him throughout the great tribulation, and they're the ones given to Him through election before the world began. Jesus's last words in this verse seem to echo Matthew 10:32–33 where, in the context of explaining the cost of following Him, He said, "So everyone who acknowledges me before men, I also will acknowledge before my Father who is in heaven, but whoever denies me before men, I also will deny before my Father who is in heaven." These words are given to be a great motivator for the saints at Sardis—they must persevere in faithfully following Jesus throughout their trials because it is ultimately not their efforts, but rather the eternal work of the Triune God in them that will see them overcome. These words ought to likewise motivate us to persevere through the various and sundry troubles we face in our twenty-first-century world, even the aforementioned cultural revolution taking place around us here in the West.[22]

---

22   See notes at 2:22–23.

Verse 6: "He who has an ear, let him hear what the Spirit says to the churches." Jesus repeats the same closing exhortation here as in His other epistles.

To the Congregation at Philadelphia

Turning His attention to the Philadelphian assembly, the Lord now begins His words particularly unto them. John records those words for us in verses 7–13.

Verse 7: "And to the angel of the church in Philadelphia write: 'The words of the holy one, the true one, who has the key of David, who opens and no one will shut, who shuts and no one opens.'" Jesus greets this congregation with a reminder of the way in which He rules the world as the Messianic King, the Son of David. The language of irreversibly opening and shutting is similar to what Jesus taught His disciples concerning His authority imparted to the local church. In Matthew 16:18–19, He declares, "And I tell you, you are Peter, and on this rock I will build my church, and the gates of hell shall not prevail against it. I will give you the keys of the kingdom of heaven, and whatever you bind on earth shall be bound in heaven, and whatever you loose on earth shall be loosed in heaven." Again, in the context of church discipline, the combined true testimony of two to three congregational witnesses before the elders as the ecclesiastical court is binding with His Messianic authority. "Truly, I say to you, whatever you bind on earth shall be bound in heaven, and whatever you loose on earth shall be loosed in heaven. Again I say to you, if two of you agree on earth about anything they ask, it will be done for them by my Father in heaven. For where two or three are gathered in my name, there am I among them" (Matt. 18:18–20). Thus, it is through the faithfulness of His local congregations that King Jesus rules the world.[23] These are remarkably encouraging words to the Philadelphian believers in their hour of suffering. It means their Lord has not ignored their suffering, but instead will rule through them—He will indeed conquer through their conquering in the midst of tribulation! How very counterintuitive are the ways of God's Messiah!

We can likewise be encouraged with this important aspect of the gospel. When we face suffering in faithfully following our Messiah, we need to remember His promise unto us: "Blessed are those who are persecuted for righteousness' sake, for theirs is the kingdom of heaven" (Matt. 5:10)!

---

23 Henry, *Commentary*, Revelation 3:7–13.

Verse 8: "I know your works. Behold, I have set before you an open door, which no one is able to shut. I know that you have but little power, and yet you have kept my word and have not denied my name." This is now the fourth congregation Christ has addressed with the words, "I know your works." To Ephesus and Thyatira, these words came as an encouragement. To Sardis, they came as a rebuke. Now to Philadelphia, they also come as an encouragement.

Christ's will cannot be thwarted by anything or anyone because it comes forth from His immutable nature, and thus the door that He has opened will remain open until the preordained time for its closing. Given the context, this open door seems to be the continuance of their presence and witness in Philadelphia. The reason for this open door is their ongoing faithfulness to Christ their King, despite many trials and tribulations. Truly, the immutable, simple, and impassible will of the triune God, emanating from His very nature, means that He really is the immovable Rock on whom we can fully depend![24] While the rest of life swirls, Yahweh remains ordered; while men are fickle, He remains constant; while all things in the universe develop imperfections over time, with Him "there is no variation or shadow due to change" (James 1:17). This is why we can fully trust Him with our whole lives!

Verse 9: "Behold, I will make those of the synagogue of Satan who say that they are Jews and are not, but lie—behold, I will make them come and bow down before your feet, and they will learn that I have loved you." The tribulation these believers face is the same as those in Smyrna, persecution from apostate Jews. Jesus promises to force them to recognize the truth of His Messiahship and that He has set His unfailing covenant love on these believers, and not on them, as they have presumed. This indictment parallels those given to national Israel in Matthew 21, particularly in His parables of the two sons and of the tenants.

---

24   2LCF, Ch. 2, Par. 1, https://www.arbca.com/1689-chapter2. Here is summarized the Lord's attributes thusly: "The Lord our God is but one only living and true God; whose subsistence is in and of himself, infinite in being and perfection; whose essence cannot be comprehended by any but himself; a most pure spirit, invisible, without body, parts, or passions, who only hath immortality, dwelling in the light which no man can approach unto; who is immutable, immense, eternal, incomprehensible, almighty, every way infinite, most holy, most wise, most free, most absolute; working all things according to the counsel of his own immutable and most righteous will for his own glory …."

Verse 10: "Because you have kept my word about patient endurance, I will keep you from the hour of trial that is coming on the whole world, to try those who dwell on the earth." This "hour of trial" will come very soon from the perspective of these believers since, if they had failed to keep His word, they would have personally participated in this trial. This is an *hour* of trial—it lasts for a relatively short period of time. This trial seems to be a period of persecution soon to come to their region in Asia Minor. In the years leading up to the desolation of Jerusalem in AD 70, persecution of Christians at the hands of the Romans was particularly severe. Because of their patient endurance, this particular congregation would be kept from personally going through these terrible circumstances.

Verse 11: "I am coming soon. Hold fast what you have, so that no one may seize your crown." Jesus explicitly indicates that His coming in judgment is imminent to those in the Philadelphian congregation. For this reason, they must be resolutely faithful with the body of doctrine they've been given so that no one can lead them away from the truth. It should be noted that both this assembly and the one in Smyrna are the only two assemblies to receive commendation without correction. What an incredible privilege to be wisely stewarded!

Verse 12a: "The one who conquers, I will make him a pillar in the temple of my God. Never shall he go out of it." This is a reference to the elect people of God as the true temple in the midst of whom God's presence dwells (see Eph. 2:18–22; 1 Peter 2:4–10). Once these individuals have become pillars in the temple, they will never be removed, which is to say they are permanently a part of the structure (see John 10:22–30; Rom. 8:31–39; Eph. 1:13–14). The assurance and security the believer experiences due to the work of the entire Godhead is something that can only produce humble gratitude.

Verse 12b: "and I will write on him the name of my God, and the name of the city of my God, the new Jerusalem, which comes down from my God out of heaven, and my own new name." For the one who conquers, the Lord promises to write three names on his forehead, indicating ownership—we know it is on the forehead because 7:3 and 14:1 explicitly reveal this. The first name inscribed is that of God the Father. The second is that of the city—that is, the new Jerusalem, which is the Bride of Christ in all her radiant beauty (cf. Heb. 12:22–24). The third name to be engraved is that of the Messiah, God the Son. In the Revelation, there are only two kinds of people: those belonging to the Father and the Son, and those belonging to Satan via his beast. This is true universally. Either a person belongs to the Father and His beloved Son or he belongs to sin and the Prince of Darkness. Either he's united to Christ in His perfect obedience and life or he's united to Adam in his disobedience and the curse of death (Rom. 5:12–21). There is no middle ground!

Verse 13: "He who has an ear, let him hear what the Spirit says to the churches.'" Following the pattern already established, Jesus closes His letter to the Philadelphian congregation with the same exhortation as to the others.

TO THE CONGREGATION AT LAODICEA

The last of the seven churches is now addressed. The apostle records our Savior's words in verses 14–22.

Verse 14: "And to the angel of the church in Laodicea write: 'The words of the Amen, the faithful and true witness, the beginning of God's creation.'" Jesus addresses the leaders of the Laodicean congregation and draws their attention all the way back to chapter 1, verse 5. First, He refers to Himself as the "Amen" to remind them that it is He who defines reality and that all that takes place in history, whether great or small, is the outworking of His eternal will. In a way, this is simply another way of expressing 1:8: "'I am the Alpha and the Omega,' says the Lord God, 'who is and who was and who is to come, the Almighty.'"

Second, Messiah calls Himself the "faithful and true witness," which is an expanded version of the title found in 1:5. This is meant to remind the Laodicean believers that He alone has revealed the Father unto them.

Lastly, He expresses the title presented in 1:5, yet with different words— "the firstborn of the dead" becomes "the beginning of God's creation"; that is, He is the first of God's *new* creation. It is vitally important to notice that this is a reference to 1 Corinthians 15 instead of Genesis 1. Indeed, Acts 13:33 interprets the Father's words to the Son in Psalm 2:7, "You are my Son; today I have begotten you," to be speaking of His resurrection from the dead. He then asks His Father for the nations as His heritage and the ends of the earth as His possession, of which He is currently in the process of receiving in full. Furthermore, Colossians 1:15–20 declares that Christ

Jesus is "the image of the invisible God, the firstborn of all creation," meaning He is the preeminent one over all creation, who has created all things everywhere. Paul then goes on to say that He is "the firstborn from the dead, that in everything he might be preeminent." This preeminence means that He has already reconciled "to himself all things, whether on earth or in heaven, making peace by the blood of his cross" in His death, and He is now in the process of bringing that into reality in His resurrected glory. Thus, this title reminds the Laodicean believers that Jesus's resurrection effected the start of both the resurrection of all true believers, and eventually the resurrection of the entire universe itself, on the Last Day.

Many well-meaning Christians have become confused on this point, thinking the Lord Jesus comes to make *all new things*, specifically on the Last Day. Yet this is the exact opposite of the biblical witness, which declares that He has come to make *all present things new* in like pattern to His own resurrection.[25] While our Lord's new creation is already at work in the world, the physical creation itself will not be finally delivered from its corruption until the day of His majestic bodily return (cf. Rom. 8:18–25).

Verse 15: "I know your works: you are neither cold nor hot. Would that you were either cold or hot!" The Reformation Study Bible explains, "Laodicea's water supply had to be provided from a distant source through pipes. The resulting water was lukewarm and barely drinkable. By contrast, the neighboring town of Hierapolis had medicinal hot springs, and neighboring Colossae was supplied by a cold mountain stream. Christ urges the church to be refreshing (cold) or medicinally healing (hot), rather than like the Laodicean water supply."[26] In other words, Christ deeply desires them to be useful participants in His kingdom rather than apathetic loafers!

Verse 16: "So, because you are lukewarm, and neither hot nor cold, I will spit you out of my mouth." The Messianic King threatens to dispossess this congregation, meaning to say that He will remove His Spirit from among them and they will no longer be counted among His lampstands. As the author to the Hebrews put it, "It is a fearful thing to fall into the hands of the living God" (Heb. 10:31)!

Verse 17: "For you say, I am rich, I have prospered, and I need nothing, not realizing that you are wretched, pitiable, poor, blind, and naked." Here

---

25 See notes at 21:5.
26 Reformation Study Bible notes, Revelation 3:15.

the Lord describes their true spiritual condition, in contrast to how they view themselves, in light of their temporal prosperity. While this evaluation may not apply to every single member, it certainly does to the congregation as a whole. They are described as "wretched," which is to say they are in great distress, having been torn apart by all their enemies: the world, the flesh, and the devil. They are also "pitiable"—they are people to feel sorry for because their condition is so terrible. Likewise they are "poor," meaning they barely have any spiritual life, if at all. As well, Jesus identifies them as "blind," which can be understood to mean that they are completely self-deceived and blinded by the deceitfulness of sin and the trickery of the devil. Lastly, the Laodicean church is described as "naked"—just like Adam their father, they are left in a condition of total shame before God because of their sin.

It is a very sad thing that Word of Faith teachers like Kenneth Copeland and Benny Hinn in America, as well as the late Prophet T. B. Joshua and Prophet Shepherd Bushiri in Africa, promote their "gospel" of health, wealth, and success in their pseudo-congregations. This is especially so since it puts them under this exact rebuke from the Lord Jesus! Messiah's rebuke unto them is actually far worse than it was unto the Laodiceans because they are not believers on the verge of apostatizing, but rather ravenous wolves in sheep's clothing who have come in to destroy the flock (see 2 Peter 2:1–3)!

Verse 18: "I counsel you to buy from me gold refined by fire, so that you may be rich, and white garments so that you may clothe yourself and the shame of your nakedness may not be seen, and salve to anoint your eyes, so that you may see." The Son of Man urges them to come to Him for three things: gold refined by fire, white garments, and anointing salve. This "gold refined by fire" seems to be a reference to Zechariah 13:7–9, where the remnant is refined and tested in the fire, as it were, so that they would call upon Yahweh and be in right relationship with Him once again. With regard to these "white garments," as throughout the rest of the Apocalypse, it is the faithful who are dressed in the pure, spotless righteousness of the Lamb. Last but not least, just as Jesus alone has the power to give physical sight to a beggar through anointing his eyes with mud, so also He alone holds the power to give sight to those born spiritually blind (cf. John 9:1). In the same way the Christ earlier said, "I am the way, and the truth, and the life. No one comes to the Father except through me" (John 14:6), here He also makes it clear that the Laodiceans can only expect to find these blessings in Him and nowhere else! In order to come to Jesus like this, humble repentance is needed. This kind of repentance is only wrought in a person by the powerful regenerating work of the Holy Spirit.

Verse 19: "Those whom I love, I reprove and discipline, so be zealous and repent." The type of love Jesus speaks of here is specifically the covenantal love that a husband shares with his wife. This is the self-sacrificial love that He expressed exclusively toward the church, His bride, when He died in her stead. Only in this context does His love demand that He reprove and discipline His people, which indeed is quite different than complete rejection. If the Laodiceans, as a congregation, wish to receive discipline instead of complete rejection, they must repent of their tremendous apathy and begin actively pursuing Christ in a hurry!

Verse 20: "Behold, I stand at the door and knock. If anyone hears my voice and opens the door, I will come in to him and eat with him, and he with me." The reason Jesus now stands outside, demanding to come back in, is because this congregation has forced Him out with their false worship and apathy. He is ready and willing to forgive them if they should repent and actively pursue Him as a congregation once again. This is how they must let their Messiah back into their midst, which is His rightful place.

Many have used this verse to call individuals to receive Christ as their personal Savior. That view pictures the Savior as though He is merely waiting patiently at the door of a person's heart to be let in, and it is dependent on that individual to decide whether or not to let Him in. Yet this letter is addressed to a *congregation* concerning their *corporate* sins in falling into apostasy—those individuals within who have brought the Laodicean assembly to this state as a whole must repent in a hurry! The issue here does not concern unbelieving sinners being called to receive the Lord for the first time, but rather those who have confessed Him for a time and now are in grave danger of their lives proving their confession to be false. The Son of Man, who walks amongst His lampstands, has thus found this lampstand greatly wanting, and now, after threatening to remove from them their lampstand, He demands to be welcomed back into His own congregation. The question is, have our assemblies become focused on the acquisition of temporal prosperity rather than enjoying in increasing measure the eternal treasure, which is Jesus and His kingdom-rule in every area of life? Have our local churches become apathetic in this way and thus need to fall prostrate in repentance before the Lord for offering up false worship, as was the case at Laodicea?

Verse 21: "The one who conquers, I will grant him to sit with me on my throne, as I also conquered and sat down with my Father on his throne." This sounds quite similar to the Savior's words to the Thyatiran believers. Jesus fully conquered all His enemies in His sufferings and then sat down on David's throne at His Father's right hand in His glory. In the same way, He promises all those who remain faithful to Him to the end of their tribulations that they also are seated with Him on David's throne and rule over all the nations with a rod of iron—that is, with the law and the gospel (see Eph. 2:4–7). This is a present reality for the faithful even as Jesus currently reigns from David's throne, progressively putting all His conquered enemies under His feet (1 Cor. 15:24–26).

Verse 22: "He who has an ear, let him hear what the Spirit says to the churches." As with the other six congregations, Jesus urges those remaining regenerate believers to pay close attention to the voice of His Spirit, both in this epistle and throughout the Revelation.

The Second Vision (4:1–5:14)

At this juncture, John receives a new set of visions, marking the beginning of a lengthy section in the Apocalypse. Chapter 4 presents Yahweh seated on His throne, chapter 5 shows the giving of the scroll and the breaking of its seals by the Lion-Lamb, and chapters 6 through 16 describe the outpouring of the judgments contained therein, along with several important interludes along the way. Thus, the curses come forth historically.

THE LORD ENTHRONED ON HIGH

Chapter 4, verse 1a: "After this I looked, and behold, a door standing open in heaven!" This continues the already established pattern of *hearing* and *seeing*. Here John turns to look, and what he sees is a vision of events in heaven.

Verse 1b: "And the first voice, which I had heard speaking to me like a trumpet, said, 'Come up here, and I will show you what must take place after this.'" This is a reference back to 1:10, meaning this is the same one speaking—we know His identity is the Lord Jesus because when John turned to see who was speaking, he saw "one like the Son of Man," clothed in all His majesty.

Now the second phrase: "I will show you what must take place after this," is a slight rephrasing of that at 1:1, which reads, "the things that must soon take place." Jesus again emphasizes the imminency of the coming events. When the Messiah promises to do a thing, He most certainly will do it! Though others may betray us, we can fully trust in our Lord because He cannot violate His own nature.

Verse 2: "At once I was in the Spirit, and behold, a throne stood in heaven, with one seated on the throne." Just as John was "in the Spirit on the Lord's day" in 1:10, so also he is brought up into the heavenly throne room "in the Spirit." There he sees the Almighty enthroned in all His majesty. It is truly hard to imagine how absolutely incredible this must have been!

Verse 3: "And he who sat there had the appearance of jasper and carnelian, and around the throne was a rainbow that had the appearance of an emerald." This is picking up on the description of Yahweh's glory in Ezekiel 1:26–28. That passage describes His throne having the "appearance like sapphire," His upper torso "gleaming [like] metal, like the appearance of fire enclosed all around'" and His lower torso having "the appearance of fire." In addition, the brightness surrounding Him had "the appearance of the bow that is in the cloud on the day of rain." This symbolic depiction of Yahweh on His throne is meant to communicate how absolutely radiant and pure and powerful His universal rule truly is.

Verse 4: "Around the throne were twenty-four thrones, and seated on the thrones were twenty-four elders, clothed in white garments, with golden crowns on their heads." This is a reference back to Daniel 7:9, where Daniel sees the Ancient of Days clothed in garments white as snow, taking His seat in the midst of thrones. Thus, these ministers serving directly in His presence have the reflection of both His purity and His wisdom. Indeed, their white garments stand in direct contrast to the Laodicean congregants who are in need of them. These elders are twenty-four in number, which are the twelve tribes of Israel together with the twelve apostles. Together they make up the foundation of the entire bride of Christ across redemptive history, just as will be depicted in chapter 21 concerning the new Jerusalem[1]—this aligns with Jesus's words to His disciples: "Truly, I say to you, in the new world [lit. in the regeneration], when the Son of Man will sit on his glorious throne, you who have followed me will also sit on twelve thrones, judging the twelve tribes of Israel" (Matt. 19:28). From John's usage here, this is not a reference to the consummation, but rather to Christ's current reign at His Father's right hand; thus, "in the regeneration" is a much better rendering

---

1   See Wilson, *When the Man Comes Around*, Kindle Location 620.

of Matthew 19:28—this is how the translators of the NKJV have rightly rendered it. This also fits since later in chapter 20, we find particular saints seated on thrones in heaven reigning together with the Lord Jesus. In this way, though every believer is united to Christ and thus reigns with Him in His current session, the twenty-four elders rule with Him in a special way as those who make up the foundation of the church.[2]

Verse 5a: "From the throne came flashes of lightning, and rumblings and peals of thunder." When Ezekiel saw his first vision by the Chebar canal, he recorded, "As I looked, behold, a stormy wind came out of the north, and a great cloud, with brightness around it, and fire flashing forth continually, and in the midst of the fire, as it were gleaming metal" (Ezek. 1:4). As well, in Exodus 19–20, thunder and lightning surrounded the top of the mountain where Yahweh's presence had descended in smoke and fire. As Beale notes, "The actual wording of 4:5a is influenced by the fiery theophanic descriptions of Ezek. 1:13 (cf. LXX), although the similar scene of Exod. 19:16 is evident to a secondary extent."[3] It is for this reason that both Deuteronomy 4:24 and Hebrews 12:28–29 identify Him as a "consuming fire." In Job, lightning is a symbol of God's power, especially in judgment. Likewise, Psalm 18 shows that God uses lightning to rout the enemy's army. This language in verse 5 seems to point in the same direction as these texts—namely, that God is so pure and so "other" that He is anything but safe, especially to those not clothed in the pure and spotless righteousness of Christ! As C. S. Lewis's Mr. Beaver told Lucy concerning Aslan, "Who said anything about safe? 'Course he isn't safe. But he's good. He's the King, I tell you."[4]

Verse 5b: "and before the throne were burning seven torches of fire, which are the seven spirits of God." These are the same seven spirits found in 1:4 where they together represented the Holy Spirit in all His completion and perfection. In connection with this, on the Day of Pentecost, the waiting disciples heard a "mighty rushing wind" that filled the room wherein they stayed, as well as receiving "divided tongues as of fire," which came to rest on them. The result was "they were all filled with the Holy Spirit and began to speak in other tongues [lit. languages] as the Spirit

---

2   See notes at 20:4.
3   See Beale and McDonough, "Revelation," 1100.
4   C. S. Lewis and Pauline Baynes, The Lion, the Witch, and the Wardrobe (#2) (HarperTrophy, 2000), 80.

gave them utterance" (Acts 2:1–4)—this seems to be a specific, localized instance of the same kind that Yahweh displayed at Mount Sinai. Truly, the third person of the Trinity is just as much an all-consuming fire as the Father and the Son, for They share the same being. They are of one nature together, coequal, coeternal, immutable through and through. Once again, the most holy character of our awesome God shines through, demanding nothing less than unceasing praise and adoration!

Verse 6a: "and before the throne there was as it were a sea of glass, like crystal." This sea of glass appears again in 15:2, where the context calls to mind Moses and the defeat of the Egyptian armies at the Red Sea. In addition, 1 Kings 7:23–26 describes a sea that Solomon built in the first temple. Thus, this radiant heavenly sea is a symbol of God's power to conquer all His enemies. Simultaneously, it stands as a heavenly version to Solomon's temple sea—in His presence is true life everlasting (cf. John 4:13–14).[5] Furthermore, this image may be drawn from Ezekiel 1:22, where Ezekiel sees an expanse of shimmering crystal over the heads of the living creatures. According to his vision, this expanse serves to separate Yahweh on His throne from the heavenly creatures, indicating His immense holiness. Therefore, we may say the same continues to be true here in John's vision of the heavenly throne room. What an amazing symbol showing forth the perfect unity of character and purpose between the Father and His Anointed King!

Verses 6b–7: "And around the throne, on each side of the throne, are four living creatures, full of eyes in front and behind: the first living creature like a lion, the second living creature like an ox, the third living creature with the face of a man, and the fourth living creature like an eagle in flight." These are clearly the four living creatures of Ezekiel chapter 1 as they're described here with similar likeness in their faces (see Ezek. 1:10).[6] These heavenly ministers are guardians of God's throne.

Verse 8a: "And the four living creatures, each of them with six wings, are full of eyes all around and within." In Ezekiel 1:6, they have four wings each, but in Isaiah 6:2, the heavenly guardians have six. It appears that this vision presents a combination thereof. Ezekiel 1:18 records that the four living creatures were stationed beside the four wheels of God's heavenly

---

5   See Reformation Study Bible notes, Revelation 4:6.
6   See Beale and McDonough, "Revelation," 1100.

chariot, each rim being "full of eyes all around." Here, though, there's no mention of a heavenly chariot carrying Yahweh's throne, yet the eyes are still present. This shows that these guardians of God's throne have such an ability as cannot be startled or taken off guard. It should be noted that "the various portraits of the living creatures in Revelation and within the Old Testament (cf. 1 Kings 6:24–28; 2 Chron. 3:13; Ezek. 1:6) argue against a strictly literal understanding of these beings"[7]—they represent actual heavenly creatures, but as given with figurative elements.

Verse 8b: "and day and night they never cease to say, 'Holy, holy, holy, is the Lord God Almighty, who was and is and is to come!'" These heavenly ministers are worshiping Yahweh incessantly with both the words of Isaiah (Isa. 6:3)[8] and the Lord's own description of Himself in 1:8—they worship God for who He truly is. Not only do these four living creatures have the immense privilege of guarding His very throne, but they also are closer to Him in proximity than nearly any other being! For this reason, they can't help but respond in relentless praise for who their Creator is!

Believers today find themselves in the glorious presence of Yahweh day by day due to their union with Jesus, who is the true temple. Does this reality lead us to respond in like kind to these heavenly creatures? Do we not have more reason than they to respond in ceaseless praise with our whole lives since "we are to judge angels" (1 Cor. 6:3) as those redeemed by the Lamb?

Verses 9–10a: "And whenever the living creatures give glory and honor and thanks to him who is seated on the throne, who lives forever and ever, the twenty-four elders fall down before him who is seated on the throne and worship him who lives forever and ever." Pictured here is all of heaven in constant response to one another's worship with their own worship unto the Lord God in a never-ending cycle of praise and magnification.

Verse 10b: "They cast their crowns before the throne." Even the very rewards for their faithfulness to the Lord are immediately cast down at His feet in worship! Truly the apostle was right when he wrote, "For from him and through him and to him are all things. To him be glory forever. Amen" (Rom. 11:36)! It is a temptation for us to think of receiving rewards as the motivation for love and good deeds, as if we are meant to permanently keep

---

7   See Beale and McDonough, "Revelation," 1100.
8   See Beale and McDonough, "Revelation," 1100.

them. However, in reality our motivation ought to be a desire to magnify the name of Jesus out of love for Him since even our rewards will end up serving that purpose for all eternity!

Verses 10c–11: "saying, 'Worthy are you, our Lord and God, to receive glory and honor and power, for you created all things, and by your will they existed and were created.'" The focus of the twenty-four elders' worship is a response to Yahweh's creative and providential acts in history (cf. Ps. 33). The Baptist Catechism explains, "Q. 13. What is the work of creation? A. The work of creation is God making all things out of nothing, by the Word of His power, in the space of six days, and all very good. . . . Q. 15. What are God's works of providence? A. God's works of providence are His most holy, wise, and powerful preserving and governing all His creatures, and all their actions."[9] These are the things for which the elders fall down in worship before the Lord of all. We must take their lead in likewise prostrating ourselves in heartfelt adoration for who Yahweh is and for the great and mighty deeds He's done in history.

THE UNOPENED SCROLL

Chapter 5, verse 1: "Then I saw in the right hand of him who was seated on the throne a scroll written within and on the back, sealed with seven seals." At this point, John is introduced to the next phase of the heavenly vision. God Almighty, being seated on His throne, and thus ruling over all things in His universe, holds the decree of the judgments that are about to come. He holds it in His right hand, the same hand with which He holds His royal scepter—that is, the hand of authority and power to do as He wills. Consequently, this is why Jesus is seated at the Father's *right hand*, not His left.

The scroll in Yahweh's hand is very unusual since it's written on both sides. Traditionally scrolls were only written on the inside to protect what was written when it was rolled up. The decree's protection comes from the right hand of the one who authored it. It seems this scroll constitutes a covenant lawsuit, or even a bill of divorce as Gentry posits, since it contains all manner of judgments against adulterous, apostate Israel.[10] The imagery

---

9 *The Baptist Catechism (1677)*, Q. 13 and 15, http://baptiststudiesonline.com/wp-content/uploads/2007/02/keachs-catechism-of-1677.pdf.

10 See Kenneth Gentry, "Revelation's Scroll: God's Divorce Decree," *Postmillennial Worldview*, December 27, 2013, https://postmillennialworldview.com/2013/12/27/

here of the scroll written on both sides is the same as what we find in Ezekiel 2:8–3:3. Not only this, but John later eats a miniature version of the scroll prior to prophesying, just as Ezekiel did (10:8–11).[11]

The seven seals are representative of God's perfect grace keeping the decree from being enacted, and thus coming to pass, until the appointed time. Yahweh is in perfect control of all things, whether great or small, gigantic or minute, such that not even a hair falls from a person's scalp apart from its divine appointment in keeping with His good and eternal decree. This ought to be a great comfort to us when things go "pear shaped" in our lives, even to the extent of a nation's government controlling its people's movements from one district to another without government-approved documents. Indeed, no matter how bad a situation might get from our perspective, none of it has happened apart from its divine appointment, and all of it has a purpose within the good counsel of our Sovereign's will. For this we can trust Him through it all.

Verses 2–3: "And I saw a mighty angel proclaiming with a loud voice, 'Who is worthy to open the scroll and break its seals?' And no one in heaven or on earth or under the earth was able to open the scroll or to look into it." This mighty heavenly messenger is declaring his message in the same way that the Son of Man did back in 1:10 and 4:1. The angel searches for a qualified person "to open the scroll and break its seals" so that the judgments will come to pass, but he finds none in all creation who is worthy or has such ability.

Verse 4: "and I began to weep loudly because no one was found worthy to open the scroll or to look into it." John's immediate response to the lack of a worthy person is deep sadness and despair. Why? Because he loves his Lord deeply and he knows that His judgments are always just and true. If the scroll cannot be opened, then two things would be true. Firstly, God's decree would fail to come to pass, and thus He would fail to be glorified through the execution thereof. Secondly, His counsel would fail, and thus His faithfulness would be in serious question.

How many of us, as twenty-first-century Christians, would have responded the same way if we were in John's place? It is a genuine concern that much of the evangelical community in the West is so man-centered

---

revelations-scroll-gods-divorce-decree.
11   See Beale and McDonough, "Revelation," 1101.

and shortsighted that all we can think about is wanting "nice" things for others when it comes to God's work in their lives. Yet the psalmist had no difficulty in praying imprecatory prayers, not out of hatred for his neighbors, but rather out of a deep love for Yahweh and a deep desire to see His justice and righteousness established in the earth. How many of us are genuinely anguished in the depths of our hearts when wickedness prevails and Yahweh seems to have forgotten His promise to establish justice and righteousness in the earth through His Messianic King? Is Psalm 13 our prayer too? Will we weep with John, longing for God's judgments to come to pass, not just His mercies? This is a challenge for us that we all must take seriously if we claim to love the Lord.

THE LION WHO IS THE LAMB

Verse 5: "And one of the elders said to me, 'Weep no more; behold, the Lion of the tribe of Judah, the Root of David, has conquered, so that he can open the scroll and its seven seals.'" One of the elders encourages John to stop weeping because of who the Messiah is. He tells him to "behold, the Lion of the tribe of Judah"—that is, to look intently at Him. In Hosea 5:14, Yahweh describes Himself as a lion in the context of bringing severe judgment on both Ephraim (the northern kingdom) and Judah (the southern kingdom) for their rebellion against Him. This language is also found in Jacob's blessing to Judah: "Judah is a lion's cub; from the prey, my son, you have gone up. He stooped down; he crouched as a lion and as a lioness; who dares rouse him?" (Gen. 49:9).[12] Judah is a ferocious warrior with whom no one should contend! Here in verse 5, this language is applied to the Messianic King in the context of bringing righteous judgment—this is the same message found in Psalm 2, Psalm 110, and 1 Corinthians 15:24–28 concerning God's Anointed One. This title also identifies Him as being a world-conquering King from the tribe of Judah: "The scepter shall not depart from Judah, nor the ruler's staff from between his feet, until tribute comes to him [Shiloh]; and to him shall be the obedience of the peoples" (Gen. 49:10). It should be noted that Shiloh means "Rest Giver," which has the same sense as the title "Prince of Peace" revealed in Isaiah 9:6.[13]

The elder also describes the Messiah as the "Root of David." This is a

---

12 See Beale and McDonough, "Revelation," 1101.
13 See R. Veldman, "The Meaning of 'Shiloh' in Genesis 49:10," The Standard Bearer, February 1, 1959, https://sb.rfpa.org/the-meaning-of-shiloh-in-genesis-4910/.

clear reference to Jesus's Messiahship since He is the Son of David, the one who sits on David's throne forever (2 Sam. 7:12; Ps. 110:1; Acts 2:32–36). It is also a reference to Isaiah 11, where He is described as a "shoot from the stump of Jesse" (Isa. 11:1) and the "root of Jesse, who shall stand as a signal for the peoples—of him shall the nations inquire, and his resting place shall be glorious" (Isa. 11:10). Later on in the same book, we learn that this "Root of Jesse" is Yahweh's servant who "will bring forth justice to the nations" (Isa. 42:1). Thus, it is through progressively conquering all His enemies, most notably in the way of subduing their rebellious hearts, that the Messianic King is establishing justice and shalom to the ends of the earth, and all the nations are streaming up to Mount Zion (see Isa. 2:1–5, esp. v. 3).

The elder continues to explain that this Messiah has already, in a sense, conquered all His enemies. He has accomplished this in His death on the cross. Colossians 2:15 speaks to the fulfillment of Genesis 3:15 when it says, "He disarmed the rulers and authorities and put them to open shame, by triumphing over them in [the cross]." This same sentiment is expressed in Jesus's words to the Pharisees when they accused Him of casting out demons by Satan's power: "But if it is by the Spirit of God that I cast out demons, then the kingdom of God has come upon you. Or how can someone enter a strong man's house and plunder his goods, unless he first binds the strong man? Then indeed he may plunder his house" (Matt. 12:28–29). The complete accomplishment of evil's cosmic defeat in Messiah's death was vindicated in His resurrection from the dead! Now, in His resurrected glory at His Father's right hand, He is gradually, but surely, bringing into historic reality all that He successfully accomplished. This is the reason why He alone is both worthy and able to break the seven seals of the scroll and bring to pass the judgments contained therein.

Oh, that this comprehensive biblical vision of Jesus's Messiahship would permeate our hearts and minds! Oh, that our understanding of His kingdom-rule would thus be radically realigned to who He truly is! Oh, that Jesus's teaching to "seek first the kingdom of God and his righteousness" (Matt. 6:33), as well as to pray, "Your kingdom come, your will be done, on earth as it is in heaven" (Matt. 6:10), would dramatically change the way we live in faithfully following Him on His narrow road!

Verse 6a: "And between the throne and the four living creatures and among the elders I saw a Lamb standing, as though it had been slain." The hearing/seeing pattern established back in chapter 1 here continues.

Verse 5 describes what John *heard* from the elder, but now he turns to *look* at Him who was described. In the place of a victorious Lion he sees "a Lamb standing, as though it had been slain." In his Gospel account, John describes Jesus as "the Lamb of God, who takes away the sin of the world!" (John 1:29). This picks up on the Old Testament expectation of one to come who would completely fulfill the role that the sacrificial system played under the old covenant, in which only through an animal sacrifice in the temple, being performed by a purified high priest, could Israel's sins be symbolically atoned for and God's wrath against it turned away. Isaiah 52:13ff explains that the victorious Servant, the Root of Jesse, would be this pure and spotless Lamb who would deal with His people's iniquities once and for all through His own slaughter.[14] The heavenly vision presents unto John this same message: the way in which the Messiah conquered all evil in the world, even death itself, was through His atoning death in the place of sinners—it was a real atonement for real sinners.

But the Lamb *stands*, "as though it had been slain" because, even though He died, behold He is alive "forevermore" (1:18).[15] Here, the direct and intimate connection between the Messiah's humiliation and exaltation is shown forth—everything He fully accomplished in His death must surely come to pass in His resurrection! This same connection is emphasized in Psalm 110. While verse 1 gives us the theme of the Messiah's total victory over all His enemies, a theme that undergirds the entire psalm, the chiastic structure leads us to the foundation of that victory in verse 4—namely, His high priestly work. We can also see this in Philippians 2:5–11, where the obedience merited for all the nations in Jesus's humiliation temporally becomes theirs in His exaltation.

Often this intrinsic, organic bond is severed in the hearts and minds of believers through an emphasis on Christ's death to the near exclusion of His resurrection. This has resulted in turning Jesus into half a high priest—we force Jesus into the unorthodox position of giving Himself as a propitiatory sacrifice in the place of one group of people, but then interceding for a subset of that group rather than the whole of it. This makes Him half a high priest to all those for whom He doesn't intercede. This severance also has resulted in extracting personal salvation from sin from the larger historical drama of how God is progressively rescuing all

---

14   See Beale and McDonough, "Revelation," 1101.
15   See Reformation Study Bible notes, Revelation 5:6.

aspects of His creation from the effects of the fall, destroying all His enemies, and establishing His just and righteous rule, and thus peace, to the ends of the earth. The gospel has become good news of personal, individual salvation almost entirely to the exclusion of Yahweh's rule in the world through His Messianic King—this despite Jesus's main message while on earth being the good news of *His kingdom*! For these things, we as the evangelical church in the West need to fall on our faces before a holy God in humble repentance. We must return to a much more biblical, historic, and holistic understanding of the gospel, which stands at the center of our faith and practice!

Verse 6: "with seven horns and with seven eyes, which are the seven spirits of God sent out into all the earth." The seven horns symbolize the totality and perfection of the Messiah's authority and dominion, both in heaven and on earth. We have evidence of this kind of Messianic imagery in the Psalter. For example, in the context of depicting David's future Son, Psalm 132 describes Him as "a horn" who will clothe His enemies with shame (cf. Ps. 132:17–18). The psalmist also calls all creation to praise Yahweh because "he has raised up *a horn* for his people" (Ps. 148:14, author's emphasis), the horn being His Anointed King who was first introduced in the Psalter back in Psalm 2. Building on this, directly following His resurrection, Jesus told His disciples, "All authority in heaven and on earth has been given to me" (Matt. 28:18). This universal authority is a vital part of His exaltation, in His resurrection, ascension, current session, and future judgment on the Last Day.

The seven eyes are interpreted for us as "the seven spirits of God sent out into all the earth." These are the same seven spirits that we already met in 1:4 and 4:5, which symbolically is the Holy Spirit.[16] This is a direct reference to Zechariah 3:9, where Yahweh promises to "remove the iniquity of this land in a single day."[17] The text specifically tells us *where* the Spirit is working: in "all the earth." The means by which the Messianic King exercises His authority on earth is through the agency of His Holy Spirit, who was sent as "another Helper . . . [to] teach you all things and bring to your remembrance all that [He has] said to you," "[to] convict the world concerning sin and righteousness and judgment," and "[to] guide you into all the truth," which comes from Jesus, who has all authority (John 14:16,

---

16 See notes at 1:4.
17 See Beale and McDonough, "Revelation," 1102.

26; 16:8, 13). Thus, as the Spirit of Christ works in and through the lives of His elect, Jesus is extending His dominion of justice, righteousness, and peace to the ends of the earth—He is actually taking possession of His promised inheritance as He rules from His Father's right hand since it has already been given to Him (see Ps. 2:7–9, esp. v. 8)! In this way, He is progressively bringing to pass in His exaltation all that He fully accomplished in His humiliation—namely, the complete defeat of all evil in every corner of the universe! Truly, the effects of Genesis 3:15 coming true are playing out in HD right before our eyes!

Verse 7: "And he went and took the scroll from the right hand of him who was seated on the throne." The Lord Jesus does what He alone can do—He takes the scroll from His Father's hand of authority and governance to break the seals. Thus, He progressively releases the judgments contained therein.

Verse 8: "And when he had taken the scroll, the four living creatures and the twenty-four elders fell down before the Lamb, each holding a harp, and golden bowls full of incense, which are the prayers of the saints." The immediate response of the four heavenly court guardians, together with the twenty-four representatives of Christ's bride throughout the ages, is worship. The Messiah should not only be worshipped for His grace in rescuing sinners from their rebellious hearts and from God's wrath against them, but also for His holy justice toward those who refuse to submit to Him. This worship is in the form of music, denoted by the harps they play.

We are also told that the incense symbolizes "the prayers of the saints" and that the bowls carrying them are full to the brim. The picture here is that of the twenty-four elders offering up all the prayers of the saints on their behalf as an act of worship. These prayers all comport with John 14:13–14. This means they are all prayers that God is glorified to answer in His Son, which means they all comport with Scripture's teaching as a whole. This likewise means they all are asked in Jesus's name, not as a magic formula with the expectation of receiving an automatic "yes" from God, but rather as a humble, glad submission to His Messiahship and all that office means. Indeed, these prayers are a sweet-smelling savor to the Lord! "This tells us how God receives the prayers of the saints. It tells us what He thinks about our prayers—they are a sweet-smelling odor to Him."[18]

---

18 Wilson, *When the Man Comes Around*, Kindle Location 738.

From the example of these saints, and from the way in which they pray, we are given a blueprint for how to appropriately approach our thrice-holy God. In reflection, do we come to the throne of Almighty God with flippancy, telling Him what we want as if He is somehow obligated to do whatever we say, especially if we tack on the end, "in Jesus's name"? Conversely, do we come before Him with humility, reverence, and thankfulness, knowing that it is only because of the spotless righteousness of Christ that we safely stand in His presence, and then, in light of this, make our requests known to God? This is a challenge for each of us as we grow in personal piety.

Verses 9–10: "And they sang a new song, saying, 'Worthy are you to take the scroll and to open its seals, for you were slain, and by your blood you ransomed people for God from every tribe and language and people and nation, and you have made them a kingdom and priests to our God, and they shall reign on the earth.'" The song is new because this is the first time the Son of Man has opened this particular scroll. The song is crafted to exalt Him for His worthiness to open it. The contents of the melody explain the reason why He is worthy. He was slaughtered as the final and greatest Lamb of the sacrificial system—truly, all former sacrifices were but a shadow pointing forward to their reality in Christ Himself! Through His sacrificial death on the cross, He bought a particular group out of slavery to sin—the ransom price being His own blood. Those He redeemed are actually, permanently set free from their personal slavery to sin. This group of ransomed sinners makes up an absolutely gigantic number since they are "from every tribe and language and people and nation." He redeemed the world (see John 3:16–17)—that is, "all the families of the earth" (Gen. 12:3), who are the spiritual offspring of Abraham as numerous "as the stars of heaven and as the sand that is on the seashore" (Gen. 22:17), who are "the nations . . . , the ends of the earth" given to Yahweh's Anointed King to be His inheritance and treasured possession (Ps. 2:8). Those Jesus ransomed have been made to be "a kingdom and priests to our God." This is almost the exact same wording as found in 1:6. This sentiment is expressed when Peter takes Yahweh's words directed toward the physical seed of Abraham at Mount Sinai (see Ex. 19:5–6) and reapplies them to his spiritual seed, the true Israel of God (1 Peter 2:9). Those He ransomed will "reign on the earth" with Him. The Thyatiran congregation has already been promised that as they conquer through their trials, they are ruling with their Lord.

Ephesians 2:6 teaches that when sinners are regenerated by the supernatural working of the Holy Spirit, God has "raised us up with him and seated us with him in the heavenly places in Christ Jesus"—union with Christ demands that whatever is true of Jesus is also covenantally true of all those in Him. And 2 Corinthians 2:14–17 explains that the regenerate are reigning with their King on earth—through proclaiming the good news of His kingdom-rule over all the nations.

If we have been united to the Lord Jesus in His death and resurrection through receiving the new birth, and we are persevering in faithfully following Him no matter the cost involved, then we are, in fact, ruling and reigning with Him in the here and now! This is a tremendous privilege for us as His saints for which we must be truly grateful. Not only that, but it's also an incredible responsibility to be well stewarded "with reverence and awe," since our spiritual warfare is meant to be worship unto God (cf. Heb. 12:28–29)!

Verse 11: "Then I looked, and I heard around the throne and the living creatures and the elders the voice of many angels, numbering myriads of myriads and thousands of thousands." The idea is that every messenger in heaven, too many to count, surrounds those already around the throne to add in their worship. This harkens back to Hebrews 12:22, which describes that when the gathered saints, being the heavenly Jerusalem, worship the Lord together, they join their praise of the Almighty with that of those creatures in heaven, "innumerable angels in festal gathering." That is precisely what is taking place in this vision given unto John the apostle.

Verse 12: "saying with a loud voice, 'Worthy is the Lamb who was slain, to receive power and wealth and wisdom and might and honor and glory and blessing!'" Everything that is truly valuable in the universe rightfully belongs to Him since it all originates in Him! Do we actually believe this to be true? Do we actually believe that Jesus has crown rights, not just over things spiritual, but also over things physical? Is it our conviction that, although this world is stained by sin and the effects of the fall, it still is good and Psalm 24:1–2 remains true and ought to affect how we live—"The earth is Lord's and the fullness thereof, the world and those who dwell therein"? Ought not this conviction transform our daily lives by the Puritan vision that *all* of life is meant to be worship unto God, that we may join both our voices *and* our lives to the praises of that myriad of myriad of angels in heaven? Is this not what is reflected in the very next verse—verse 13?

Verse 13a: "And I heard every creature in heaven and on earth and under the earth and in the sea, and all that is in them." Now every other creature in heaven and in all of creation joins the throng in worshipping the Lamb. Unlike with the myriad of angels, whom John a moment earlier *saw* join the host, with these he *hears* them joining in. Truly, all of creation is now in the throes of white-hot worship to the Lamb for His tremendous worth!

Verse 13b: "saying, 'To him who sits on the throne and to the Lamb be blessing and honor and glory and might forever and ever!'" This indeed is the truth the psalmist brings to us when he says, "The heavens declare the glory of God, and the sky above proclaims his handiwork" (Ps. 19:1ff). The fact that all creation is constantly declaring the glory and greatness of Yahweh, and we so often fail to do so, is surely a strong indictment against our wickedness. It calls us to repent and join this innumerable throng in worshipping the Lamb for all He's worth. As the Westminster Shorter Catechism puts it, "Q. What is the chief end of man? A. Man's chief end is to glorify God and enjoy Him forever (1 Cor. 10:31; Ps. 73:25–26)."[19] The call to join this host is not something other than our intended purpose—*it is* the reason for which we were created!

Verse 14: "And the four living creatures said, 'Amen!' and the elders fell down and worshiped." The four guardians nearest to Yahweh's throne affirm the truthfulness of their worship in relation to the worthiness of the one being worshipped. The twenty-four representatives of the church militant continue to lead the massive host in heaven and on earth in worshipping the Lamb for His worthiness to break the seals of the scroll and bring out the judgments decreed therein. Their celebratory declaration, "Amen!" denotes their absolute confidence in the surety of these judgments coming to pass.

---

19   *Baptist Catechism*, Q. 2; Westminster Shorter Catechism, Q. 1.

The Third Vision (6:1–8:5)

THE FIRST SEAL

Chapter 6: verse 1, "Now I watched when the Lamb opened one of the seven seals, and I heard one of the four living creatures say with a voice like thunder, 'Come!'" Again, the interplay between what John sees versus what he *hears* is shown forth at this point. What he *sees* is the Lamb breaking the first of the seven seals. What he *hears* is a powerful, authoritative command from the first living creature for the first judgment to come to pass—we learned in 4:7 that this living creature looks like a lion.

Verse 2: "And I looked, and behold, a white horse! And its rider had a bow, and a crown was given to him, and he came out conquering, and to conquer." This image first appears in Zechariah 1:8[1] as one of the four heavenly patrol officers who patrolled the earth announcing there was peace (see Zech. 1:11).[2] It soon after appears in Zechariah 6:3. Here, the image symbolizes how Jesus Christ the Righteous is conquering the whole world. While He certainly is doing this through the spread of His gospel, the focus seems to be on the other way in which He does so, which is through providentially orchestrating the utter demise of His enemies. Hendriksen points out that the same language is utilized in both chapters 5 and 6. At 5:5, Messiah is said to be "the Lion of the tribe of Judah, the Root of David, [who] has conquered." Now here at 6:2, this Rider comes out "conquering, and to conquer." Given that one vision follows the other, it would be

---

1 See Reformation Study Bible notes, Revelation 6:1–8:1.
2 See Beale and McDonough, "Revelation," 1103.

quite strange indeed for the subject to suddenly change.[3] Furthermore, in chapter 19, we again see Jesus coming out riding on a white horse. In that passage, He is said to be defeating all His enemies as He rules them with a rod of iron, an image lifted directly out of Psalm 2 (see Rev. 19:11, 15). Thus, the "conquering" here is Christ's utter defeat of unrepentant enemies, just as will be seen in 19:17–21. The following three horses and their riders must be understood in light of this, for they are meant to be taken together.

Often we can have a view of Jesus as being presently distant and uninvolved—now that He is resurrected and ascended, He's just "hanging out" at His Father's right hand until He comes again at the end of history. Such a view is contrary to reality. In the same way that Jesus is far more committed to our personal sanctification than we are, He is far more devoted to the success of His gospel and His kingdom in the earth than we could ever be! He is unstoppably building His church over the centuries in such a way that each and every barrier the devil erects as a "no-go zone" will most certainly be torn down by the power of His gospel (cf. Matt. 16:18). The apostle Paul taught the Corinthian believers, "For the weapons of our warfare are not of the flesh but have divine power to destroy strongholds. We destroy arguments and every lofty opinion raised against the knowledge of God, and take every thought captive to obey Christ, being ready to punish every disobedience, when your obedience is complete" (2 Cor. 10:4–6). He also taught the saints at Rome, "I want you to be wise as to what is good and innocent as to what is evil. The God of peace will soon crush Satan under your feet" (Rom. 16:19–20). Many groups today have this attitude in promoting their worldview: "Total victory! No compromise!" This most notably is true of the Neo-Marxists who have slowly hijacked academies in the West ever since the Cold War and now flood public discourse on every level with their deeply divisive, revolutionary, and totalitarian ideas of equity, critical theory, and intersectionality. Yet according to Scripture, such unbelieving worldviews will only end in ruin, while the gospel-shaped worldview of the one true and living King will in fact prevail and triumph! Since we have the truth, shouldn't we as followers of the Lord Jesus be the ones living with a joyful, hope-filled, sanctified attitude of "Total victory! No compromise!"?

---

3 See Hendriksen, *More Than Conquerors*, 94.

THE SECOND SEAL

Verse 3: "When he opened the second seal, I heard the second living creature say, 'Come!'" Upon seeing the Messiah break the second seal, John hears the second living creature call out for the second judgment to come—this is the living creature with the appearance of an ox (4:7).

Verse 4: "And out came another horse, bright red. Its rider was permitted to take peace from the earth, so that people should slay one another, and he was given a great sword." This image also is derived from Zechariah 1:8,[4] and later Zechariah 6:1–3,[5] but reapplied here in the context of judgment. This horse and its rider represent war. Messiah taught that His disciples should expect that He did "not come to bring peace, but a sword.... And a person's enemies will be those of his own household" (Matt. 10:34, 36). Those who hate Him will hate those loyal to Him and will even fight with each other as they openly rebel against Him. The open rejection of God's Anointed One is, after all, the entire reason for Jerusalem's fall soon to take place, which comports with His prediction that "nation will rise against nation, and kingdom against kingdom" (Matt. 24:7; Luke 21:10).

THE THIRD SEAL

Verse 5a: "When he opened the third seal, I heard the third living creature say, 'Come!'" At this point it's obvious that a pattern has been formed. When John sees the Lord Jesus breaking the third seal, he immediately hears the third living creature loudly summoning forth the third judgment—the one doing this is the creature with the face like a man (4:7).

Verses 5b–6: "And I looked, and behold, a black horse! And its rider had a pair of scales in his hand. And I heard what seemed to be a voice in the midst of the four living creatures, saying, 'A [khoinix] of wheat for a denarius, and three [khoinikes] of barley for a denarius, and do not harm the oil and wine!'" Though a black horse fails to appear in Zechariah 1:8 as in 6:2 and 6: it is clear from the established pattern that this symbol is a takeoff on those given in that passage.[6] First, a particular first-century measurement is mentioned. A *khoinix* was a "dry measure equal to

---

4   See Reformation Study Bible notes, Revelation 6:1–8:1.
5   See Beale and McDonough, "Revelation," 1103.
6   See Reformation Study Bible notes, Revelation 6:1–8:1.

about a quart,"⁷ which is marginally more than one liter in metric units. Next, a certain price is given according to the local currency. A *deinariou* "was a day's wage for labor"⁸ in the Greco-Roman world. This means that, under this judgment, supply and demand is so bad that people are forced to spend an entire day's wage on an inconsequential amount of grain. This economic disaster is further underscored by the concluding words of verse 6—even the most common, everyday necessities like oil and wine need to be rationed! This is a situation of severe famine in the land, comporting with Jesus's prophecy that "there will be famines and earthquakes in various places" (Matt. 24:7; see Luke 21:11).

THE FOURTH SEAL

Verse 7: "When he opened the fourth seal, I heard the voice of the fourth living creature say, 'Come!'" Once again, as John looks upon the Lamb breaking the fourth seal, he hears the booming voice of the fourth living creature beckoning this judgment to come forth. We learned in 4:7 that this particular creature has the appearance of an eagle in flight.

Verse 8, "And I looked, and behold, a pale horse! And its rider's name was Death, and Hades followed him. And they were given authority over a fourth of the earth, to kill with sword and with famine and with pestilence and by wild beasts of the earth." In Zechariah 1:8 and 6:3, the fourth horse is sorrel, (a light chestnut hue) yet here the horse has become pale. It seems the reason for this shift in shade is due to its rider being Death, followed closely by the current destination of the damned, Hades. Wherever Death and Hades ride throughout the land—that is, the land of Israel—they only bring death to the unrepentant as a form of judgment. This agrees with Jesus's prophecy that those who fail to flee to the mountains when Jerusalem is surrounded by armies—but instead delay—will be slaughtered in the greatest tribulation history has ever known (see Matt. 24:15–21; Luke 21:20–24). This time of tribulation is called "great" (Rev. 7:14), not because it was the most gruesome of all trials known to man, but rather because it meant the complete cessation of Israel as a nation in covenant with Yahweh, and thus the entire old covenant as an economy came to a jolting and permanent halt (cf. Heb. 8:13). In addition, comporting with

---

7   See ESV notes, Revelation 6:5.

8   See ESV notes, Revelation 6:5.

Jesus's words in Matthew 24:22, the amount of people who die under this judgment is limited, denoted here by "a fourth of the earth." This ought to be taken symbolically of the limitation at this point in the judgments against apostate Israel. The reason Jesus gives in the Olivet Discourse for the days of this judgment being cut short is for the sake of the elect.

For many today, the very idea of a God filled with holy fury against the ungodly, such that He actually takes vengeance out on them, is nothing short of shocking. Indeed, for many evangelicals, it is acceptable that Jesus would wield His just sword against the wicked on the Last Day, but that He would actually see fit to do so within human history at His appointed time is simply unthinkable! Yet these preparatory judgments leading up to Jerusalem's utter ruin teach us that the Messiah is under no obligation to be kind or lenient with anyone, either prior to or following the final judgment. If the Lord of lords were to bring the United States or Canada to their knees for the bloodguiltiness caused by the unbridled and celebrated genocide of our unborn neighbors, and do so as a means of continuing to put His enemies under His feet, then He would be completely just to do so. Truly, it is right for us to grieve over the wickedness of the land and boldly call for nationwide sackcloth, ashes, and repentance. At the same time, the Messiah ought to be worshipped for the exercise of His holy and just wrath upon His enemies for two reasons. First, it means the demonstration of His infinite perfections, and second, it means the expansion of His dominion in the earth. Are we as His people happily willing to do both?

The Fifth Seal

Verse 9: "When he opened the fifth seal, I saw under the altar the souls of those who had been slain for the word of God and for the witness they had borne." These are the saints who had been martyred for their testimony and faithfulness to Christ, just as Jesus predicted they would be in His sermon on the Mount of Olives (Matt. 24:9; Luke 21:12–19). The souls of these saints are now under the altar in heaven. Indeed, through their deaths, they faithfully bear witness to their Lord and Savior, as the Greek term *marturian* indicates.

Verse 10: "They cried out with a loud voice, 'O Sovereign Lord, holy and true, how long before you will judge and avenge our blood on those who dwell on the earth?'" Their expectation is that the Lord would bring judgment on the earth in order to avenge their deaths as martyrs for Him. They know their deaths were unjust, and therefore they look to their holy God to bring justice on the wicked quickly.

Verse 11: "Then they were each given a white robe and told to rest a little longer, until the number of their fellow servants and their brothers should be complete, who were to be killed as they themselves had been." Because they are true and faithful saints, they are given white robes to show the pure and spotless obedience of the Messiah that already defines them. They are "told to rest a little longer" because the avenging of their martyrdom is about to happen. This is a repetition of the opening words of the Revelation—"to show His servants the things that *must soon take place*." and "blessed are those who hear, and who keep what is written in it, for *the time is near*" (1:1, 3; author's emphasis). In addition, the one speaking gives them an event indicator in conjunction with this time indicator. They are told that when the number of those saints appointed to martyrdom, as per Jesus's prophecy (Matt. 24:9; Luke 21:12–19), reaches its full measure, then their blood will be vindicated. Furthermore, 17:6 indicates that it is Jerusalem, riding in dependency on Rome, who is the culprit in view here.[9] The words from the angel are a great comfort to these saints in heaven since they must wait only a little longer for this to take place.

Again, we gladly affirm that at the great white throne, Jesus will right every wrong and vindicate those who have suffered for righteousness' sake in this life. However, the notion that He is actively avenging the sufferings of His people within human history, even as we speak, is far too uncomfortable for many to accept. Yet this is precisely what these martyred saints were promised, and it came to pass exactly on time in the destruction of the temple and all it represented. Our conception of Jesus the Messiah needs to be radically reformed back to what Holy Writ actually presents to us in all its fullness. If this fails to happen, we will find ourselves worshipping a "Jesus" of our own liking, and thus become guilty of breaking the second commandment. Are we willing, with Spirit-created heartfelt willingness, to imitate those saints in calling the Lord our God for our own vindication when we suffer for righteousness' sake? Not only does the gospel teach us to pray for our persecutors to experience the same gracious change of heart that we have experienced, but it also teaches us to expectantly look to the Lord for His holy justice to come to bear in our lives. Perhaps this

---

9   See notes at 17:6.

God-ordained vindication will come to pass quickly, or perhaps several years after the fact. Perhaps it will not take place until the Last Day. Whatever the timing, it most likely will take place in a way other than that which we might expect. When coming to the Lord for vindication, we must not come with a demanding or vindictive attitude, but rather with a humble heart full of love for Yahweh and love for our enemies.

THE SIXTH SEAL

Verses 12–14: "When he opened the sixth seal, I looked, and behold, there was a great earthquake, and the sun became black as sackcloth, the full moon became like blood, and the stars of the sky fell to the earth as the fig tree sheds its winter fruit when shaken by a gale. The sky vanished like a scroll that is being rolled up, and every mountain and island was removed from its place." This is the language used in both Matthew's and Mark's versions of the Olivet Discourse, which speaks of the time of Jesus's coming in judgment upon the covenant-breakers through destroying the temple and bringing Jerusalem to her knees at the hands of the Romans in AD 70 (cf. Matt. 24:29–30; Mark 13:24–26). This is the first large group of enemies He was appointed to put under His feet as ruling over all the nations from His Father's right hand.[10] In saying "the sky vanished like a scroll . . . and every mountain and island was removed from its place," the apostle surely does *not* mean this literally, but rather picks up the same hyperbolic prophet language from Isaiah 13:10 as utilized by the Lord in the Olivet Discourse. Truly, the two speak of the same events in the same way. Likewise, the wording here also picks up that of Joel 2:28–32,[11] which Peter applies to his day in the first century (see Acts 2:17–21), and prophesies national Israel's end.

Verses 15–17: "Then the kings of the earth and the great ones and the generals and the rich and the powerful, and everyone, slave and free, hid themselves in the caves and among the rocks of the mountains, calling to the mountains and rocks, 'Fall on us and hide us from the face of him who is seated on the throne, and from the wrath of the Lamb, for the great day of their wrath has come, and who can stand?'" Everyone, from the most powerful in society to the very weakest, responds to the coming of this great day of Yahweh's judgment against them with absolute terror such

---

10   See notes at 1:7.
11   See Wilson, *When the Man Comes Around*, Kindle Location 879.

that, if it were possible, they would have mountains themselves fall on them. This is the response of those who know their guilt before a holy God, but would rather find a way to escape His justice than fall at His feet in heartfelt repentance.

Oh, that Yahweh our God would break us over any such stubbornness and hardness of heart that yet remains in us! Oh, that His almighty Spirit would bring us to our knees in repentance with a broken and contrite heart, like He did for King David of old! Oh, that we would actively mortify persisting sins in our lives lest we should receive the judgment of being handed over to our hard-heartedness!

AN INTERLUDE

At this point the Apocalypse momentarily shifts gears, as it were. Chapter 7 acts as an interlude between the breaking of the sixth and seventh seals.

Chapter 7, verse 1: "After this I saw four angels standing at the four corners of the earth, holding back the four winds of the earth, that no wind might blow on earth or sea or against any tree." The visions now shift and John sees four angels. John Gill connects these four angels with the four spirits of heaven found in Zechariah 6:5.[12] In that context, the spirits patrolled the earth riding on chariots with horses having the same colors as those found in the first four seals: red, black, white, and dappled—like the sorrel horse of Zechariah 1:8, the dappled horse becomes pale in the Revelation. Here, these angels stand at the four corners of the earth, holding back the judgments from consuming the saints who are patiently enduring through them. This aligns with Jesus's prophecy that "He will send out his angels with a loud trumpet call, and they will gather his elect from the four winds, from one end of heaven to the other" (Matt. 24:31).

Often, as Christ followers, we can find ourselves drifting along through life, intellectually agreeing with the promises of God, even experiencing emotional euphoria upon focused contemplation. Yet we can fail to truly believe them such that they actually reform our thought and behavioral patterns. Are we a people who walk by faith and not by sight in confession only, or does this confession radically affect how we live under the rulership of our Lord and Savior?

---

12 See Gill, *Exposition*, Kindle Location 356115.

Verse 2,: "Then I saw another angel ascending from the rising of the sun, with the seal of the living God, and he called with a loud voice to the four angels who had been given power to harm earth and sea." A fifth angel now enters the vision and calls out to these four angels.

Verse 3: "saying, 'Do not harm the earth or the sea or the trees, until we have sealed the servants of our God on their foreheads.'" He commands his fellow angels to do what they are already engaged in—to protect those saints who are passing through the severe tribulations, which were just described. This comports with Jesus's words in Luke 21:17–19: "You will be hated by all for my name's sake. But not a hair of your head will perish. By your endurance you will gain your lives." Thus, their protection is of the eternal sort that belongs to those made citizens of Christ's kingdom by the power of the Holy Spirit.

In order for saints to be protected, they must be identified or marked out as true bondservants of God. The mark on their foreheads is a symbol that God owns them. This is in contrast to those owned by the beast in 13:16. It seems this image is taken from Deuteronomy 6:8, where national Israel was exhorted to take Yahweh's commands and "bind them as a sign on [their] hand, and they shall be as frontlets between [their] eyes" (cf. Ezek. 9:4–6).[13] Even in the days of Moses, this was not meant to be taken literally, but rather God wanted His law to be the driving force in everything to which they would put their minds and hands. This is exactly what was expressed four verses earlier in the *sh'ma* (Deut. 6:4–5).

For those who belong to the Lord Jesus, we have had this very law written anew on our hearts through conversion, such that now we are both willing and able to truly love Yahweh and love our neighbor as ourselves (see Jer. 31:31–34). Not only this, but the Spirit of the living God has sealed each and every one of us with His presence so that He Himself is the guarantee that we will come into our inheritance as coheirs with our elder Brother (Eph. 1:13–14). These are amazing truths to be celebrated as those who have come to see and enter into the dominion of Jesus by the regenerating work of the Holy Spirit! Hallelujah to our King!

Verses 4–8: "And I heard the number of the sealed, 144,000, sealed from every tribe of the sons of Israel: 12,000 from the tribe of Judah were sealed, 12,000 from the tribe of Reuben, 12,000 from the tribe of Gad, 12,000

---

13   See Beale and McDonough, "Revelation," 1106.

from the tribe of Asher, 12,000 from the tribe of Naphtali, 12,000 from the tribe of Manasseh, 12,000 from the tribe of Simeon, 12,000 from the tribe of Levi, 12,000 from the tribe of Issachar, 12,000 from the tribe of Zebulun, 12,000 from the tribe of Joseph, 12,000 from the tribe of Benjamin were sealed." Numbers often carry symbolic value throughout the Apocalypse. In this case, twelve is used as a symbol of completion or totality, corresponding to the twelve tribes of Israel. The idea communicated here is that of the totality of those true believers, the true and spiritual sons of Abraham (Rom. 9:6–8; Gal. 4:21–31). These are God's elect, the true Israel of God (Gal. 6:16; Eph. 2:12).[14] What the angel tells John here stands in direct contrast to the apostasy of national Israel, which is about to be judged as the opening of the first six seals has just depicted. It should be noted that these are the things which John *heard* from the fifth heavenly messenger.

Verse 9: "After this I looked, and behold, a great multitude that no one could number, from every nation, from all tribes and peoples and languages, standing before the throne and before the Lamb, clothed in white robes, with palm branches in their hands." Now upon turning to *look* at that of which the angel spoke, this is what John saw. He saw the same thing about which the four living creatures and twenty-four elders were singing around Yahweh's throne (5:9–10), but this time with an emphasis on their being uncountable. This is reflective of passages going all the way back to the Abrahamic covenant, when God promised that through Abraham "all the families of the earth shall be blessed" (Gen. 12:3) and that through his son, "I will surely bless you, and I will surely multiply your offspring as the stars of heaven and as the sand that is on the seashore" (Gen. 22:17, in reference to Gen. 15:5).[15] This promise is progressively built upon in the context of Abraham's greater Son, the Messiah, throughout the Scriptures.[16]

Here, this vast number of saints is clothed in white robes, indicating that they have been made righteous by the perfect obedience of Jesus in their place and that God the Father has fully accepted them on that basis. In addition, they are waving palm branches, just as the Jews did in welcoming their Messianic King into Jerusalem. Matthew commented that Jesus entered riding on a donkey, which fulfilled Zechariah 9:9 (Matt. 21:1–10).

---

14 Wilson, *When the Man Comes Around*, Kindle Location 938.
15 See Beale and McDonough, "Revelation," 1108.
16 See Ps. 2:7–8; 72:5–11; Isa. 2:1–5; 9:1–7; 11:1–10; Dan. 2:31–45 (esp. vv. 35, 45); 7:13–14; Hab. 2:14; Zech. 9:9–13; Matt. 8:10–12; 28:18–20; Rom. 1:1–6; 16:25–27; etc.

It should be noted that the very next verse in Zechariah 9 describes that the Messiah would rule over all the nations "from sea to sea, and from the River to the ends of the earth" (Zech. 9:10). The parallel between the cross-canonical thinking in Matthew 21 and here in Revelation 7 is strikingly similar, likely due to the fact that John was present in both circumstances.

As part of maturing in faithfully following Jesus and becoming more biblically minded, it is crucial that we learn to think God's thoughts after Him. This is not some esoteric truism, but rather is a deeply practical discipline. In short, it means we need to learn to resolve in ourselves that God's logic is best even if it doesn't fit our "common sense" approach to reason. We cannot outsmart the Creator and Sustainer of all things; thus, we must learn to submit ourselves to *His* line of reasoning as revealed in His Word. Boot explains, "The replacement of biblical law (and the positive law derived from the general principles of biblical law), with 'man's law,' was a product of Deism and the Enlightenment tradition, both of which were virulently hostile to Christianity, where the law of God was sacrificed on the altar of 'reason' and public opinion. Nonetheless, the Enlightenment vision only gained general ascendency after World War I, and arguably triumphed only after the second world conflagration."[17] While this comment was made in the context of discussing society and legislation, it certainly applies to the way many Christians attempt to read Scripture—they approach Holy Writ on their own common-sense terms rather than seeking to read God's Word on *its* own terms.

Scripture is meant to be read as one unified story that points to the Lord Jesus and His righteous rule over all things in heaven and on earth. It is meant to be read from front to back with later revelation defining and clarifying former revelation. We must learn to utilize the Word in the same ways in which the biblical authors do, even if it rails against our preconceived understanding—we must be conformed to the Word of God, not the other way around. For example, we can see this in both Hosea's and Paul's interpretations of Adam's broken prelapsarian (that is, pre-fall) relationship with Yahweh in the garden of Eden (Hos. 6:7; Rom. 5:18–19). They understand that relationship as a God-imposed covenant with the terms of "Obey My law and you will gain eternal life, but if you fail, you will gain the curse of death," and therefore, so must we. We can also see

---

17   Joseph Boot, *The Mission of God: A Manifesto of Hope for Society* (Toronto: Ezra Press, 2016), 92.

how this works in Matthew's utilization of Zechariah 9 and then, in turn, how Matthew 21 informs John's understanding of the massive, innumerable host of saints standing before the throne of Yahweh and His Lamb. Scripture's usage of itself ought to form our hermeneutic, build our theological system, and create the categories by which we think through every area of life. We cannot live wisely in God's world in the fear of Him, and think His thoughts after Him, according to any other model!

Verse 10: "and crying out with a loud voice, 'Salvation belongs to our God who sits on the throne, and to the Lamb!'" These are almost the same words that were sung by all of heaven and earth back in chapter 5 in response to the Lamb's worthiness to open the scroll and break its seals. The ones here singing are all the redeemed of the Lamb, the nations that have come to be blessed in Him—"Blessed are all who take refuge in him" (Ps. 2:12).

As those sealed by the Holy Spirit and belonging to this myriad of myriads of worldwide saints, believers today find themselves awestruck by the same divine Persons seated on Their throne and are moved to respond in blessing Their name. Worship in spirit and in truth is the only response fitting for such a matchless Creator, Sustainer, Rescuer, and Sovereign over all!

Verses 11–12: "And all the angels were standing around the throne and around the elders and the four living creatures, and they fell on their faces before the throne and worshiped God, saying, 'Amen! Blessing and glory and wisdom and thanksgiving and honor and power and might be to our God forever and ever! Amen.'" At this point we learn that the apostle is still in front of the throne in heaven viewing the massive worship service there. In 5:11–12, the myriads of angels gather around the four living creatures and twenty-four elders to join their worship, but now they prostrate themselves in reverent humility before their Lord. Their song lyrics follow suit with what they sang before.

Verse 13: "Then one of the elders addressed me, saying, 'Who are these, clothed in white robes, and from where have they come?'" This is a very strange question since he is one of the twenty-four elders, those representatives of the Old Testament and New Testament churches together as one body in Christ. For this reason, John replies, "Sir, you know" (v. 14a).

Verse 14b: "And he said to me, 'These are the ones coming out of the great tribulation. They have washed their robes and made them white in the blood of the Lamb.'" In agreement with the apostle, the elder explains thus. Given the context of the Revelation thus far, the "great tribulation" refers to the judgment soon to come on Jerusalem, which Jesus predicted in the Olivet Discourse (Matt. 24:21; Mark 13:19; Luke 21:22). Yet since John's vision in this chapter is of the full mass of the redeemed, not just those saints in the first-century known world, by extension this seems to speak to the tribulation that believers experience in every age until the end of the world. These have conquered through their sufferings by keeping their eyes fixed on Christ, their Savior and King. They have been justified by God through their faith in Christ's perfect obedience, specifically His death, as depicted here in washing "their robes . . . in the blood of the Lamb." This is what Jesus promised the Sardisian congregation—namely, that their conquering would testify that their faith in Him was real to begin with (3:5).

Our expectations of the future have a direct impact on how we live in the present. They affect how we make plans and with what kind of fervor we execute them. In light of this, it would be very helpful for Christian involvement in kingdom building in the world if we would abandon the popular notion of a future great tribulation period toward the end of history in favor of a much more biblical understanding—namely, that it *already* took place in AD 70. As has been explained above, this does not negate the fact that faithful followers of Jesus will experience periods of trials and sufferings throughout the centuries, but it does lead us to wholeheartedly embrace Jesus's own promises that His dominion will gradually expand and penetrate until it has enveloped the whole earth (cf. Matt. 13:31–33). As a way of demonstration for how this plays out in Christian activity, two poignant examples would be the lives of William Carey (1761–1834) and David Livingstone (1813–1873), through whom Yahweh worked to open up both the Indian Subcontinent and Sub-Saharan Africa to far-reaching gospel advancement.

Verses 15–16: "Therefore they are before the throne of God, and serve him day and night in his temple; and he who sits on the throne will shelter them with his presence. They shall hunger no more, neither thirst anymore; the sun shall not strike them, nor any scorching heat." Ephesians 2:21–22 teaches that all true believers are growing together "into a holy temple in the Lord . . . [and] being built together into a dwelling place for God by the Spirit." In this sort of way, the saints serve the Lord day and night before His throne. In addition, Psalm 2:12 gloriously declares, "Blessed are all who take refuge in him." Truly, only in Messiah's presence, united to Him by faith, is there permanent safety from the holy wrath of the Almighty, which burns against sinners everywhere day and night. Not only this, but verse 16 attributes new creation language to these saints, which sounds very much like that found in Isaiah 11 and 65. Jesus promised that those who come to Him for their true satisfaction would neither hunger nor thirst (John 4:10–15; 6:35).[18] In addition, the language of not being scorched by the sun comes from Psalm 1:3 and Jeremiah 17:7–8 in describing the righteous, most especially the Anointed One to whom the righteous are united.

Verse 17: "For the Lamb in the midst of the throne will be their shepherd, and he will guide them to springs of living water, and God will wipe away every tear from their eyes." The word *hoti* ("for") indicates that the elder is now giving John the reason these things are true for those who have conquered through the great tribulation. He says that "the Lamb … will be their shepherd." Yahweh as the Good Shepherd is a theme running throughout Scripture. Psalm 23 brings this truth out in poetic form. However, the most in-depth explication of it is found in John 10, where Jesus taught that He is "the good shepherd [who] lays down his life for the sheep" (John 10:11). As that Good Shepherd, "he will guide them to springs of living water." This again refers to John 4, where the Son of Man taught the Samaritan woman that "the water that I will give him will become in him a spring of water welling up to eternal life" (John 4:14). Furthermore, the elder explains, "God will wipe away every tear from their eyes." Here the imagery picks up directly from Isaiah 65:19 concerning saints in the new creation, which is again repeated in the same context in Revelation 21:4. The fact that the elder combines present realities in Christ with consummate new-creation language shows that, in some sense, the new heavens and new earth are already a reality in the lives of believers. This new creation is gradually growing in the world as saints fulfill their calling to invade every sphere of culture with the law and the gospel and transform the so-called "secular" into the sacred,[19] bringing to bear

---

18 See Beale and McDonough, "Revelation," 1109.

19 Nothing can truly be called "secular," or irreligious, since one's religious beliefs inherently drive the way he seeks to build culture. He either does so in opposition to the one true and living God or in honoring Him. There is no neutrality.

the crown rights of our Lord and Savior throughout (see 2 Cor. 5:16–20). This also means that Isaiah 65:17–25 is describing the conditions of the nations *prior* to Christ's second advent—this can clearly be seen in verses 20 and 23, which speak of death and childbearing, two things that Jesus says won't exist in the eternal state (cf. Matt. 22:29–30; 1 Cor. 15:51–55). More will be said on this point in chapters 21 and 22. Thus, this new-covenant, new-creational order began with Messiah's resurrection and subsequent exaltation on high. All those united to Him by the regenerating work of the Spirit have been transformed into new creations, being made members of the new covenant, who then go out into the world with their King's terms of surrender. However, this new creation will not reach its completed, eternal state until the Last Day, when our Lord returns.

Therefore, let us rejoice and be glad that the new creation has broken into history because of Christ's resurrection from the dead! Let us go out and live like it's a present reality—because it is! Let us follow Jesus by faith and not by sight.

At this point in the Apocalypse, the vision shifts back to the breaking of the seventh seal. This seal acts as a point of transition into the seven trumpet judgments.

THE SEVENTH SEAL

Chapter 8, verse 1: "When the Lamb opened the seventh seal, there was silence in heaven for about half an hour."

"The silence may indicate that heaven stands in awe at His presence (Hab. 2:20; Zech. 1:7)."[20] This fits the context since the last seal to be broken released terrible judgment on all the unrepentant covenant-breakers. In chapter 19, the saints also praise God for His justice poured out upon the wicked. Are we likewise willing to give heartfelt thanks to the Lord when He brings to bear His perfect justice upon wicked men, enslaved by their rebellion just as we once were?

Verse 2: "Then I saw the seven angels who stand before God, and seven trumpets were given to them." The seven trumpets are introduced on the same basis as were the seven seals—namely, the victorious death and resurrection of the Lion-Lamb.

---

20 Reformation Study Bible notes, Revelation 8:1.

Verses 3–4: "And another angel came and stood at the altar with a golden censer, and he was given much incense to offer with the prayers of all the saints on the golden altar before the throne, and the smoke of the incense, with the prayers of the saints, rose before God from the hand of the angel." In 5:8, the apostle learned that the bowls of incense offered *are* the prayers of the saints. The same is true here. The prayers rise before God as they are offered, showing that they are continually offered unto the Father and are pleasing to Him. What prayers could be pleasing to the Father except those that glorify Him by aligning with His revealed will and that are prayed in the name of His Son (cf. John 14:13–14)? These are the sort we must offer unto Him.

Verse 5: "Then the angel took the censer and filled it with fire from the altar and threw it on the earth, and there were peals of thunder, rumblings, flashes of lightning, and an earthquake." The fire that lit the incense now is thrown down in judgment on the earth via the censer, the same instrument by which the incense is offered up. It is in response to the prayers of the saints that the Messiah now brings judgment on the earth.[21] It is noteworthy to mention that the same symbolic language of vengeance used when the sixth seal was broken (see 6:12–17) is utilized here, as well, yet in preparation for the release of the trumpet judgments about to follow.

---

21 See Reformation Study Bible notes, Revelation 8:2–6.

The Fourth Vision (8:6–11:19)

THE FIRST TRUMPET

Chapter 8, verse 6: "Now the seven angels who had the seven trumpets prepared to blow them." These are the same angels who each received a trumpet in verse 2. Now they are prepared to sound them, and thus deliver seven judgments from the hand of Christ their King.

Verse 7: "The first angel blew his trumpet, and there followed hail and fire, mixed with blood, and these were thrown upon the earth. And a third of the earth was burned up, and a third of the trees were burned up, and all green grass was burned up." This judgment of hail and fire is drawn from Exodus 9:22–26, which in that time was on the whole land of Egypt, save the region of Goshen.[1] Beale explains, "Both Exod. 9 and Rev. 8:7 present an affliction of hail together with fire sent from heaven against three parts of creation: the earth or land, the trees, and the grass."[2] However, in this judgment, the hail and fire are mixed with blood since the object of its destruction is the *land*, the third portion of creation Yahweh originally set in order to be a good and suitable place wherein man could dwell (cf. Gen. 1:9–13, 24–25). The fact that the figurative portion has shifted from one fourth to one third indicates an increase in intensity in Messiah's judgment against the covenant-breakers of Israel. Beale again

---

1 See Gill, *Exposition*, Kindle Location 356600. Although Gill interprets this plague as referring to the Arian heresy, with which there is disagreement, he does recognize the connection back to the plagues upon Egypt described at Exodus 9.
2 Beale and McDonough, "Revelation," 1112.

notes that just as with the judgment upon Egypt, this act of vengeance affects food supplies in the land.³

The Second Trumpet

Verses 8–9: "The second angel blew his trumpet, and something like a great mountain, burning with fire, was thrown into the sea, and a third of the sea became blood. A third of the living creatures in the sea died, and a third of the ships were destroyed." This judgment of water turning to blood is drawn from Exodus 7:14–24, which was upon all the waterways of Egypt.⁴ Here, though, the object of its destruction is specifically the *sea*, the second great section of creation Yahweh ordered and then subsequently filled (Gen. 1:6–10, 20–23). Once again, the transition from one fourth to one third shows a distinct growth in intensity. Indeed, the mountain being thrown therein is Mount Zion, upon which Jerusalem was built, which represents the temple together with the holy city. Jesus said this would happen if His disciples were to "have faith and do not doubt" (Matt. 21:20–22).⁵

The Third Trumpet

Verses 10–11: "The third angel blew his trumpet, and a great star fell from heaven, blazing like a torch, and it fell on a third of the rivers and on the springs of water. The name of the star is Wormwood. A third of the waters became wormwood, and many people died from the water, because it had been made bitter." This judgment is turning fresh, useable water into bitter, sickening water. It has as its object the other major water source, that being *fresh water*. It seems this is merely a continuance of the previous trumpet judgment.

The Fourth Trumpet

Verse 12: "The fourth angel blew his trumpet, and a third of the sun was struck, and a third of the moon, and a third of the stars, so that a third of

---

3   Beale and McDonough, "Revelation," 1112.

4   See Daniel L. Akin, *Exalting Jesus in Revelation.* (*Christ-Centered Exposition Commentary*) (Nashville: Holman, 2016), Kindle Location 3640.

5   See Wilson, *When the Man Comes Around*, Kindle Location 1050. See also Beale and McDonough, "Revelation," 1113. Although he indicates at chapter 17 that Babylon is emblematic of "the anti-God forces in the world," with which there is disagreement, Beale does draw a connection between this trumpet and the judgment on Babylon, the "great city" of Revelation 11–18.

their light might be darkened, and a third of the day might be kept from shining, and likewise a third of the night." This judgment of darkness is drawn from Exodus 10:21–23, in which darkness covered all the land of Egypt.[6] The object of this judgment is the *sky*, specifically illuminating bodies, an allusion back to Scripture's first narrative account, describing the way in which the sky was set in order and then filled with living creatures at Yahweh's direction (Gen. 1:3–5, 14–23).

It is important to see that all four of these judgments are limited in scope and intensity, signified by the use of one third. However, this round is not quite as limited as was the seal judgment of death, which was signified by one fourth (cf. 6:8). In the apocalyptic imagery presented, this does not necessary indicate entirely separate and discrete acts of vengeance on Jerusalem, but more likely they represent growing levels of intensity in the same events. These trumpet judgments follow the same form as did the seal judgments in chapter 6—judgments 1–4 have their pattern, judgments 5–6 have theirs, and then judgment 7 appears only after a lengthy interruption given to encourage the suffering saints who are meant to receive this Apocalypse.

This round of judgments brings up an important worldview question—namely, "How do we interpret natural disasters?" There seem to be two extremes within the purview of Christians. On the one hand, many charismatics would want to look for a demon under every rockslide, around every tornado, and behind every tsunami. In their way of thinking, there is a one-to-one correlation between demonic activity and these kinds of events. Thus, the proper response would be to have a twenty-four-hour prayer vigil to cast out the demon. On the other hand, many fundamentalist-minded believers see natural disasters as broadly under God's sovereignty, but specifically in naturalistic terms—there is *no* correlation between spiritual entities and the spiritual state of those living in the affected area and the physical devastation they experience. Thus, the response is to sadly accept the reality of living in a fallen world. Yet is this how Scripture, in its totality, answers this question? It seems this passage would lead us to view the universe in which we live with much more overlap between the spiritual and physical realms than most in the West are accustomed to think. While not every disease or devastating event can be interpreted as God's judgment on

---

6 Beale and McDonough, "Revelation," 1113. See also Akin, *Exalting Jesus in Revelation*, Kindle Location 3663.

sinners for their rebellion—as Jesus indicated in John 9 with regard to the man born blind—there are times where the correlation between sin, sickness, death, famine, fires, etc. and a subsequent judgment is quite strong. For example, Paul explains that improperly partaking of the Lord's Supper could very well result in illness and death, as was the case in the Corinthian congregation (1 Cor. 11:29–30). As well, we have the example in this passage of national Israel's rebellion mounting up in the sight of Yahweh until it finally reached its full measure in their rejection of the Messianic King whom He sent. The result is the Lord's vengeance coming upon them in very physical terms. Thus, we shouldn't automatically assume natural disasters, famine, and disease to be acts of Christ's judgment against the wicked. However, if such events do come upon us in His providence, and we know that we have been rebellious against His law—personally, corporately, or even nationally—the only proper response is heartfelt repentance and contrition before our thrice-holy God. Only in the righteous life and death of His beloved Son can we find mercy, forgiveness, and new life!

THE EAGLE

Verse 13: "Then I looked, and I heard an eagle crying with a loud voice as it flew directly overhead, 'Woe, woe, woe to those who dwell on the earth, at the blasts of the other trumpets that the three angels are about to blow!'" The eagle announces that these last three judgments are three woes that "explicitly differentiate between the righteous and the wicked, as did the earlier Egyptian plagues."[7] This indicates that the judgments are greater in intensity to even these. Morris expounds on this point: "The solemn words of the eagle show that the plagues to come are worse than those already experienced. There is a deepening of intensity."

Much in the same way that Matthew 24 has oft been abused by cult leaders, so also has chapter 9 of the Apocalypse that now lays before us. Even amongst evangelicals, there have been wild and crazed interpretations put forth. For example, among cult leaders, Charles Manson used this text to convince his followers of a coming race war where blacks would wipe out all whites, save for the Manson family. Likewise, many dispensationalists have interpreted these texts to indicate a seven-year great tribulation just prior to Christ's return where the locusts coming forth from the abyss

---

7   Morris, Leon, *The Book of Revelation: An Introduction & Commentary*, Leicester, UK: Inter-Varsity Press, 1999, pg. 122.

represent Apache helicopters. For this reason, if for no other, it is of great importance that we carefully examine this passage in the way in which it's given. Verses 1–11 describe the fifth trumpet judgment, first with contextual details and then with whom the tormentors are permitted to torment. Finally, they provide a description of the tormentors themselves.

THE FIFTH TRUMPET

Chapter 9, verses 1–2: "And the fifth angel blew his trumpet, and I saw a star fallen from heaven to earth, and he was given the key to the shaft of the bottomless pit. He opened the shaft of the bottomless pit, and from the shaft rose smoke like the smoke of a great furnace, and the sun and the air were darkened with the smoke from the shaft." We will meet this language of cosmic imprisonment again in chapters 12 and 20. In both of those passages, Satan is being cast down and bound, which is a symbolic expression of Jesus's teaching in Matthew 12:28–29 and John 12:31–32—namely, that Satan must be bound and cast out so that all the nations would become His inheritance as was promised Him. Already in Revelation 1:18, Jesus presents Himself as the one who has "the keys of Death and Hades," and in 2:28 as "the morning star." Yet here, it's a "star fallen" that opens this cosmic prison, releasing the instruments of the Messiah's judgment upon the wicked (cf. Luke 10:18, which communicates the same idea as being bound and cast out). This fallen star is Satan, the adversary of all that is good and righteous and just, who is being sent at the Lord God's command.

"He was given the key" means "he receives power to open the abyss and let the demons out." This power comes from the risen Christ, the one who restrains him. Truly, the deceiver often disguises himself as a messenger of light, even the Light Himself. Though we must never underestimate the devil's schemes and devises, for his trickery has been well-honed over the millennia, we must also never forget that all his deeds are subservient to the risen Lord Jesus and unwittingly accomplish His purposes in the world. In the same way that Joseph's brothers meant evil against him, but simultaneously God meant it for good (Gen. 50:20), so, too, is the case with evil spirits. This ought to be a great comfort to us as Christ's sheep, since it is written, "Little children, you are from God and have overcome them, for he who is in you is greater than he who is in the world" (1 John 4:4)!

The first thing to come forth from the bottomless pit is great billows of smoke that darken the entire sky. This is an image meant to set John's readers up to expect something very terrible to follow.

Verses 3–6: "Then from the smoke came locusts on the earth, and they were given power like the power of scorpions of the earth. They were told not to harm the grass of the earth or any green plant or any tree, but only those people who do not have the seal of God on their foreheads. They were allowed to torment them for five months, but not to kill them, and their torment was like the torment of a scorpion when it stings someone. And in those days people will seek death and will not find it. They will long to die, but death will flee from them." The image of plaguing locusts is drawn from Joel 1:2ff, which was a precursor to a great judgment on Judah, described in chapter 2 as the Day of Yahweh. Wilmshurst notes that locusts are presented in Joel as destroyers of life.[8] It is also likely drawn from Exodus 10:3–15 where locusts were one of the ten plagues that came upon Egypt as a means of Yahweh's hardening of Pharaoh's heart—this fits the pattern established in the trumpet judgments up to this point.[9] In the same way, this judgment of demonic destroyers, symbolically depicted here as locusts, is a precursor to an even greater act of judgment yet to come in the Apocalypse. In addition, we learned from chapter 7 that the elect are those who symbolically have been branded with God's seal of ownership on their foreheads. They are the ones who are forbidden from receiving the torment of the aforementioned demoniac. The torment here is presented as the infliction of some kind of excruciating pain, although whether physical or metaphysical is unclear. Indeed, it causes its victims to desire death as a means to stop it, but without finding the relief they crave. This judgment is given to the wicked as a small taste of the eternal judgment in hell reserved for them, which is to come about on the Last Day. Nevertheless, this foretaste lasts only a relatively short period of time, represented in the text as "five months." Our most holy God will not be mocked—His very nature will not allow it!

Verses 7–9: "In appearance the locusts were like horses prepared for battle: on their heads were what looked like crowns of gold; their faces were like human faces, their hair like women's hair, and their teeth like

---

8   See Steve Wilmshurst, *Revelation: The Final Word*, Westminster Commentary Series (Darlington, England: Evangelical Press, 2008), Kindle Location 1370.
9   See Beale and McDonough, "Revelation," 1114.

lions' teeth; they had breastplates like breastplates of iron, and the noise of their wings was like the noise of many chariots with horses rushing into battle." At this junction, John is doing the same thing as did Ezekiel when seeing various visions; namely, he's trying to describe what he sees in the only terms he knows as a first-century Jew living in the Roman Empire. Twice these locust creatures are described as horses heading into battle, both in behavior and in their sound. They are like horses prepared for battle for several reasons. Firstly, they wear what appears to be golden crowns on their heads, as though they are the royal army of Christ, but in fact are ot. Secondly, they have the beauty of humans, as though they are bearers of God's image, but in reality are not. The text indicates that their teeth are like those of lions, as though they have the ability to devour and destroy whatever lay in their path. Yet in fact, they are limited to whatever the Messianic King permits. Finally, they wear what looks to be breastplates of iron—they are meant to appear as invincible, immune to every attack and defensive maneuver, but truly they are not. Indeed, they are very eager to speed out into battle, much like a restless horse being restrained at the battle line, wanting desperately to charge ahead.

Verses 10–11: "They have tails and stings like scorpions, and their power to hurt people for five months is in their tails. They have as king over them the angel of the bottomless pit. His name in Hebrew is Abaddon, and in Greek he is called Apollyon." These strange demonic creatures are described as stinging their victims for the appointed time as a scorpion does with its tail. When a scorpion stings, the poison causes not only extreme pain, but also a temporary paralysis to the poisoned area. Depending on the strength of the poison, it can paralyze the entire nervous system, bringing death to its victim. The Lord Jesus is restraining these demonic spirit beings from killing their victims, but He has authorized them to torment with different kinds of extreme pain such that their victims cannot think clearly.

Furthermore, the fallen star is now depicted as the "angel of the bottomless pit." Isaiah 14:12–15 describes the king of Babylon as having the same attitude with which the serpent first tempted Eve in the garden (Gen. 3:1–5)—he was acting out what his father the devil had first exemplified in his initial rebellion. Satan is not the ruler of the bottomless pit, but is rather its chief prisoner. By binding Satan, the Messiah has also bound his spirit servants. His name is revealed, both in Hebrew and in Greek, *Abaddon* and *Apollyon*, respectively, coming from the verb meaning "to destroy." This is a descriptive title meaning "destroyer," just as "Satan" means "adversary." As well, in bringing up the title *Apollyon*, "there may be an ironic allusion to Nero or Domitian, both of whom saw themselves as similar to the Greek god Apollo."[10] Nero fits the time period instead of Domitian—his reign lasted AD 81–96, which occurred after the fall of Jerusalem.[11] In addition, Mounce notes that "the allusion [to the powers of the underworld] is strengthened by the observation that the locust was one of the symbols of the god Apollo."[12] Likewise, this destroyer is described as being "king over them"—that is, the demonic creatures symbolically portrayed here as locusts. They are loyal subjects of this one demonic spirit who rules over them all.

While we ought not ascribe greater abilities or influence to the demoniac than revealed in Holy Writ, we cannot think their Christ-inflicted bonds mean they exert no sway in the hearts and minds of men whatsoever. The apostle Paul writes, "For we do not wrestle against flesh and blood, but against the rulers, against the authorities, against the cosmic powers over this present darkness, against the spiritual forces of evil in the heavenly places" (Eph. 6:12). Within the context of his epistle as a whole, he speaks primarily of ideologies that lead folks into subtle, if not outrightly hostile, opposition against the Lord Jesus and His people. In his day, such examples would be the teachings of the Judaizers, the proto-Gnostics, and the Nicolaitans. In our day, the likes of neo-Gnosticism, neo-Marxism, and the new age have presented the church in the West with deceptive ideas that must be defended against in order to remain loyal to our Messianic King. This is how the devil is seeking to gain a foothold amongst Christ's ranks in our modern era. We must not be fooled into agreeing with the atheist, who is, in fact, a fool (Ps. 14:1)—there is no neutrality!

Verse 12: "The first woe has passed; behold, two woes are still to come." This is merely a narrative comment to remind the reader as to the place in the order of the giving of the trumpet judgments. This interjection is likely given since the description of the fifth trumpet was significantly longer than the first four.

---

10   Reformation Study Bible notes, Revelation 9:11.

11   See John Donahue, "Titus Flavius Domitianus (A.D. 81–96)," https://rome.us/roman-emperors/domitian.html.

12   Robert H. Mounce, "The Book of Revelation," in *The New International Commentary on the New Testament* (Grand Rapids: Eerdmans, 1997), 191.

THE SIXTH TRUMPET

Verses 13–15: "Then the sixth angel blew his trumpet, and I heard a voice from the four horns of the golden altar before God, saying to the sixth angel who had the trumpet, 'Release the four angels who are bound at the great river Euphrates.' So the four angels, who had been prepared for the hour, the day, the month, and the year, were released to kill a third of mankind." This is the same altar under which are the souls of the martyrs (see 6:9).[13] The image of the golden altar with four horns is drawn from Exodus 37:25–28, which describes in what manner the altar of incense was meant to be constructed. The reason this golden altar cannot be the altar of whole burnt offerings is that the once-for-all-time Lamb has already been sacrificed and subsequently exalted. In addition, that this is a symbolic representation of the incense altar fits with the offering of incense in heaven already mentioned in Revelation 5:8 and 8:3–4.

The voice coming from the incense altar is that of the angel standing "at the altar with a golden censer" (8:3). He instructs the sixth trumpet-holding angel to "release the four angels who are bound at the great river Euphrates." These angels are God's messengers of destruction who are appointed to drive the Roman army to attack and lay siege upon Jerusalem. Wilson puts it this way: "When the sixth angel sounded his trumpet, the Roman legions were released, described here under the figure of four angels of destruction."[14] While there is disagreement with Wilson on the identity of the four angels—the author of this commentary would take them to be God's destruction messengers standing behind the Roman army driving them along, not the Tenth Legion itself—the point remains the same. This point is that the Tenth Legion under General Vespasian's leadership, and later his son Titus's, is the means by which the Messiah is bringing a judgment of death upon a limited portion of mankind, figuratively denoted here by the use of one third, in order to harden the Jewish covenant-breakers in their already hard hearts (cf. vv. 20–21). We can see Yahweh working in like manner in the life of Pharaoh (Ex. 4:21; Rom. 9:17–18), as well as through the preached gospel in the hearts of the reprobate (see Matt. 13:11–17; 2 Cor. 2:14–16). Truly, the Lord is sovereign over all the affairs of men, even what their hearts desire, so that He orchestrates all things to accomplish His appointed ends, to the praise of His glory!

---

13 See Wilson, *When the Man Comes Around*, Kindle Location 1182.
14 See Wilson, *When the Man Comes Around*, Kindle Location 1182.

Verses 16–19: "The number of mounted troops was twice ten thousand times ten thousand; I heard their number. And this is how I saw the horses in my vision and those who rode them: they wore breastplates the color of fire and of sapphire and of sulfur, and the heads of the horses were like lions' heads, and fire and smoke and sulfur came out of their mouths. By these three plagues a third of mankind was killed, by the fire and smoke and sulfur coming out of their mouths. For the power of the horses is in their mouths and in their tails, for their tails are like serpents with heads, and by means of them they wound." The Romans evidently have a massive army since their mounted troops alone are "twice ten thousand times ten thousand." Taken literally, this would indicate that their cavalry is two hundred million strong. Yet in Greek, the literal meaning is "myriads of myriads," which is like saying "gazillion" in English.[15] Thus, the number is meant to represent a vast army that seemingly cannot be counted by the citizens of Judea as they're seen coming. Now as before, this is what John *hears* from the angel, but when he turns to look at the subject matter, he *sees* something far more amazing.[16]

The nature of the horsemen and their horses prepared for battle shows how ferocious the Roman army was to the Jews, even slaughtering a significant, but limited, number of Jews with great power and viciousness—this limitation in scope is again indicated here by one third. This victory occurred during the First Jewish-Roman War of AD 68–70. The horsemen are protected with breastplates colored like fire, sapphire, and sulfur, which correspond to the fire, smoke, and sulfur that comes from the horses' mouths, bringing great destruction. This shows that the riders and their mounts are united with one mind and one spirit. Similarly, the horses' tails are used to wound their victims since they are "like serpents with heads." It seems the horses' mouths represent the Roman legionaries, while the tails symbolize their auxiliaries, which are comprised of heavily armored cavalry rather than mere foot soldiers.

Wilson brings out an important point in his concluding remarks to this section. He says, "This is all connected to the sixth trumpet, the middle of the last three trumpets. We are not yet at the horrifying end of the Battle of Jerusalem. We are still in the build-up to that climax."[17] This is very true.

---

15 See Wilson, *When the Man Comes Around*, Kindle Location 1190.
16 See Wilson, *When the Man Comes Around*, Kindle Location 1203.
17 See Wilson, *When the Man Comes Around*, Kindle Location 1209.

It is important to recognize we are still in the trumpet judgments at this point in the Revelation and have yet another round of increased intensity in the bowl judgments before apostate Israel is finally eliminated from the face of the earth altogether.

Verses 20–21: "The rest of mankind, who were not killed by these plagues, did not repent of the works of their hands nor give up worshiping demons and idols of gold and silver and bronze and stone and wood, which cannot see or hear or walk, nor did they repent of their murders or their sorceries or their sexual immorality or their thefts." The result of this great defeat for the nation of Israel, brought on by their ruler Rome, was an overall deepening in their idolatry, various abominable practices, and breaking of God's law rather than repentance. Some commentators take the fifth and sixth trumpets as warnings, but the text presents them as actual judgments. For this reason, it seems this result is what the Messiah was intending to accomplish all along in accordance with what was written in the scroll, which He Himself is actively bringing to pass through His various and sundry unwitting agents.

There are several interpretative traditions that see the sixth and seventh trumpets, along with the sixth seal (6:12–17) and the sixth and seventh bowls (16:12–21), as the end of human history, the cosmic deconstruction of this sin-corrupted universe, and the transition to a newly created new heavens and new earth. However, this cannot be the case since in each round of judgment there remains those who respond with greater hardness of heart in their rebellion against Yahweh than before. It is important for this to be mentioned since a plethora of failed "end of the world" prophecies have used this type of interpretation to substantiate their claims. The result has been that devoted followers of such leaders have gone bankrupt through selling all their possessions, have committed heinous murders, and some have committed mass suicide. This demonstrates that theology tremendously matters as it has deep and abiding consequences in people's everyday lives. Therefore, deriving our theology from a close and careful study of the text is vital to faithfully following Christ.

An Interlude

Revelation 10:1–11:14 forms a lengthy interlude in order to encourage the suffering believers to whom John writes. This follows the same pattern as the breaking of the seals, where chapter 7 jumps in to provide the same sort of encouragement.

Chapter 10, verse 1: "Then I saw another mighty angel coming down from heaven, wrapped in a cloud, with a rainbow over his head, and his face was like the sun, and his legs like pillars of fire." The vision shifts at this point so that John is now back on earth, but still in the Spirit. The text indicates the angel comes *down* from heaven, and in verse 2, he stands on the land and the sea, showing that John is close by.[18] This angel is surrounded by images identical to those surrounding God's throne in chapter 4—"around the throne was a rainbow" (4:3) and "before the throne were burning seven torches of fire" (4:5). Some interpreters see this angel as the Lord Jesus Himself, given the similarities in description. However, so far throughout the Revelation, the Messiah is either referred to as the "Son of Man" or the "Lamb," while heavenly messengers are referred to as "angels." Thus, the "mighty angel" in this verse should be taken at face value—that is, as a heavenly messenger. As to the majestic images spoken of here, they harken back to Ezekiel chapter 1, which reveals, "And downward from what had the appearance of his waist I saw as it were the appearance of fire, and there was brightness around him" (Ezek. 1:27). Furthermore, it describes the area around Yahweh's throne: "Like the appearance of the bow that is in the cloud on the day of rain, so was the appearance of the brightness all around" (Ezek. 1:28).[19] Thus, this angel comes forth from spending the majority of his time very close to God's throne in His direct presence. What an absolutely incredible experience that must be for all those heavenly servants to whom has been given such a privilege! What a privilege for us as His saints, here and now, to enter into God's presence each Lord's Day and worship around the throne of grace!

Verse 2a: "He had a little scroll open in his hand." This seems to be a miniature version of the scroll that the Lamb took from His Father's hand to break its seals. The book is laid open because Christ has already broken its seals and is now in the midst of setting in motion the judgments decreed therein.

Verses 2b–3: "And he set his right foot on the sea, and his left foot on the land, and called out with a loud voice, like a lion roaring. When he called

---

18   See Moses Stuart, *A Commentary on the Apocalypse, Vol. 1* (London: Wiley and Putnam, 1845), 203.

19   See Beale and McDonough, "Revelation," 1116.

out, the seven thunders sounded." With the authority of the Almighty who sent him, this heavenly messenger places his right foot on the sea and his left on the land, symbolically showing that all creation is under Yahweh's authority and no part of it can escape His righteous judgments. He speaks with the authority of the one who sent him, like a roaring lion, since that one is the Lion of the tribe of Judah. At his command, the seven thunders sound, which are a symbol of the seven acts of vengeance yet to be revealed. This becomes evident in the following verses. This also shows that all three rounds of seven judgments were decreed in the scroll and are being brought to pass by the Messianic King Himself.

It is often thought that the sole reason Jesus died on the cross was to save sinners from their sins. Yet here and throughout the Apocalypse, we're presented with the reality that divine judgment in this life against those who would persist in raising their fists against Yahweh and His Anointed was also accomplished therein. This can be seen in how all these judgments flow out of the scroll, which only Messiah Jesus is able to open.[20] This is an excellent example of how we must always be willing to allow God's Word to refine and sharpen our understanding rather than foisting our preconceived ideas upon the text. This is what submission to Christ's lordship is all about—we must die to self in order to rise again in Him.

Verse 4: "And when the seven thunders had sounded, I was about to write, but I heard a voice from heaven saying, 'Seal up what the seven thunders have said, and do not write it down.'" This shows that John did not write down the whole Apocalypse at once, but rather bit by bit as he experienced the visions. Stuart comments, "The intimation here plainly is, that John was employed in writing during the intervals of his visions."[21] Immediately, a voice from heaven commands him to seal up what was just revealed, indicating that the time for their publication had not yet come. This is the voice that continues to speak to the apostle until we discover it to be the voice of Yahweh Himself in 11:3, where He "grant[s] authority to [*his*] two witnesses" (author's emphasis). The instructions given to John here are the same as were given unto Daniel concerning his visions: "But you, Daniel, shut up the words and seal the book, until the time of the end" (Dan. 12:4). John immediately obeys as he continues in the Spirit.

---

20 See notes at 5:1–6.
21 Moses Stuart, *A Commentary on the Apocalypse*, 207.

Verses 5–7: "And the angel whom I saw standing on the sea and on the land raised his right hand to heaven and swore by him who lives forever and ever, who created heaven and what is in it, the earth and what is in it, and the sea and what is in it, that there would be no more delay, but that in the days of the trumpet call to be sounded by the seventh angel, the mystery of God would be fulfilled, just as he announced to his servants the prophets." In response to the heavenly instruction, the angel near to John swears by the Creator, who is faithful and good in all He does. In recording these things, the apostle uses the Hebraic threefold division of creation in connection with the one by whom is sworn—namely, sky, land, and sea. This draws his readers' attention back to Genesis 1:3–25 and Exodus 20:11, wherein the Spirit of God first utilizes this division through the pen of Moses. Furthermore, this directly links the Revelation, and thus the entire New Testament, back to the *Tanakh*—that is, to the entire Jewish canon of Scripture (the Jewish Old Testament): *Torah* (Law), *Nevi'im* (Prophets), and *Ketuvim* (Writings).

Now quite to the contrary to what was told Daniel, John is given only a short time period for which to await the unveiling and the fulfillment of those things contained within the little scroll. The angel calls these seven judgments "the mystery of God." He promises on the surety of God's own character that these judgments will be unveiled and come to pass "in the days of the [seventh] trumpet call"—this doesn't necessarily mean "at the exact moment of the seventh trumpet call," but certainly at a time in close proximity to that avenging act.

By way of application, there are some teachers today who would advise that we must follow suit with Christ and His apostles by "unhitching" the Old Testament from the New Testament, especially on an ethical front, which is quite the opposite to what John the apostle does here in the Revelation under the moving of the Holy Spirit. They would argue this in order to make the gospel message as simple as possible for modern-day non-Christians to accept—we just need the death, burial, and resurrection of Jesus. Full stop. Probably the loudest voice at the present in this regard is Andy Stanley, the son of the popular evangelical preacher Charles Stanley. In a sermon entitled "Aftermath, Part 3: Not Difficult," preached on April 29, 2018, he argued passionately for this point from a rather ahistorical rendering of Acts 15.[22] That view is not only dangerous, since no part of the

---

22   Andy Stanley, "Aftermath, Part 3: Not Difficult," YouTube Video, April 30, 2018, https://www.youtube.com/watch?v=pShxFTNRCWI.

New Testament treats the Old Testament in such a fashion, but it serves to reignite the ancient Marcionite heresy once again.[23] While all sides of the debate within orthodoxy would concur that there are elements of discontinuity between the old and new covenants, to treat the Scriptures as if there is no continuity (or very little) between them is to completely ignore the way the Bible treats itself. This has led to such erroneous ideas as identifying the God of the Old Testament as a God of wrath but the God of the New Testament as a God of grace. Such "minced-meat making" of the text of Holy Writ is something any person wishing to faithfully follow the Lord Jesus ought to avoid with all their might! May we imitate the apostle John in holding the Scriptures together as a unified whole.

Verses 8–9a: "Then the voice that I had heard from heaven spoke to me again, saying, 'Go, take the scroll that is open in the hand of the angel who is standing on the sea and on the land.' So I went to the angel and told him to give me the little scroll." In the Spirit, John again receives instruction from Yahweh, who spoke to him in verse 4. He's commanded to take the little scroll from the angel's hand, and he obeys by requesting the messenger to give him the book.

Verses 9b–10: "And he said to me, 'Take and eat it; it will make your stomach bitter, but in your mouth it will be sweet as honey.' And I took the little scroll from the hand of the angel and ate it. It was sweet as honey in my mouth, but when I had eaten it my stomach was made bitter." This is the same thing Ezekiel was previously instructed to do, the result being "it was in [his] mouth as sweet as honey" (Ezek. 3:1–3).[24] Wilmshurst notes that this is a "very similar command to another exiled prophet about 680 years before (Ezek. 2:9–3:3)."[25] Wilson adds, "That ancient prophet was addressing the destruction of Jerusalem (also), as accomplished by the Babylonians in 586 BC."[26] Like Ezekiel, the scroll is initially sweet in the disciple's mouth, but then becomes bitter in his stomach. The acts of vengeance decreed in the scroll are sweet because through them the Lord is pleased to accomplish the counsel of His will in His justice and holiness.

---

23 See Kevin DeYoung, "Marcion and Getting Unhitched from the Old Testament," The Gospel Coalition, May 11, 2018, https://www.thegospelcoalition.org/blogs/kevin-deyoung/marcion-getting-unhitched-old-testament/.

24 See Beale and McDonough, "Revelation," 1117.

25 Wilmshurst, *Revelation: The Final Word*, Kindle Location 1520.

26 Wilson, *When the Man Comes Around*, Kindle Location 1300.

Yet simultaneously, they are bitter because there is much hardship and suffering involved. This is what John experiences as he is in the Spirit.

Verse 11: "And I was told, 'You must again prophesy about many peoples and nations and languages and kings.'" The Lord again speaks from heaven, just as He did in verses 4 and 8. This is the main point of this particular vision. It is given as an encouragement to the apostle that he has much more to prophesy unto God's people concerning the way in which the Messiah must conquer to the ends of the earth and take all the nations as His treasured possession. Here is the same language used in 1:5, 5:9–10, and 7:9, and thus continues the already established pattern. In this way, the fall of Jerusalem comes as the definitive closure to the old covenant system (cf. Heb. 8:13), giving way to the fullness of the covenant of grace in the new covenant to progressively take root worldwide—truly, the gospel of the kingdom is a gospel unto the whole world![27] This is revealed as he receives and writes down the rest of the Apocalypse, which includes the seven thunder judgments contained in the scroll. All praise and honor and strength to the Father and the Son who faithfully keep Their word, and not one iota or dot could ever be thwarted! Hallelujah to the Lord God Most High!

Chapter 11, verses 1–2: "Then I was given a measuring rod like a staff, and I was told, 'Rise and measure the temple of God and the altar and those who worship there, but do not measure the court outside the temple; leave that out, for it is given over to the nations, and they will trample the holy city for forty-two months.'" Being in the Spirit, John continues to speak with the angel who's standing on the land and the sea, meaning the visions at this point are taking place on *earth*, not in heaven. Nevertheless, the one speaking at this point to him is again the Lord Almighty. Now the apostle is transported to the temple in Jerusalem, where he is told to measure the temple and everything in it, including the worshippers. This seems to be a reference to the temple described in Haggai 1:12–2:8, which is the second temple, rebuilt under the leadership of Joshua the high priest and Zerubbabel the governor. Just as Ezekiel described the glory of Yahweh leaving the first temple to the east just prior to its destruction (Ezek. 10), so also Jesus left the second temple to the east, leaving it to become desolate (see Matt. 23:37–24:3). Most importantly, verse 8 confirms that this "holy city" is in fact the "great city . . . where their Lord was crucified"—this is

---

27 Wilson, *When the Man Comes Around*, Kindle Location 1316.

further confirmed in 14:14–20, 17:15–18, and 19:15–24, as these later passages all refer to the same city. Therefore, this is speaking of the temple in Jerusalem, which was still standing as John penned these words.

"To measure" in this context means "to evaluate"—in this case, the condition of the entire center of worship in Israel, including those who worship therein. John is instructed to evaluate the inner courts, while Jesus has already evaluated the outer court, the court of the Gentiles (nations). The court of the Gentiles had become a kind of bazaar instead of being the sacred place of worship it was built to be. In keeping Leviticus 14:33–47, our Lord came to the temple to evaluate it as the authoritative High Priest. He first came to the temple at the beginning of His ministry looking for disease; He found it and so cleansed His Father's house (John 2:13–17). He came again at the end of His ministry and the spiritual disease was still there (Matt. 21:12–13). Therefore, He condemned that house and ordered that it should be torn down completely (see Matt. 23:37–39).[28] This is why John is instructed *not* to measure the outer court, which has been given over to the nations that will trample Jerusalem for forty-two months. This is exactly what Jesus prophesied would happen—that is, "They will fall by the edge of the sword and be led captive among all nations, *and Jerusalem will be trampled underfoot by the Gentiles*, until the times of the Gentiles are fulfilled" (Luke 21:24, author's emphasis). Notice that "and [the nations] will trample the holy city" is nearly a direct quotation of Jesus's words!

There is a time frame of forty-two months given in verse 2. This is equivalent in value to the 1,260 days in the following verse and in 12:6, as well as to the three and a half years mentioned at 12:14. This timeframe is derived from Daniel 7:25.[29] All these refer to the same historic time period, that being the First Jewish-Roman War, which lasted approximately three and a half years. The siege of Jerusalem began April 14, AD 70, and the conquest of the city ended September 8 of the same year—a little under five months. The surrounding fortresses of Herodium, Machaerus, and Masada continued to be run by Judean rebels until the last of the three, Masada, was finally taken in AD 73. Josephus writes that Masada's defenders committed mass suicide before the Romans breached the entrance.[30]

---

28 See Matt. 21:18–22, 28–44; 22:1–14; 23:1–39; 24:1–35.

29 See Reformation Study Bible notes, Revelation 11:2; see also Beale and McDonough, "Revelation," 1118.

30 See Flavius Josephus, trans. William Whiston, *The Complete Works of Josephus, Wars of the*

Verses 3–4: "'And I will grant authority to my two witnesses, and they will prophesy for 1,260 days, clothed in sackcloth.' These are the two olive trees and the two lampstands that stand before the Lord of the earth." These two witnesses take spiritual leadership under God's authority during the entire period of tribulation, "until the times of the [nations] are fulfilled" (Luke 21:24), which symbolically is the length of 1,260 days. They are much like Joshua and Zerubbabel during the time of the temple's rebuilding when the remnant returned from Babylon, mentioned in Zechariah 3–4.[31] Furthermore, they wear sackcloth as a sign of humility and grief for the nation, much akin to Elijah and, later, John the Baptizer.

John's interpretation of these two in verse 4 points us back to Zechariah 4, where we learn that the seven-branched lampstand represents "the eyes of Yahweh, which range through the whole earth," and the two olive trees on either side thereof "are the two anointed ones who stand by the Lord of the whole earth" (Zechariah 4:10, 14).[32] "The two anointed ones," literally rendered from Hebrew, mean "the two sons of new oil,"[33] which is a reference to the fruits in a believer's life resulting from the new birth (cf. Matt. 25:1–4). Yet here we read of *two* lampstands, which are one and the same as the two olive trees, a symbolic description of the two witnesses who "stand by the Lord of the whole earth." In addition, the following verses show them performing amazing, supernatural feats, including belching forth fire from their mouths that consumes their enemies—this ought to be taken as symbolic language. It seems these two witnesses together represent the believing remnant of Israel who have endured much suffering for the name of the Messiah, even some being put to death, yet have remained faithful to the end. Acts 4:32–37 shows how the Jerusalem believers took great care of one another as they prepared for the coming sign to "flee to the mountains" (Matt. 24:16). Hendriksen observes, "Just as 'the two olive trees and two candle sticks,' Joshua and Zerubbabel(?) (*cf.* Zc. 4), represented the offices through which God blessed Israel, so throughout the gospel era He blesses His church through the offices—that is, through the preaching of the Word and the administration of the sacraments."[34] Other than on the point of timing, this seems to accurately represent what is being

---

Jews, 7.8–9 (Grand Rapids: Kregel, 1981).
31 See Beale and McDonough, "Revelation," 1119.
32 See Reformation Study Bible notes, Revelation 11:3.
33 ESV notes, Zechariah 4:14.
34 Hendriksen, *More Than Conquerors*, Kindle Location 2247.

communicated in this passage. This means that the supernatural feats of the church militant, symbolically portrayed in verses 5–6 as belching forth fire from their mouths and commanding rain to cease, comes through their faithful public worship in the assembly and their faithful witness in preaching the gospel of Messiah's kingdom-rule in both the familial and civil spheres.

Worship is warfare. When the local church congregates together for public worship, not only are we joining the heavenly beings around Yahweh's throne in heaven in exalting Him for who He is, but we are also advancing the rule of Jesus in the world. When God commanded the children of Israel to take Jericho, it was not through brute force, but rather through worship (see Josh. 5:13–6:21). The apostle Paul tells us that "the weapons of our warfare are not of the flesh but have divine power to destroy strongholds" (2 Cor. 10:4). What are the "weapons of our warfare" but the right preaching of the Word and the right administration of the sacraments? These are indeed the central acts of public worship, and for this reason, the great Genevan pastor John Calvin rightly gave much weight and emphasis to these things. Of such importance were they to him that he was willing to guard the Lord's Table with swords to prevent those unworthy coming forward! For many a Reformed believer, the right teaching and preaching of the Word is of utmost concern. But too often the sacraments, those soul-nourishing means of grace, end up underemphasized, sidelined, and hurried through without the proper reflection on the fullness of what the Scriptures reveal with regard to the Lord's Supper and baptism. It would be unthinkable to many a Christian to attempt public worship without singing the Word back to God in praise. However, we relegate seeing the Word in Holy Communion to once a month at best, sometimes even quarterly or biannually. Doing so could lead some to consider worship through singing as more central than worship through keeping the ordinances. Not only that, but we may trivialize what some see as a New Testament precedent in breaking bread together each and every time we assemble ourselves for public worship (e.g., Acts 20:7), and thus treat it as an optional element of worship rather than the Christ-prescribed element it is.

The main issue here is one of heart attitude. Do we actually believe the sacraments are a central element of public worship? Do we truly believe that entering into heaven every Lord's Day to worship round the throne is a most holy privilege, and thus must be done exactly the way He has commanded, no more and no less, lest we end up like Nadab and Abihu (see Lev. 10:1–3)? Do we really view the ordinances as equally central to right worship as the Word preached? Do we actually trust God's Word when it indicates that the public worship of the saints is, in fact, warfare? Are we convinced that through our faithful, physically assembled acts of service, "the God of peace [is] crush[ing] Satan under [our] feet" (Rom. 16:20) and that His Messiah is, in fact, destroying the enemy's strongholds through us? May the Lord challenge us to the depths of our beings in this regard.

Verse 5: "And if anyone would harm them, fire pours from their mouth and consumes their foes. If anyone would harm them, this is how he is doomed to be killed." Throughout the Apocalypse, fire is used in the context of judgment. Thus, Christ's saints have been given His authority to bring judgment on His enemies through their prophetic witness.[35] Indeed, the preaching of the law and the gospel is "the aroma of Christ to God among those who are being saved *and* among those who are perishing, to one a fragrance of death to death, to the other a fragrance from life to life" (2 Cor. 2:15–16, author's emphasis). They have been given this authority directly from the one who has "all authority in heaven and on earth" (Matt. 28:18).

What an incredible privilege is ours, having been joined to our Savior in death and resurrection by the regenerating work of His Spirit! May we steward it well unto His honor and glory. May we do so always remembering that it is *His* power at work through us, not any strength of our own!

Verse 6: "They have the power to shut the sky, that no rain may fall during the days of their prophesying, and they have power over the waters to turn them into blood and to strike the earth with every kind of plague, as often as they desire." Like Moses and Elijah, they are given power to bring plagues of vengeance on the Messiah's enemies. Elijah brought a severe drought as judgment upon Israel (1 Kings 17:1). Likewise, Moses turned water into blood as judgment upon the land of Egypt (Ex. 7:14–24).[36] In the same way, when enemies of Christ persistently reject the faithful preaching of His gospel message, believers have real authority to judge and condemn them in His congregation. In fact, Jesus assures His

---

35 See Beale and McDonough, "Revelation," 1119–1120.

36 See Beale and McDonough, "Revelation," 1120. Beale's notes here are helpful in seeing the allusion to both Elijah and Moses.

disciples that their judgments are His judgments in the context of the local church (see Matt. 16:19; 18:18–20).[37]

In our politically correct culture, manifested in the evangelical world as a need to avoid violating the "Eleventh Commandment: You shall be nice" at all costs, such a proposition is simply unacceptable. This has led to congregations refusing to properly apply scriptural teaching on church discipline, which has resulted in a tolerance of ungodliness and worldliness amongst the saints. It has also resulted in a severe lack of concern for Christ's bride to be presented unto Him on the Last Day pure and without blemish. Yet all of the above are conspicuously taught in Holy Writ, and thus must be fully accepted and acted upon with gladness of heart. The Word of God, when rightly understood on its own terms, is not subject to our disagreements—rather, we are the ones who must change and submit ourselves to divine revelation as unto the Triune God Himself.

Verses 7–8: "And when they have finished their testimony, the beast that rises from the bottomless pit will make war on them and conquer them and kill them, and their dead bodies will lie in the street of the great city that symbolically is called Sodom and Egypt, where their Lord was crucified." The events of these verses take place *after* "they have finished their testimony." The persecution and martyrdom of these saints are things appointed, not random or without purpose, since God decrees all such trials and sufferings in all their specifics (see Phil. 1:29; Heb. 9:27). Yet the one through whom He is working to bring this about is the beast, who rises from the same place from whence came the locusts in the fifth trumpet judgment. This is the abyss, which symbolizes a kind of imprisonment for evil spirits.

Now, "In Scripture, beasts are persecuting political powers."[38] We learn in chapter 13 that the beast of the sea generically represents Rome and specifically Caesar Nero, who reigned from AD 54 to 68. Here in verse 7, the beast likely refers to Rome in general.[39] The beast is also demonically possessed and takes his cues from Satan. He hates all followers of Christ because they insist that there is only one Lord over all, who is Jesus, *not* the emperor (cf. Acts 4:12; Rom. 10:8–10). Therefore, he attacks the saints in Israel and

---

37 See Hendriksen, *More Than Conquerors*, Kindle Location 2258. Hendriksen brings this out in his notes at this juncture in the text.

38 Wilson, *When the Man Comes Around*, Kindle Location 1382.

39 See Kenneth L. Gentry Jr., *He Shall Have Dominion: A Postmillennial Eschatology* (Chesnee, SC: Victorious Hope, 2021), 420.

throughout the Empire, killing many of them for their faith in the Messiah—this comports with Jesus's words in Matthew 24:9 (and the parallel accounts in Mark 13:12–13 and Luke 21:12–19). The epicenter of this is the great city, which is clearly Jerusalem, since this is "where their Lord was crucified." It is symbolically called Sodom and Egypt because its vile rebellion against Yahweh and His Anointed King parallels that of those ancient communities, Sodom and Egypt, which both came under judgment.[40]

Verses 9–10: "For three and a half days some from the peoples and tribes and languages and nations will gaze at their dead bodies and refuse to let them be placed in a tomb, and those who dwell on the earth will rejoice over them and make merry and exchange presents, because these two prophets had been a torment to those who dwell on the earth." It is a great disgrace for someone's dead body to be left without a proper burial, especially in the middle of a public roadway of all places! Indeed, the goal of the nations' refusal of Messiah's followers was in order to publicly shame them. The reason the nations celebrate their deaths is that they had been tormented day and night by their preaching of the good news of His kingdom. We have an example of this in Acts 6:12–15. That passage demonstrates that even though false witnesses were trying to slander Stephen at his trial, it is quite evident that he and others were boldly preaching against the Jewish leadership, warning them of Jesus's soon coming in judgment against them. Here, the nations' celebration over their seeming defeat continues for three and a half days, which is symbolically forty-two months, or three and a half years. Most of the time, in the apocalyptic imagery of John's visions, this time period of three and a half days represents the whole duration of the First Jewish-Roman War, the height of which was the fall of Jerusalem and the destruction of its temple. This is exactly what Jesus predicted would come to pass. However, at this particular juncture, it speaks to the period between when Nero blamed Christians for the fires in Rome, which he himself instigated, and when he was cornered into committing suicide during a coup—historically, this period of persecution lasted from November of AD 64 to June of 68, a period of 42 months.[41] This took place actually as John prophesied. Truly, the Word of the living God can be fully trusted!

---

40 See Beale and McDonough, "Revelation," 1120–1121.
41 See Wilson, *When the Man Comes Around*, Kindle Location 1347.

Verse 11: "But after the three and a half days a breath of life from God entered them, and they stood up on their feet, and great fear fell on those who saw them." Immediately following the coup in Rome, the church would gain strength and stability once again as persecution waned for a season, such that they would have a gospel influence in society as salt and light (see Matt. 5:13–16). This would have been a great surprise to their persecutors, and thus great fear fell on them all, just as it was for Jonah's shipmates when they discovered they were, in fact, opposing the living God (Jonah 1:9–16).[42] Truly, in all manner of trial the Lord sends our way, "we are more than conquerors through him who loved us" (Rom. 8:37)! As the Heidelberg Catechism puts it, "1. Q. What is your only comfort in life and death? A. That I am not my own, but belong with body and soul, both in life and in death, to my faithful Savior Jesus Christ. He has fully paid for all my sins with His precious blood, and has set me free from all the power of the devil. He also preserves me in such a way that without the will of my heavenly Father not a hair can fall from my head; indeed, all things must work together for my salvation. Therefore, by His Holy Spirit He also assures me of eternal life and makes me heartily willing and ready from now on to live for Him."[43] What a tremendous comfort this truly is for those who are His!

Verse 12: "Then they heard a loud voice from heaven saying to them, 'Come up here!' And they went up to heaven in a cloud, and their enemies watched them." This is as Jesus said it would be: "By your endurance you will gain your lives" (Luke 21:19). This is a clear confirmation of all that He promised unto each of the seven congregations back in chapters 2 and 3 on the condition of conquering through all their tribulations. These martyrs, as those who have been vindicated, are a part of the great multitude in chapter 19 singing aloud, "Hallelujah!" in response to the judgments. Their spirits have entered Paradise for the intermediate period until the time of their physical resurrection on the Last Day, which is symbolically given here in the words, "and they went up to heaven in a cloud."

Verse 13: "And at that hour there was a great earthquake, and a tenth of the city fell. Seven thousand people were killed in the earthquake, and

---

42 See Beale and McDonough, "Revelation," 1121.

43 Zecharias Ursinus, "The Heidelberg Catechism (1563, 1619)," https://www.apuritansmind.com/creeds-and-confessions/the-heidelberg-catechism-by-zacharias-ursinus/.

the rest were terrified and gave glory to the God of heaven." The earthquake symbolizes the great vengeance that fell upon Jerusalem in that hour, with the exact number of people slaughtered at the hands of the Romans, according to what had been decreed in the scroll. The value "seven thousand" represents the complete number of those appointed to be killed. This attack on the holy city was not that led by Vespasian and Titus, but rather an earlier attempt led by Gaius Cestius Gallus, proconsul of Syria. However, the Zealots under the leadership of Simon bar Giora managed to fend them off with great ferocity. Through this initial conflict at the outset of the Jewish-Roman War, Yahweh took a tithe of the city, indicating that He would surely claim the rest as well.[44] One might ask why they were terrified. They were sore afraid that judgment would also fall on them, and so quickly they "gave glory to the God of heaven," clearly motivated by self-preservation. However, as the rest of the Revelation indicates, this self-serving response had zero effect in deterring their God-ordained demise. The eternal counsel of the Lord stands firm and can in nowise be thwarted by another!

Verse 14: "The second woe has passed; behold, the third woe is soon to come." This is simply a way for John to return his readers' attention back to the trumpet judgments. Behold, the seventh trumpet.

THE SEVENTH TRUMPET

Verse 15: "Then the seventh angel blew his trumpet, and there were loud voices in heaven, saying, 'The kingdom of the world has become the kingdom of our Lord and of his Christ, and he shall reign forever and ever.'" At this point, the visions return to heaven, from whence the Son of Man reigns, which is indicated by the rejoicing and worship taking place in heaven. Although Jesus's reign officially began in His ascension, the scene here seems to be in direct response to the completion of the previous six trumpets, including the first Roman attack on Jerusalem under Cestius. This is the first portion of the first major act of the Messianic King putting His enemies under His feet since His exaltation and, in so doing, transforming the very fabric of society and culture from being defined by sin to being defined by the rule of God on earth! "He shall reign forever and ever!" is a sentiment that's been expressed throughout Scripture concerning the rule of the Messiah over all the nations (e.g., 2 Sam. 7:12–13, 16; Isa. 9:7),

---

44 See Wilson, *When the Man Comes Around*, Kindle Location 1420.

so it should by no means surprise us to find such a joyous announcement at this juncture in redemptive history. Such a glorious abundance of good news can do nothing less than elicit endless rejoicing from all His sheep worldwide! That ought to be our response as well when we see the Lord Jesus subduing His enemies, just as He said He would!

Verses 16–18: "And the twenty-four elders who sit on their thrones before God fell on their faces and worshiped God, saying, 'We give thanks to you, Lord God Almighty, who is and who was, for you have taken your great power and begun to reign. The nations raged, but your wrath came, and the time for the dead to be judged, and for rewarding your servants, the prophets and the saints, and those who fear your name, both small and great, and for destroying the destroyers of the earth.'" The leaders of the entirety of Christ's body, who are reigning with Him as He reigns, also worship Him for this great victory, falling prostrate before Him. They thank Him and address Him by His self-given title, as revealed in 1:8—namely, the one "who is and who was and who is to come, the Almighty." They worship Him because he has taken his "great power and begun to reign." This does not mean that Yahweh was not reigning from all eternity—for surely He was (cf. Ps. 103:19)—but rather that He now reigns in a new and special way through His Anointed King. Christ was given "all authority in heaven and on earth" in His exaltation (Matt. 28:18) which began with His resurrection from the dead and formally took place at His enthronement upon returning to heaven, having completed all that the Father gave Him to do (see John 6:35–44; 17:5; 19:30).[45]

The twenty-four elders celebrate that "the nations raged, but your wrath came." This is an allusion to Psalm 2, which the apostles applied to all those involved in murdering the Son of Man, most particularly the Jews (cf. Acts 2:23; 4:24–28). They rejoice because the Anointed One is doing what He was given to do—that is, to "break [his enemies] with a rod of iron and dash them in pieces like a potter's vessel" (Ps. 2:9). For this reason, He sat down on the Davidic throne at His Father's right hand. As Psalm 110 explains, "[Yahweh] sends forth from Zion your mighty scepter. Rule in the midst of your enemies! . . . The Lord is at your right hand; he will shatter kings on the day of his wrath. He will execute judgment among the nations, filling them with corpses; he will shatter chiefs over the wide earth. He will drink from the brook by the way; therefore he will lift up his head"

---

45 See Wilson, *When the Man Comes Around*, Kindle Location 1438.

(110:2, 5–7). This results in the judging of the wicked and rewarding of all those who fear God. Contrary to what many assert, this cannot be referring to the final judgment, which is depicted in Revelation 20. There is a textual reason in that Revelation 20:11 states that "earth and sky fled away," indicating the end of human history, while Revelation 11:19 uses the same cosmic deconstructive language as before, signaling that further judgments are yet to come on the covenant-breakers of Israel.

Their song ends with praising Yahweh "for destroying the destroyers of the earth" in His wrath. The Pharisees' elevation of what would be called the *Mishnah*, (that is, the oral tradition of the elders—which they saw as theoretically on par with the Scriptures but functionally over and above them) caused them to destroy people's lives by leading them into all manner of spiritual ditches. This is precisely why Jesus condemned them in Matthew 15:1–20. This also led to their prideful rejection of their own Messiah, though the entire *Tanakh* (the Jewish Old Testament) was clear in speaking of Him and though He was right in front of them in flesh and blood! The Pharisees were undoubtedly the very epitome of Israel in her greatest and final apostasy, for which King Jesus is now in the process of judging.

This ought to be a great warning to us as Christ's saints. There have been many who have unwittingly imitated the Pharisees in elevating a secondary source to the same level as God's Word, and thus have ended up forcing the latter to become subservient to the former. Poignant examples may be offered. For example, the Papists attempt to justify a plethora of dogmatized teachings—purgatory, papal infallibility, and the immaculate conception of Mary, to name but a few—by appealing to the oral traditions of the church and then loading already formulated conclusions into individual verses like Luke 1:46–47 and 1 Corinthians 3:13. Not only this, but for the Mormons, the visions of Joseph Smith led him to teach that the god of our planet is an exalted *man*, having once been a man just as we are, but now we are his spirit children, capable of attaining exaltation just the same as he. In his King Follett Discourse, Smith taught, "God himself was once as we are now, and is an exalted man, and sits enthroned in yonder heavens! That is the great secret."[46] Yet earlier in this funeral sermon, Smith quotes John 17:3, evidently filling those God-breathed words with his own meaning. A final example, perhaps not so far afield to many of us, is the

---

46   Philippines Olongapo Mission, "King Follett Discourse by Joseph Smith," https://sites.google.com/site/philippineolongapomission/messages/king-follett-discourse-by-joseph-smith.

charismatic teaching of receiving a "word of knowledge" or "prophecy" from the Lord. Most often this is treated as a direct, personal communication from God, and thus authoritative and binding on the recipients thereof. Appeals to such instances as Paul receiving divine instruction to go to Macedonia (Acts 16:9) are used to substantiate treating these extrabiblical revelations as functionally on par with Scripture itself. It is noteworthy that in all three of these examples, there is a denial of the sufficiency of Scripture for all of faith and practice; in their minds, the canon isn't closed! This is an incredibly dangerous stance to take, as has been demonstrated above.

Verse 19: "Then God's temple in heaven was opened, and the ark of his covenant was seen within his temple. There were flashes of lightning, rumblings, peals of thunder, an earthquake, and heavy hail." It must be noticed that this verse speaks of God's *heavenly* temple with His *heavenly* ark of the covenant, which is not the same as the earthly temple mentioned in verses 1–2. Into the Most Holy Place of *this* temple Jesus entered with the blood of His sacrifice and sat down for all time (see Heb. 9:23–24). The temple here symbolizes God's true covenant people in heaven, the church, comprised of the spirits of those martyred for the sake of the Lamb (see Eph. 2:19–22; Heb. 12:22; 2 Peter 2:4–8). The ark of the covenant, however, represents God's presence among them[47] since they are forever united to Christ (cf. John 1:14, which speaks of Jesus as the true tabernacle/temple since only in Him can we directly experience the presence/glory of God).

As noted above, the second half of verse 19 contains the same language of cosmic undoing as was seen earlier, meaning that further acts of vengeance are yet to be unveiled as John continues on in his Spirit-induced out-of-body experience. Not only this, but as the author to the Hebrews put it, "At that time his voice shook the earth, but now he has promised, 'Yet once more I will shake not only the earth but also the heavens.' This phrase, 'Yet once more,' indicates the removal of things that are shaken—that is, things that have been made—in order that the things that cannot be shaken may remain" (Heb. 12:26–27). In other words, in order for the new covenant age to remain, having been established in Christ's blood on Calvary, the old covenant age must come to an end, which took place historically in AD 70.

---

47 See Beale and McDonough, "Revelation," 1122.

The Fifth Vision (12:1–14:20)

Here begins the most significant interlude in this large central section of the Revelation. This interlude may be divided into two parts: the first consisting of chapters 12–13 and the second, chapter 14. Here we are introduced to the spiritual forces at work behind their human expressions.

THE WOMAN AND THE CHILD

Chapter 12, verse 1: "And a great sign appeared in heaven: a woman clothed with the sun, with the moon under her feet, and on her head a crown of twelve stars." John continues to be shown things in heaven. Here is a woman who is absolutely radiant since she is clothed with the sun, which seems to symbolize her radiant purity and beauty as having been clothed with the seamless obedience of her Lord. In this way, she foreshadows the new Jerusalem of chapter 21.[1] As for the moon, it seems best to understand it as representing the ceremonial law, with its new moons and festivals, in which the light of the gospel was dimly seen. Gill explains, "There was some light in it, and it gave light to the saints in the night of Jewish darkness; it pointed out Christ to them, and was their schoolmaster to teach and lead them to him; yet, like the moon, it was the lesser light, the light it gave was interior to that which the Gospel now gives; and as the moon has its shots had that its imperfections; had it been faultless, there had been no need of another, and a new dispensation, but that could make nothing perfect;

---

1 See Henry, *Commentary*, Revelation 12:1–11.

and, as the moon, it was variable and changeable; it was but for a time, and is now done away; it is not only waxen old like the moon in the wane, but is entirely vanished away."[2] This "vanishing away" historically took place in AD 70 with the destruction of the temple. In addition, the lady wears a crown of twelve stars, representing the twelve tribes of Israel. Thus, the woman herself represents the Messianic community, the spiritual seed of Abraham, while still a part of the old covenant nation of Israel.[3]

Verse 2: "She was pregnant and was crying out in birth pains and the agony of giving birth." Spiritual Israel is on the verge of giving birth to the Messiah, as it were. This is meant to be taken in metaphorical terms since a community cannot *physically* give birth to a child, but only a single lady therein. It is not Mary who is said to be "crying out in birth pains," but the Messianic community itself.

Verse 3: "And another sign appeared in heaven: behold, a great red dragon, with seven heads and ten horns, and on his heads seven diadems." In verse 9, John gives us the identity of this red dragon: "that ancient serpent, who is called the devil and Satan, the deceiver of the whole world." He's pictured here as a *red* dragon because he's absolutely outraged that the one who has been promised of old to crush his head is about to come on the scene. This "indicates the beginning fulfillment of Gen. 3:15."[4] In chapter 13, he gives power to the beast, who also has seven heads and ten horns (13:1). Chapter 17 reveals an angel telling John that the seven heads represent seven mountains, which is allegorically understood to be Rome, the "City on Seven Hills." Similarly, the angel explains that the ten horns are ten kings—that is, the magistrates of the ten Roman provinces who, for a short time, will loyally assist the beast in making war on the Lamb (17:9–14). The text continues its description of the dragon thus: "on his heads [are] seven diadems." These heads are interpreted by the angel in chapter 17 as symbolizing seven kings of Rome, five having fallen, one who is, and one who is yet to come (17:9–10). History confirms the accuracy of Holy Writ.[5] In this way, at this point in the visions, Rome and its ten provinces are under Satan's sway because he has dominance over them.

---

2   See John Gill, *Exposition*, Kindle Locations 358062–358067.
3   See Reformation Study Bible notes, Revelation 12:1.
4   Beale and McDonough, "Revelation," 1123.
5   See notes at 17:9–10 for a more detailed discussion.

Verse 4: "His tail swept down a third of the stars of heaven and cast them to the earth. And the dragon stood before the woman who was about to give birth, so that when she bore her child he might devour it." As the Messianic community is on the verge of birthing a child, the devil busies himself with making those believers anxiously awaiting the coming of their King "as useless as he could."[6]—Although I would disagree with Henry in interpreting the dragon as Rome, it seems the dragon's effects on believers is still in view in his notes. The adversary's success is significant, but quite limited as only one third of the stars were swept down, symbolically a limited portion of the Messianic community. We learn in the next verse that this male child is, in fact, the promised Messiah, the Son of Man. The devil's intent is clear—he wishes to completely destroy the child before He can have influence on others and success in His mission. His intent is none other than to prevent Genesis 3:15 from coming about! Yet his power and influence are restrained by his Creator's wise providence in the world—what a great comfort is this fact to those who are Christ's!

Verse 5: "She gave birth to a male child, one who is to rule all the nations with a rod of iron, but her child was caught up to God and to his throne." Here is yet another allusion to Psalm 2:7–9, demonstrating the Messiah King is in view in this vision. Ruling "all the nations with a rod of iron" is His job description as God's Anointed One, and Satan desperately wants to prevent this from happening. The focus is clearly on the Messiah's ascension and enthronement at His Father's right hand since His entire earthly ministry, death, and resurrection are skipped over in one gigantic jump from incarnation to ascension. In this way, the Lord's eternal purposes are accomplished while Satan's intentions are thwarted, which brings great glory and honor to the name of the one true and living God.

Many a well-meaning Christian has been given a cosmology wherein the powers of good and the powers of evil have relatively equal strength, and are thus forever "duking it out." Much like the situation presented in the *Star Wars* series, there is no eternal decree being worked out in time and space, there is no ultimate purpose to the conflict, and there is no real assurance as to which side will win. Yet this is not at all the view of Scripture. Much like rebellious men, who are also creatures, Satan and his minions make plans and enact them, but theirs is merely that of secondary causation, not primary. The primary mover in all things is the Triune God,

---

6   Henry, *Commentary*, Revelation 12:1–11.

who does all that He pleases in the heavens and on the earth, accomplishing all His good and eternal purposes, and no one can stay His hand or insolently ask, "What have You done?"

Verse 6: "and the woman fled into the wilderness, where she has a place prepared by God, in which she is to be nourished for 1,260 days." Jesus instructed His disciples, "But when you see Jerusalem surrounded by armies, then know that its desolation has come near. Then let those who are in Judea flee to the mountains, and let those who are inside the city depart, and let not those who are out in the country enter it" (Luke 21:20–21). Eusebius, a fourth-century church historian, recorded that when Jerusalem was surrounded by Roman armies, all the Christians escaped and fled to the town of Pella, where they remained during the war.[7] In this way the Messianic community was kept safe in the wilderness for 1,260 days, or three and a half years, which was the entire duration of the Jewish-Roman War. History itself corroborates the truthfulness of these words! Truly, our Lord is most trustworthy!

Just as the Lord saw fit to protect His people in the first century from the reach of Satan, as enacted through the agency of Rome, He continues to be a refuge unto them throughout the ages. The psalmist expresses that truth in this way: "LORD is my rock and my fortress and my deliverer, my God, my rock, in whom I take refuge, my shield, and the horn of my salvation, my stronghold. I call upon the LORD, who is worthy to be praised, and I am saved from my enemies" (Ps. 18:2–3). For the one who truly belongs to Jesus by the regenerating power of the Holy Spirit, though we may not be kept from experiencing the temporal effects of satanically influenced groups or ideologies in the exact same way our first-century Judean brethren were, our confidence lies in Yahweh our God to aid us in overcoming therethrough and to safeguard us in our eternal experience. May this truth be a great comfort to us and may we follow our King with the eyes of faith set squarely on Him!

THE DRAGON CAST DOWN

Verses 7–9: "Now war arose in heaven, Michael and his angels fighting against the dragon. And the dragon and his angels fought back, but he

---

[7] See Eusebius, trans. Kirsopp Lake, *Ecclesiastical History, Volume I: Books 1–5*, 3.5.3, Loeb Classical Library 153 (Cambridge: Harvard University Press, 1926).

was defeated, and there was no longer any place for them in heaven. And the great dragon was thrown down, that ancient serpent, who is called the devil and Satan, the deceiver of the whole world—he was thrown down to the earth, and his angels were thrown down with him." This cannot be referring to Satan's expulsion from heaven sometime prior to mankind's fall into sin, as some have supposed. Why? Because the context is of the Messiah's rule over all the nations, which He began to exercise at His enthronement. This seems to parallel verses 4–5 and serves to further explain the spiritual conflict concurrent with the birth, life, death, and resurrection of the Lord Jesus. The entire cosmos is convulsing as the Son of God prepares to take on flesh and tabernacle among us (see John 1:14). Yet God's purposes in history cannot be thwarted, and so Satan's accusations are cast down. The triumph that Jesus accomplished over all His enemies in His death at Calvary (see Col. 2:15)[8] is a present reality in heaven, and thus any accusation against him has been excommunicated therefrom. However, these accusations still remain in the earth, where Messiah is in the process of overcoming them as He gradually subdues all His enemies under His feet in His resurrected glory. Is this not what we are praying for when we request, "Your kingdom come, your will be done, on earth as it is in heaven" (Matt. 6:10)?[9] As this takes place on earth historically, Michael stands in heaven to bear witness to this victory before the throne—his relationship to the Son of Man here parallels that described in Daniel 10.[10]

Verse 10: "And I heard a loud voice in heaven, saying, 'Now the salvation and the power and the kingdom of our God and the authority of his Christ have come, for the accuser of our brothers has been thrown down, who accuses them day and night before our God.'" They rejoice in the reality of what Jesus announced immediately before His ascension: "All authority in heaven and on earth has been given to me" (Matt. 28:18). The Son is now free to accomplish His purpose as the appointed Messianic King now that the accuser, which is what *Satan* means in Hebrew, "has been thrown down," which is the equivalent of saying that the strong man's house can be plundered since he has now been bound (see Matt. 12:29; John 12:30–32).[11] Through His death and resurrection, the Lord

---

8   See Wilmshurst, *Revelation: The Final Word*, Kindle Location 1785.
9   See Wilson, *When the Man Comes Around*, Kindle Location 1507.
10 See Beale and McDonough, "Revelation," 1124–1125.
11 See Reformation Study Bible notes, Revelation 12:7–12.

Jesus prevents Satan from bringing accusations against His people before the Father in heaven; thus, any accusations that come their way on earth are rendered meaningless. We are truly "more than conquerors through him who loved us" (Rom. 8:37)!

It's important to remember that history is defined by the fulfillment of Yahweh's promises and the effects of His Messianic King's humiliation and exaltation rather than by the work of the Evil One or the hardships of this life. To summarise a common Puritan sentiment, "The effects of the resurrection in history far outweigh the effects of the fall!" While what we often see around us is the latter, our lives are to be characterized by walking by faith in the former and not by sight, just like the Old Testament saints of Hebrews chapter 11. May our daily prayer be to live more and more in light of this biblical view of history by faith, and to do so in the power of the Spirit, who indwells all true saints, even us who are Christ's sheep!

Verse 11: "'And they have conquered him by the blood of the Lamb and by the word of their testimony, for they loved not their lives even unto death.'" The brothers—that is, those who have the Lamb's name on their foreheads—conquer the devil through their gospel preaching and discipling of all the nations, treasuring their Lord above all, even their own lives. Indeed, this is the Great Commission in action (Matt. 28:18–20)! These are true disciples of Christ since they have counted the cost of faithfully following Him to the end (see Matt. 10:16–39; Luke 14:25–33) as a result of His death in their place. This substitutionary death for sinners is also the reason why Satan can no longer accuse them, as was discussed at verse 10. The picture here ought to be a holy example to every believer and every congregation under the sun! This is what biblical Christianity looks like!

Verse 12: 'Therefore, rejoice, O heavens and you who dwell in them! But woe to you, O earth and sea, for the devil has come down to you in great wrath, because he knows that his time is short!" Now that Satan is bound—as it were, on the end of a short chain—he is immeasurably more vicious and wild than he was before Messiah's crucifixion. Henry elaborates, "The rage of Satan grows so much the greater as he is limited both in space and in time."[12] He knows he's a defeated foe and that, at any moment, Christ could put another one of His enemies under His feet through the power of the gospel. For this reason, he desperately seeks to inflict as much

---

12   Henry, *Commentary*, Revelation 12:12–17.

suffering and discouragement as possible on the saints who dwell on earth lest they should trample his actors underfoot through their faithful testimony (see Rom. 16:20). The devil is insane, since he continues to deny reality, and insanely vindictive, as evidenced by his myriad of schemes.

Verse 13: "And when the dragon saw that he had been thrown down to the earth, he pursued the woman who had given birth to the male child." Before the saints in Jerusalem and Judea, the devil seeks to do all he can to destroy them, both through physical suffering and through various and sundry discouragements. Satan's goal is to take followers of Jesus out of the race, but our weapons of warfare are vastly superior to his since we belong to the King of kings and Lord of lords! For this reason the apostle Paul wrote, "Finally, be strong in the Lord and in the strength of his might. Put on the whole armor of God, that you may be able to stand against the schemes of the devil" (Eph. 6:10–11).

Let these words be strength to carry us when we're downcast and in the depths of despair, just as many a faithful saint has been. As the devil joins forces together with the world and the flesh to assail the faithful follower of Christ, our only hope to overcome these enemies of the soul on a daily basis is the Lord our God and His most precious Word. Even men such as Charles H. Spurgeon and David Brainerd suffered much melancholy but found great comfort in knowing that when we are weak, our Savior is very strong! Therefore, let us preach the truth to ourselves lest we lose heart and give up![13]

Verse 14: "But the woman was given the two wings of the great eagle so that she might fly from the serpent into the wilderness, to the place where she is to be nourished for a time, and times, and half a time." In verse 6, we learn that the saints fled into the wilderness to be protected and encouraged by their Lord throughout the duration of the war. This place of refuge was the town of Pella. We also learn in that verse that the saints are "nourished [there] for 1,260 days," which is expressed here as "a time, and times, and half a time," or three and a half years. This is how Christ rescued them from the snares of the Evil One in keeping with His words in the Olivet Discourse (cf. Matt. 24:15–21; Mark 13:14–19; Luke 21:20–24).

---

13 It must be noted that great melancholy and depression can be caused by chemical imbalances in lieu of, or in addition to, external influences, either human or demonic. Nevertheless, the Lord providentially brings all these things about for good, to accomplish His eternal purposes in our lives to the praise of His glory.

We must be careful in how we seek to apply this teaching to our lives today in the twenty-first century. The promises and instruction given in the Olivet Discourse were specific to the generation of believers standing before Jesus at that time, and He certainly did keep His word to them. However, it does not follow that He has promised to do the same thing for us in the same way. We are not meant to make a one-to-one comparison such that we should be packing our bags, selling our possessions, and looking for a small mountain community to which to retreat. In fact, our Lord teaches us to do the exact opposite as we wait for His physical return on the Last Day since "[we] know neither the day nor the hour" (Matt. 25:1–13)! However, Jesus has promised to be with us through our vital union to Him and the indwelling of His Spirit's presence. He has promised to be with us to ensure our success in discipling all the nations and teaching them to obey all He has commanded. He has promised to carry on the good work of salvation He has begun in us through working in us to will and do according to His good pleasure. And so, as we see God's faithfulness in keeping His word to protect His people in the first century in the specifics, we likewise can fully trust Him to keep His promises to us in the specifics.

Verses 15–16: "The serpent poured water like a river out of his mouth after the woman, to sweep her away with a flood. But the earth came to the help of the woman, and the earth opened its mouth and swallowed the river that the dragon had poured from his mouth." Since Satan could not destroy the church within Jerusalem and Judea, he now attempts to do so through deceit and slanderous accusations.[14] This effort also fails as the Lord protects His people in the wilderness from this pernicious attack, symbolized here as "the earth open[ing] its mouth and swallow[ing] the river." That the devil now tries to use his cunning against the saints fits well with what verse 9 teaches about his character—he is "the deceiver of the whole world."

No matter what the Evil One may throw our way, the Son of Man will not allow His own to be harassed beyond the measure which He has decreed. He will most assuredly protect His elect, ensuring His church is built and His dominion of justice and peace is established to the ends of the earth! This ought to be a great comfort to us when we face suffering for faithfulness to Jesus coming in various degrees and sundry kinds. We have nothing to fear because "he who is in [us] is greater than he who is in the world" (1 John 4:4)!

---

14 See Reformation Study Bible notes, Revelation 12:13–17.

Verse 17a: "Then the dragon became furious with the woman and went off to make war on the rest of her offspring, on those who keep the commandments of God and hold to the testimony of Jesus." The devil doesn't care if faithful followers of Jesus are ethnically Jewish, like those in Jerusalem and Judea, or if they are Gentiles. If he can't destroy one portion of the body of Christ, he'll go around to the other side and attack her there instead. Why? Because he abhors the Messiah's bride since she's an extension of her Lord and Bridegroom. He despises her very existence and desires to make it as miserable as possible!

Verse 17b: "And he stood on the sand of the sea." Now in what way do Satan and his demonic armies attack the entire Messianic community from all sides during the first century? This final phrase of verse 17 functions as a bridge to move the reader from generalities to specifics, which are provided in the next set of visions.

Much akin to chapter 9, this passage in chapter 13 has suffered much creative exegesis over the years, most notably from many dispensationalists. To this day, there are many who look for a coming Antichrist leader to unite the world in all-out rebellion against God. Every time the numbers "6–6–6" appear or an economically related electronic chip is inserted into a product, a prophecy teacher somewhere has a theory about the rise of the Antichrist and the coming great tribulation. Yet key to properly understanding this passage, and others in like vein, is the Bible's own distinction between "antichrists" and "beasts."

Firstly, just as the apostle John defines "sin" for us as "lawlessness" (1 John 3:4), he also provides a very specific definition for the term "antichrist." In fact, the only two places where the term is used in all of Holy Writ are 1 John 2:18–23 and 2 John 1:7. In the former, the apostle teaches that an antichrist is one who "denies the Father and the Son." He then adds, "No one who denies the Son has the Father." In the latter, he says they are "deceivers... gone out into the world, those who do not confess the coming of Jesus Christ in the flesh." Thus, by definition, an antichrist is one who denies the divinity and Messiahship of Jesus and is purposefully seeking to lead others astray in this regard. Furthermore, John indicates that the way his first-century readership knows it is the "last hour" in their day is that "now many antichrists have come." According to the apostle, there were *many* antichrists, not merely a single person, and this means *they* were living in the last hour of the old covenant age. All of this points to a very Jewish first-century context, which is the same context found here in the Apocalypse.

Secondly, outside of the Revelation, there is only one other passage where that "beast" imagery is used representatively. This passage is Daniel 7—all other Old Testament references to beasts concern physical animals. In the second half of the chapter, verses 15–27, the angel very explicitly interprets the vision of the four beasts to Daniel as symbolizing pagan, godless kingdoms. Thus, beasts are quite different in nature from antichrists since they are kingdoms, not a single person, and they are primarily politically oriented, not acting as an explicitly religious leader. This biblical distinction is paramount for properly understanding how they are symbolized throughout the Revelation unto John the apostle.

Chapter 13, verse 1: "And I saw a beast rising out of the sea, with ten horns and seven heads, with ten diadems on its horns and blasphemous names on its heads." Here is the same beast introduced in 11:7. Its description is similar to that of the dragon's in 12:3; however, instead of wearing seven diadems on its heads, it is wearing ten diadems on its horns, which are the ten magistrates of the ten Roman provinces—these are one and the same as the ten kings of 17:12.[15] In addition, the seven heads symbolize the seven emperors during the first aeon of the Roman Empire.[16] The beast rises from the sea because, from the vantage point of Israel looking across the Mediterranean, Rome looked as though it was rising out of the sea.

Verse 2: "And the beast that I saw was like a leopard; its feet were like a bear's, and its mouth was like a lion's mouth. And to it the dragon gave his power and his throne and great authority." This harkens back to Daniel 7, where Daniel has visions of four beasts arising from the sea, one like a lion with eagles' wings, one like a bear, one like a leopard with four bird wings, and one terrible in nature with ten horns and one little horn.[17] In Daniel 7:15ff, an angel explains that these four beasts are, in fact, four kings ruling four kingdoms. Out of the fourth kingdom would come ten kings, and another would arise amongst the ten who would mock the Most High and make His saints to suffer "for a time, times, and half a time" (Dan.

---

15 See notes at 17:12.
16 See Wilson, *When the Man Comes Around*, Kindle Location 1556.
17 See Beale and McDonough, "Revelation," 1127.

7:25)—amazingly, this is the exact timeframe mentioned here in Revelation chapters 11–13! Yet Daniel is told that all the kingdoms of this world would become the kingdom of our God, and He will reign forever and ever. In Daniel 7:13–14, we learn that this everlasting dominion has been given to His Messianic King at His enthronement on high.

Now John sees all four beasts combined into one arising out of the sea, nevertheless continuing to have ten horns. In both passages, the beast is a symbol for a powerful political entity. As expounded above, many have conflated Revelation 13's beast with the "Antichrist," a word that only appears in 1 John 2:18 and 2 John 1:7. Thus, beasts and antichrists are scripturally not in the same category. The picture given here is that of a very powerful political kingdom, that is completely under the control and influence of Satan. This is depicted through the dragon giving the beast his throne. We learned back in 2:13 that the devil's throne was located in Pergamum, which had the oldest temple devoted to the imperial cult in all of Asia Minor. This is yet another confirmation of the beast of the sea's true identity as the Roman Empire.

Verse 3: "One of its heads seemed to have a mortal wound, but its mortal wound was healed, and the whole earth marveled as they followed the beast." Rome received a deadly blow when Nero committed suicide and civil war thus ensued. The confusion was so bad that it looked as though the Empire was beyond recovery. This is evidenced by the three succeeding emperors collectively lasting just over one year—Galba, Otho, and Vitellius all reigned and were assassinated during AD 69![18] However, because the Evil One had given it his authority (v. 4), Rome "miraculously" recovered.

Verse 4: "And they worshiped the dragon, for he had given his authority to the beast, and they worshiped the beast, saying, 'Who is like the beast, and who can fight against it?'" Through worshiping the beast, folks are actually worshiping the dragon. The imperial cult(emperor worship,) was mandated throughout the Empire during the first century and Nero was particularly extreme in his demands. Rome cared not if one worshiped other deities in addition to Caesar, but ultimate allegiance was required of the people unto their head of state through offering a pinch of incense on a designated altar. This is why declaring *"Yesous Kurios,"* while refusing

---

18   See Britannica, "List of Roman Emperors," https://www.britannica.com/topic/list-of-Roman-emperors-2043294.

to admit "*Kaisar Kurios*" (cf. Acts 4:12; Rom. 10:9), was officially an act of treason. Not only was the demoniac the source of Rome's power, but also the object of its citizens' worship. They considered Rome to be invincible in the face of all its enemies! This is much like Edom's attitude related in Obadiah 1:3.

At the root of idolatry is an arrogance that thinks we have the right to redefine reality on our own terms, or justify giving into the demands for false worship from others. The Teacher instructs us, "Pride goes before destruction, and a haughty spirit before a fall" (Prov. 16:18). The half-brother of our Lord, the apostle James, expresses the same point: "God opposes the proud but gives grace to the humble" (James 4:6). Arrogance is a multi-headed monster growing within the hearts of men, and it feeds on their innate desire for self-determination, self-promotion, and self-justification. When three heads have been lopped off, in faith, two more arise behind the Christian's back. And when those two have been found out and executed in the power of the indwelling Holy Spirit, the three previously crucified have found a way to resurrect themselves and pull themselves off the cross to which they were nailed. Yahweh loathes hubris because He alone is supreme! For this reason, the theological advisor to Oliver Cromwell, John Owen, oft said, "Be killing sin or it will be killing you!"[19] This is a necessary exhortation for any saint to take to heart if he wishes to faithfully serve his Master as the new creation he has been recreated to be. Was this dying to self not the response of our first-century brothers when they refused to offer the pinch of incense on the altar to Caesar or when they refused the subsequent *libellus* (certificate) in order to participate in Roman society? What about when this resulted in them becoming human torches for Nero's garden parties or when they became tied-up spectacles in the arena for crowds to cheer as Nero attacked their genitals while clad as a wild beast? Humility means glad submission and loyalty to Christ Jesus, no matter the cost.

Verse 5: "And the beast was given a mouth uttering haughty and blasphemous words, and it was allowed to exercise authority for forty-two months." Just as Satan and his demonic ranks can only reach as far as the Lord allows (cf. Job 1–2), the same is true with the beast under his sway. The timeframe is forty-two months, which is the same as given in 11:9–10

---

19 John Piper, "How to Kill Sin: Part 1, John Owen on Mortification of Sin," Desiring God, February 3, 2002, https://www.desiringgod.org/messages/how-to-kill-sin-part-1.

and 12:6. Although it is possible this refers to the length of the Jewish-Roman War, centering on the destruction of Jerusalem and her temple, it makes more sense to take this as the period of Nero's intense persecution of Christians following his setting fire to parts of Rome. There are two reasons for this. The first is that this idea has already been presented in visionary form back in 11:9–10.[20] In addition, verse 6 speaks to the reality that the beast brings accusations and actions against believers unjustly. This means they must be present to be persecuted, which they're not during the siege on Jerusalem—at that time they flee to the mountain community of Pella. Secondly, verse 18 gives good reason to believe that the beast is not only generically Rome, but specifically Nero.[21] This means that Nero must be alive in order to persecute the Christians, something he is not by the time we arrive at the year 70—he committed suicide in June AD 68. Thus, this is speaking of the forty-two months of Nero scapegoating Christians in the Empire after instigating many fires throughout its capital city.

Verse 6: "It opened its mouth to utter blasphemies against God, blaspheming his name and his dwelling—that is, those who dwell in heaven." In this way, the dragon makes "war on the rest of [the woman's] offspring" (12:17). The beast utters "blasphemies against God," which both "implies speaking out against God through self-deification (as with the Roman emperors [see Suetonius, *Dom.* 13]) . . . [and bringing] accusations or actions against Christians, who have God's name written upon them."[22] In addition, the Messianic community is said to be "his dwelling," which can also be translated as "his tabernacle."[23] This comports with Ephesians 2:18–22 and 1 Peter 2, which teach that the church is the true temple because of her union with her Bridegroom, who Himself is the fulfillment of the tabernacle/temple's role (cf. John 1:14; 2:18–22). Furthermore, the Messianic community is described as "those who dwell in heaven," which comports with Ephesians 2:6, where the apostle speaks of believers' heavenly union with Christ resulting from their regeneration at the hands of the Holy Spirit. Truly, wherever Jesus is, there we are as well, covenantally, since we are bound to Him with an unbreakable bond! This means that even now His saints dwell with Him in a certain non-corporeal way.

---

20   See notes at 11:9–10.
21   See notes at 13:18.
22   Beale and McDonough, "Revelation," 1128.
23   See ESV notes, Revelation 13:6.

Verses 7–8: "Also it was allowed to make war on the saints and to conquer them. And authority was given it over every tribe and people and language and nation, and all who dwell on earth will worship it, everyone whose name has not been written before the foundation of the world in the book of life of the Lamb who was slain." "The beast compels worship (v. 8), and when the saints refuse to submit, they are martyred. But despite their apparent defeat, martyrs enjoy victory with Christ both immediately (6:9–11) and when their prayers for the final defeat of the beast are answered (19:11–21)."[24] Previously in 5:9, the phrase "every tribe and language and people and nation" referred specifically to the whole world redeemed unto Messiah. In this case, though, it refers to all the redeemed from every corner of the Empire. The dragon has given the beast authority to torment the saints when they refuse to bow the knee in worship to the emperor. This took the form of Nero scapegoating followers of Messiah, who were considered "atheists" for worshiping only the Triune God as ultimate, after he instigated destructive fires throughout the city of Rome. Indeed, the rest of the known world participated in the imperial cult—those who had not been included in the Lamb's book of life, and that before time began. It is the "book of life" because in it are recorded the names of all those whom the Father gave to the Son and joined unto Him before the foundation of the world. It belongs to the "Lamb who was slain" since, through the Lamb's death, He secured everlasting life for all those recorded therein.

The saints' ultimate protection is found not in their circumstances, but rather in their election. This is why Paul could say while chained up in a Roman prison, "I know how to be brought low, and I know how to abound. In any and every circumstance, I have learned the secret of facing plenty and hunger, abundance and need. I can do all things through him who strengthens me" (Phil. 4:12–13). He knew that his union with Jesus was not contingent on what he was experiencing or feeling in the moment, but rather was founded in the unshakeable objective work of the Triune God! That union with the Savior—established for the elect by the Father in eternity past, accomplished in their stead by the Son at Calvary, and applied directly to them by the Spirit at the appointed time—is the only solid rock upon which a saint may stand and rejoice during the most trying of times!

It seems the Lord has seen fit to send us, as Western Christians, through similar tribulations to those under Nero's reign. The cultural revolution has

---

24 Reformation Study Bible notes, Revelation 13:7.

taken over the West at an unprecedented pace! In chasing hard after revolutionaries like Gramsci and Marcuse, since the Cold War, cultural Marxists have sought to slowly transform the minds of the Western populous by way of taking over public institutions. By gaining power through controlling the dictionary (postmodernism) and by convincing large segments of society that granting the microphone solely to those suffering from envy and hysteria and silencing all dissent (critical theory) is an acceptable tool for ridding ourselves of alleged power imbalances, these radical ideologues have successfully prepared the soil for revolution at a foundational level. The results are all around us! For example, Bill C-4 was unanimously passed in both the Canadian Parliament and Senate and became criminal code on January 8, 2022. This piece of legislation explicitly mocks biblical teaching on sexual ethics as "myths" and brings Canada's heaviest judicial hammer down on anyone who would teach against or counsel to change the lifestyles and behavior of those identifying as homosexual and/or transgender. In response, whether it be a wicked cultural revolution or some other enemy of Christ we face, let us hasten to prepare ourselves by grounding ourselves in these most precious truths concerning our union with Christ so that when the gales of affliction violently whip about us, we may be able to stand fast in Christ our King and conquer through them.

Verses 9–10: "If anyone has an ear, let him hear: If anyone is to be taken captive, to captivity he goes; if anyone is to be slain with the sword, with the sword must he be slain. Here is a call for the endurance and faith of the saints." Verse 9 opens with a reminder from John to the regenerate in the seven congregations to whom he writes. He instructs them to pay close attention to the Spirit-given words, both that are about to follow, as well as those throughout the Apocalypse. This refrain, "If anyone has an ear, let him hear," harkens back to Jesus's closing words to each of those same assemblies.[25] John reminds his recipients that not only have they been appointed to repentance, but they have also been appointed to suffer, as was their Master (see Matt. 10:16–25). Likely, at this junction, he is specifically thinking of Paul's words in Philippians 1:29: "For it has been granted to you that for the sake of Christ you should not only believe in him but also suffer for his sake in coming to follow Jesus, not only as Savior, but also as Lord (see Luke 14:25–33). The question is, has each of us obeyed the Messiah in coming to Him on *His* terms? Do we continue to count

---

25 See 2:7, 11, 17, 29; 3:6, 13, 22.

the cost of following Him in His narrow way each and every day, to die to our rebellious selves in order to rise again in Him? Our Lord warns that whoever attempts to come to Him in any other way is not worthy of Him and cannot be His disciple. This is a most solemn warning indeed!

The apostle encourages these believers to continue persevering in faithfully following their Messianic King, keeping their eyes fixed on Him, since He "endured the cross, despising the shame, and is seated at the right hand of the throne of God" (Heb. 12:2). He comforts these believers in the same way the author to the Hebrews encourages his audience with the following words: "Consider him who endured from sinners such hostility against himself, so that you may not grow weary or fainthearted" (Heb. 12:3). We also must keep in mind such heartening lest we grow fatigued of the battle, fall asleep by the wayside, and forget our kingdom charter—which is the Word of God—as did Bunyan's Christian on the hill called Difficulty.

THE BEAST OUT OF THE LAND

Verse 11: "Then I saw another beast rising out of the earth. It had two horns like a lamb and it spoke like a dragon." This particular beast rises out of the land (Greek: *ge*, meaning a "tract of land" or "country"),[26] which thus far has consistently been in reference to the first-century land of Palestine. As to its character, elsewhere it is referred to as the "false prophet" (16:13; 19:20; 20:10), and thus ought to be thought of in such religious terms, rather than as a political personality. This shift away from the meaning of "beast" is due to the rest of the Revelation consistently referring to this particular beast, which arises from the land, as the "false prophet." Although it has two horns, it only has one head, unlike the beast rising from the sea. This indicates that while it has authority over others, it represents a single person. It has "two horns like a lamb," which seems to be a reference to the sacrificial system given to Israel under the old covenant. Given the image of "false prophet," it can be ascertained that this person functions as a recognized religious leader. Revelation 16:13–14 shows that the false prophet works together hand in hand with the beast, which is Rome, to deceive the whole world to come together for battle through sign-performing demonic spirits—they are separate entities, but fully cooperative with one another

---

26 "Genesis," The NAS New Testament Greek Lexicon, https://www.biblestudytools.com/lexicons/greek/nas/genesis-5.html.

under the control and direction of the dragon, who is Satan. Revelation 19:20 describes how the beast and false prophet are captured together by the Messiah and then thrown into everlasting punishment. Finally, 20:10 indicates that their master, the devil, will also meet the same end on the Last Day.

Given these clues from the text of Revelation itself, it would be unfitting to take the false prophet as representing the temple priests of the imperial cult, whose system was a part of the Roman Empire, not something separate. History informs us that the imperial cult did not end in AD 70, but continued on into the third century.[27] Both Gentry and Wilson understand the beast of the land to symbolize the highest leader in Jewish ecclesiology, the high priest, which certainly fits the textual clues and is most likely the truth of the matter.[28] Concurrent with Nero's reign, Hanan ben Hanan (known also as Ananus ben Ananus) ruled the Sanhedrim as high priest and was the instigator of the execution of Jacob (known in English as "James"), the half-brother of our Lord.[29] However, at the time of the War, Phannias ben Samuel was high priest, indeed the last of them all, and died at the hands of Roman soldiers during the siege. He was unlawfully appointed by lot from amongst the Zealots who had taken issue with the previous high priest, Mattathias ben Theophilus. Thus, this land beast/false prophet represents one holding the office of high priest in that time in general and Hanan ben Hanan in specific. Although the Jewish high priest appeared innocent, in reality he sounded exactly like his father the devil—full of deception and cunning. Not only this, but this second beast acts as a propagandist for the first, as will become evident in the following verses.[30]

At this point it is necessary to "square the circle," as it were, with regard to how the false prophet would be in league with the beast while simultaneously fighting against it. Although this may seem like a historical contradiction on the surface, it is a complicated paradox. International relations have long involved such paradoxes, so it is not difficult to suppose this to be the case two thousand years ago.

---

27 See "Overview: Imperial Cult," Oxford Reference, https://www.oxfordreference.com/view/10.1093/oi/authority.20110803095959201.
28 See Gentry, *He Shall Have Dominion*, 450–451, and Wilson, *When the Man Comes Around*, Kindle Location 1626.
29 See Josephus, *Antiquities of the Jews*, 20.9.1.
30 See Reformation Study Bible notes, Revelation 13:11–18.

On the one hand, Jerusalem's leadership was cooperative with Rome for two reasons. First, as the capital of a Roman colony, in a major way it was economically dependent on Rome for its continuance, and thus presented itself to the crown as "cheerfully" cooperative. Second, both Rome and Israel hated Christians, though for differing reasons. The former viewed those of the Way as treasonous atheists since they both denied Caesar to be the ultimate authority and denied all deities outside of Yahweh to exist. The latter viewed the same as blasphemous apostates. Thus, they both were convinced that those loyal to Jesus of Nazareth deserved to die.

On the other hand, the Jewish leadership was fully supportive of, and instrumental in, the nationalistic rebellion against Rome. How would this be possible without the Roman leadership discovering the truth of the matter? The key to this clever deception lay in the fact that in the eyes of Rome, the rebellion concerned the Zealots, while the Jewish priesthood concerned the Sadducees. Thus, it would have been possible for the Sanhedrim to present itself as uninvolved in the uprising, even seeking to quell it in the eyes of Rome, while simultaneously working to advance it with their Zealot allies behind the scenes. Playing on this distinction between the two Jewish groups was possible up until the point when the Zealots forcibly removed Mattathias ben Theophilus, replacing him with their own man in direct violation of Levitical code. Phannias ben Samuel's unlawful appointment took place at the height of the Jewish-Roman War, and thus maintaining the former distinction no longer mattered to the cause since at that point, the entire city was in the throes of battle against the Romans. In this way, it would have been possible for the Jewish high priest to be happily cooperative with Rome, while at the same time actively rebelling against her.

Verses 12–14: "It exercises all the authority of the first beast in its presence, and makes the earth and its inhabitants worship the first beast, whose mortal wound was healed. It performs great signs, even making fire come down from heaven to earth in front of people, and by the signs that it is allowed to work in the presence of the beast it deceives those who dwell on earth, telling them to make an image for the beast that was wounded by the sword and yet lived." Via demonically empowered wonders, the false prophet convinces the masses to worship the beast, who was resurrected from its bloody near-death.[31] Vespasian managed to establish the Flavian

---

31 See notes at 13:3.

Dynasty as the conclusion to a yearlong civil war in AD 69, being incited by Nero's tragic suicide.

Verse 15: "And it was allowed to give breath to the image of the beast, so that the image of the beast might even speak and might cause those who would not worship the image of the beast to be slain." This seems to point to some kind of divination and magic arts employed by the Jewish high priest and his companions as part of their deception. He not only promotes loyalty to the emperor, and thus also emperor worship, but he also rounds up all those who refuse to bow the knee and hands them over to the Roman officials to be put to death. Josephus reported that Hanan was instrumental in fighting with the Zealots for this very reason[32]—he was convinced that appearing cooperative before the crown was vital to their cause, while evidently, at least some Zealots did not agree. Again, refusal to bow the knee in the prescribed manner was equivalent to treason, especially in the mind of Nero.

Verses 16–17: "Also it causes all, both small and great, both rich and poor, both free and slave, to be marked on the right hand or the forehead, so that no one can buy or sell unless he has the mark—that is, the name of the beast or the number of its name." The image of being "marked on the right hand or the forehead" comes from Deuteronomy 6:8, where Moses instructed Israel to be entirely devoted to Yahweh, both in all their thinking and in all their labor.[33] Now the Roman Empire is forcing this kind of loyalty in the place of the one true and living God, even making participation in its economic system contingent on its worship. The mark on the forehead with the name of the beast is opposite to the mark borne by the saints with the name of God (see 7:3; 9:4)—this is a symbol of ownership and ultimate allegiance.

If we are truly honest—naked, as it were—before Almighty God, to whom are our thoughts, decisions, and activity actually loyal? Put another way, whom does our heart ultimately love and treasure? Is it Yahweh, the Triune God of Scripture, or something else? Perhaps that something else is the state, as it was for the Jewish ecclesiastical elites. Please allow a test for accurately determining the answer: (1) What/whom do I treat as my ultimate authority, such that I'm willing to sacrifice greatly in order to gain

---

32 See Josephus, *Antiquities of the Jews*, 20.9.1.
33 See Beale and McDonough, "Revelation," 1130.

his approval? and (2) What/whom do I treat as my ultimate provider, such that I'm willing to entrust the preservation and advancement of my life into his hands? Each and every one of us must carefully and soberly consider these things in our private prayer closet before the Lord.

Verse 18: "This calls for wisdom: let the one who has understanding calculate the number of the beast, for it is the number of a man, and his number is 666." By beginning this verse with "this calls for wisdom," John indicates that he knows the identity of the beast and he expects his clever readers to figure it out based on the numeral he provided—namely, 666. In both ancient Greek and Hebrew, they did not use symbols to stand for numerals as we do in English, but rather the letters of the alphabet—*aleph* stood for "one," *beth* for "two," *gimel* for "three," etc. It seems that the apostle intended his code to be obvious enough for his readers to perceive, but not so obvious for Romans transporting his rather seditious letter from Patmos to the mainland.[34] Thus, 666 is the numerical value of "Nero Caesar" in Hebrew, not Greek—*Nrwn Qsr*, being pronounced as *Neron Kaisar*.[35] He is the only one living at the time that John wrote his letter to the seven Asia Minor congregations that "fits the bill," as it were. Not only does the Hebraic number correspond to this particular emperor, but he was also described by many in his day as a "beast" for his most vile ways. Furthermore, Latin manuscripts changed 666 to 616, which is his name's numerical value in Latin.[36] The earliest known manuscript to make this numerical alteration is P115. Irenaeus rejected this particular manuscript as erroneous, but it is, in fact, the oldest fragment of Revelation 13.[37] What all this demonstrates is that the beast of the sea must be taken as both representative of the Roman Empire as a whole, and of Emperor Nero in particular.

In closing this portion of the Apocalypse, there remains a pertinent question: "If all these things transpired so very long ago, how are they relevant to us today?" Truly, they are relevant: not through modern-day fulfillment, but rather through appropriate application. As we consider history,

---

34 See Wilson, *When the Man Comes Around*, Kindle Location 1666.
35 See Gentry, *He Shall Have Dominion*, 420.
36 See Gentry, *He Shall Have Dominion*, 420.
37 "Papyrus Reveals New Clues to Ancient World," National Geographic News, April 25, 2005, https://web.archive.org/web/20080110172555/http://news.nationalgeographic.com/news/2005/04/0425_050425_papyrus_2.html.

there have been many beast-like civil governments down through the ages. Just as Nero, and Rome in general, sought to use his power to take direct shots at the rule of God and the bride of His Anointed One, others have followed suit. For example, Islamic forces stormed through North Africa during the seventh and eighth centuries and, within a hundred years, transformed this vast region from a predominantly Christian area to a predominantly Muslim one with the edge of the sword. To this day, following Christ in these countries is outlawed and severely punished by the state, even through execution. A more recent beast-like government would be that of China. Not only does it hate the Lord Jesus, His unchanging moral standard, and His people, but it also has sought to deify itself, just as Roman emperors did. This can be seen in how the Chinese Communist Party has set itself up as the unquestionable ultimate authority in the land and its edicts as the ultimate standard by which to live. Just as believers in the first century had to count the cost in order to faithfully follow their Master without compromise, so also is this true for saints living in Islamic countries and Maoist China. Through these beast-like magistrates, Satan strategically works in an effort to extinguish the witness of those faithful to the Lord Jesus in those nations. Yet it is through the blood of the martyrs that the church grows and the kingdom advances—we win through dying, just like our Master! As the apostle puts it, "Here is a call for the endurance and faith of the saints" (13:10). We may extend this application to any civil government or kingdom that follows in the footsteps of Caesar Nero and the Roman Empire.

The Lamb on Mount Zion

Chapter 14, verse 1: "Then I looked, and behold, on Mount Zion stood the Lamb, and with him 144,000 who had his name and his Father's name written on their foreheads." The apostle *sees* the same group described in 7:3–8, which is the totality of true believers, the Israel of God. These are those throughout history with the same faith as Abraham, the true members of the covenant of grace. In chapter 7, the seal of servitude to Yahweh is on their foreheads, whereas here the names of both the Lamb and His Father are thereon, signifying Their true and permanent ownership of these believers. This stands in direct contrast to the previous passage, especially 13:16–17.[38] The Messiah and His people are standing on Mount

---
38 See notes at 13:16–17.

Zion because He is the head of His church and they are members thereof (cf. Isa. 2:1–4; Heb. 12:21ff).

Verses 2–3: "And I heard a voice from heaven like the roar of many waters and like the sound of loud thunder. The voice I heard was like the sound of harpists playing on their harps, and they were singing a new song before the throne and before the four living creatures and before the elders. No one could learn that song except the 144,000 who had been redeemed from the earth." He now *hears* the voices of all these believers singing their peculiar song before the entire heavenly court, both Yahweh on His throne, His four throne guardians, and all twenty-four representatives of the Messianic community. The apostle hears these things rather than seeing them because he is on the earth in the Spirit while the rejoicing is taking place in heaven.

The apostle explains that the voice of the worshipers is compared to three things. He says it is "like the roar of many waters and like the sound of loud thunder," both of which communicate the same concept of extreme force and deafening volume. Furthermore, it is like "the sound of harpists playing on their harps." This analogy conveys the extreme sweetness and trueness of their song.

Verses 4–5: "It is these who have not defiled themselves with women, for they are virgins. It is these who follow the Lamb wherever he goes. These have been redeemed from mankind as firstfruits for God and the Lamb, and in their mouth no lie was found, for they are blameless." The reason these saints sing so sweetly and with such purity is that they have been purified in every way through their redemption in the Lamb's blood. Their Spirit-wrought purity is here symbolized by virginity. They faithfully cling to Him alone and follow Him wherever He leads. John utilizes the imagery of saints as sheep from Jesus's words in John 10. The Good Shepherd leads His elect people with great care, and "my sheep hear my voice, and I know them, and they follow me" (John 10:27).

Often we forget the depth of beauty of our relationship with the Lord Jesus. We have been marked out for Him as His sheep by the Father. We have been ransomed out of slavery to sin at the high, high cost of His own blood. We have been given His own purity and obedience, and thus declared forever just and at peace with our Maker by our Maker. We hear our Shepherd's voice and faithfully follow Him because we are *His* sheep.

Finally, our response to all of this unbelievably amazing news is heartfelt, deafening, gorgeous songs of praise to our God and to the Lamb. May we live in light of this reality day by day, that our lives would be a giant signpost of worship pointing back to His goodness and righteousness and that the world would know us by our sheepliness.

Babylon's Fall Predicted

Verse 6: "Then I saw another angel flying directly overhead, with an eternal gospel to proclaim to those who dwell on earth, to every nation and tribe and language and people." The transition here is the same as in chapter 7—that is, first a discussion concerning the 144,000 (7:3–8) and then one about those "from every nation, from all tribes and peoples and languages" (7:9ff)—first John *hears* the angel describe the 144,000 and then, in turning to look at the subject, *sees* an innumerable multitude from every language, ethnicity, and nation. Thus, this message of glad tidings concerning the Messiah's kingdom-rule in the earth is proclaimed to the same group.

Verse 7: "And he said with a loud voice, 'Fear God and give him glory, because the hour of his judgment has come, and worship him who made heaven and earth, the sea and the springs of water.'" The believing world is commanded to "fear God"—that is, to give Him His due for who He is as Yahweh. They are also commanded to "give him glory" and honor and praise, for He alone is worthy as the Creator of all. Noteworthily, the same creational divisions of sky, land, and sea are also found here (cf. Gen. 1; Ex. 20:8–11). The reason the saints ought to do these two things is "because the hour of his judgment has come," which is the hour of His judgment against the city of Jerusalem and her covenant-breaking people therein. This theme of praise in response to divine judgment will reappear in chapters 18 and 19 in full force, enough to capsize the dinghy in which many a modern Christian finds himself paddling around! The apostle John teaches us loud and clear that Yahweh must be praised, not only for His acts of lovingkindness, but likewise for His acts of justice in history against the ungodly.

Verse 8: "Another angel, a second, followed, saying, 'Fallen, fallen is Babylon the great, she who made all nations drink the wine of the passion of her sexual immorality.'" Just as the nation of Israel was described by Yahweh as a whoring, unfaithful wife in Ezekiel 16, so also here she is portrayed as the most notorious of rebellious nations against Him—namely, Babylon.

In 17:4, the whore, Babylon, wears the same colors as the Levitical priests: gold, purple, and scarlet (see Ex. 28). Wherever she goes, she persuades others to become drunk with the same spiritual adultery she commits daily against her God, specifically the rejection of His Anointed One, the Messianic King prophesied of old. While commentators have long disputed the identity of Babylon the whore, one of the seven angels who holds one of the seven bowls of vengeance explicitly says in 17:18 that this lady "is the great city that has dominion over the kings of the earth." The only "great city" consistently spoken of throughout the Revelation is Jerusalem, being first introduced at 11:8 as "symbolically... called Sodom and Egypt, where their Lord was crucified."[39] Thus Jerusalem, specifically, and apostate national Israel, generally, is here symbolized as a great and terribly illicit prostitute. May the Lord graciously protect each of us from imitating national Israel's apostasy in any way lest its punishments from the hand of King Jesus fall on us as well!

Verses 9–10: "And another angel, a third, followed them, saying with a loud voice, 'If anyone worships the beast and its image and receives a mark on his forehead or on his hand, he also will drink the wine of God's wrath, poured full strength into the cup of his anger, and he will be tormented with fire and sulfur in the presence of the holy angels and in the presence of the Lamb'" This is a warning to all those who think it is acceptable to give themselves in allegiance and servitude to Rome as the ultimate authority, which the imperial cult demanded. The end result of this idolatrous approach is promised to be the fullness of God's holy wrath poured out in torment. This takes place "in the presence of the holy angels and in the presence of the Lamb" so that Yahweh will be praised and glorified for His perfect justice executed upon the wicked. By extension, the same eternal torment awaits all those who continue on in their rebellion against Him, no matter how devoutly religious the expression of that rebellion may take. Let this be a standing warning lest we hear those dread words from our Lord on the Last Day, "I never knew you; depart from me, you workers of lawlessness" (Matt. 7:22–23; see also Luke 13:26–28).

Verse 11: "And the smoke of their torment goes up forever and ever, and they have no rest, day or night, these worshipers of the beast and its image, and whoever receives the mark of its name." Those in view here are

---

39 See notes at 11:8.

specifically worshippers of the Emperor Nero, and by extension, the Empire as a whole, who have pledged their minds and labor to his service. It is they who are punished eternally for their idolatry at the hands of Almighty God.

Some have said that the torment of the unrepentant in hell will come to an end when all their sins have finally been sufficiently punished. This view is known as "conditionalism" and is a type of annihilationism.[40] Yet here we see that "the smoke of their torment goes up forever and ever" because the torment itself is eternal—people cannot be tormented if they have already been extinguished. The reason is that all men arrive at the great white throne on the Last Day having the same nature as at the time of death (e.g., 20:11ff)—their nature doesn't change in eternity. The main problem with the conditionalist view is that it assumes this is not true—that is, that the unrepentant cease rebelling against their Creator upon entrance into hell, and thus God's wrath can only be exhausted upon those sins committed in this life. Nevertheless, the fact of the matter is that just as the elect will sinlessly rejoice in Christ their Savior for all eternity, having been given new hearts of flesh, so also the unrepentant will continue on in unbridled rebellion against their Judge forever and ever, since they have remained in their sin, never having had their heart of stone removed. Such is their just but most tragic end.

Verse 12: "Here is a call for the endurance of the saints, those who keep the commandments of God and their faith in Jesus." John is here given a repetition of the encouragement proffered unto the suffering saints back in 13:10. As they persevere in obeying God and keeping their eyes fixed on Jesus, they are conquering the beast with the true King over all kings! This is a theme going all the way back to 1:9, where John identifies himself as a contemporary with these suffering saints in the "patient endurance that [is] in Jesus." For what are they patiently waiting but the avenging of the blood of the martyrs who have been killed at the hands of Babylon the great (cf. 6:9–11; 17:6)?

If we are honest with ourselves, we are a weak people in great need of this type of encouragement. We need the Spirit to develop in us a backbone of steel to persevere through severe trials brought on in response to our faithfulness to the lordship of Christ. We need Jesus to be branded on our eyeballs and beloved brethren to walk alongside us and remind us of

---

40 e.g., See Christopher Date's biography at https://rethinkinghell.com/author/chris-date with links to both his published works and online work.

this branding when the trail becomes difficult and the temptation to give up is upon us. Likewise, we must bear the burdens of others with them that they might also conquer "by the blood of the Lamb and by the word of their testimony, for they loved not their lives even unto death" (12:11). Let us not relax in such things even for a second lest the devil should gain a foothold in our minds and distract us from the narrow path set before us.

Verse 13: "And I heard a voice from heaven saying, 'Write this: Blessed are the dead who die in the Lord from now on.' 'Blessed indeed,' says the Spirit, 'that they may rest from their labors, for their deeds follow them!'" All those who conquer and are faithful to their Messianic King to the end of their lives, though they may be martyred, are blessed and have true rest in Him.

Verse 14: "Then I looked, and behold, a white cloud, and seated on the cloud one like a son of man, with a golden crown on his head, and a sharp sickle in his hand." While there has been debate over whether "son of man" at this juncture is a reference to some kind of heavenly being, the most natural reading would bring us to the conclusion that John is seeing Jesus in this vision (see Dan. 7:13–14). This is also the most consistent understanding since the apostle sees this same Son of Man in the initial vision he receives (see 1:12ff), which is the only other occurrence of this Messianic title in the Apocalypse.

The Messianic King is seen here holding a sickle in His hand, indicating that He is about to bring in a "harvest" of sorts. This harvest is expounded upon in the next two verses for the understanding of the first-century audience to whom John writes—that is, the seven congregations in Asia Minor. The effect of this divinely orchestrated harvest is the safekeeping of God's elect so that the covenant-breakers may be taken in judgment, which is precisely what our Lord prophesied would happen in Matthew 24:36–44.

Verses 15–16: "And another angel came out of the temple, calling with a loud voice to him who sat on the cloud, 'Put in your sickle, and reap, for the hour to reap has come, for the harvest of the earth is fully ripe.' So he who sat on the cloud swung his sickle across the earth, and the earth was reaped." Gill points out that this "must be understood not as commanding, nor even directing what should be done, but as beseeching and entreating: see Ps. 132:8."[41] The angel's words must be taken in this manner lest he be

---

41 Gill, *Exposition*, Kindle Location 359226.

uttering disrespect unto his Lord and God, which is nowhere hinted at in the context. Indeed, the Son as the God-Man is functionally subordinate to His Father and no other.[42] The timing of this harvest is indicated by the angel coming "out of the temple," meaning that it is happening while the second temple still stands, but immediately before the same is destroyed—the confirmation of this understanding is found in verse 20, where John describes the great and terrible bloodshed that occurred in the fall of that city, which is Jerusalem. Here is given a description of the gathering and removal of all saints—that great harvest from the four corners of the land of Israel[43]—from the terrors about to befall the city, just as Jesus had predicted. Indeed, He had commanded His disciples to flee when they saw armies surrounding the city (cf. Luke 21:20–22).

Verses 17–18: "Then another angel came out of the temple in heaven, and he too had a sharp sickle. And another angel came out from the altar, the angel who has authority over the fire, and he called with a loud voice to the one who had the sharp sickle, 'Put in your sickle and gather the clusters from the vine of the earth, for its grapes are ripe.'" This part of the vision portrays a second gathering, this time for judgment, as indicated by the "angel who has authority over the fire" coming forth. The fire is reminiscent of that which came forth to consume Nadab and Abihu for trying to approach Yahweh with unacceptable worship (Lev. 10:1–3). That this divinely initiated gathering is indeed unto judgment is brought out more fully in verses 19–20.

Verses 19–20: "So the angel swung his sickle across the earth and gathered the grape harvest of the earth and threw it into the great winepress of the wrath of God. And the winepress was trodden outside the city, and blood flowed from the winepress, as high as a horse's bridle, for 1,600 [stadion]." The objects of divine retribution are thrown "into the great winepress of the wrath of God," which symbolizes the fiery judgment of Yahweh upon the covenant-breakers. The text goes on to say that "the winepress was trodden outside the city," indicating the location of this terrible judgment—namely, the now whoring city of Jerusalem. Furthermore,

---

42 See G. K. Beale and David H. Campbell, *Revelation: A Shorter Commentary* (Grand Rapids: Eerdmans, 2015), 310.

43 As previously noted, *ge* means a "tract of land" or "country," whether it be specified or not, not "the entire surface of the globe." Throughout the Revelation, this term is most often used in reference to the land of Israel.

the "blood flowed from the winepress, as high as a horse's bridle, for 1,600 [stadion]." This portrays how very great and thorough is the judgment. This is in direct fulfillment of how Jesus describes the way in which His kingdom-rule advances in the world in the similitude of the wheat and the darnel (see Matt. 13:24–30) and His own interpretation thereof (Matt. 13:36–43).

Now Romans liked using Arabian horses, which average 14–15 hands (145–155 cm) in height at the withers,[44] which is approximately how high the blood the covenant-breakers at Jerusalem is portrayed to flow. In addition, 1,600 *stadion* is equivalent to 296 km (1 *stadion* = 185 m),[45] the distance the blood of those slain is here presented to have flowed out from the city—this comports with the ESV footnote at Revelation 14:20. It is worth noting that the number forty, the number of judgment used throughout the Jewish Old Testament,[46] when squared equals 1,600. This grotesque imagery is drawn from Isaiah 63:1–6 to portray the sheer horror of God's vengeance against His most unfaithful wife.[47]

In agreement with the biblical witness, Josephus records that due to the siege, the famine in the city was so severe that wherever a morsel of food was found, a small war instantly commenced. He reports that robbers stumbled around delusional, tripping over corpses in the streets, chewing on whatever they could. One lady, crazed with hunger, killed her own infant son, eating half of him and hiding the other half from robbers[48]—cannibalism is specially mentioned in Deuteronomy 28:52–57 as one of the curses for Israel breaking the covenant Yahweh had made with her. Truly, outside Jerusalem, where the "winepress of the wrath of God" is said here in the text to be "trodden," there were so many Jews crucified that one literally had to walk through a forest of crosses in order to travel in any direction![49] Such was the desperateness of the situation.

---

44   See "Arabian," U.S. Equestrian, https://www.usef.org/compete/breeds/arabian.
45   See "Stadion (Unit)," Wikipedia, https://en.m.wikipedia.org/wiki/Stadion_(unit).
46   E.g., Israel's wandering for forty years in the wilderness as judgment for unbelief. Cf. Deut. 1:19ff; Heb. 3:7ff.
47   See Wilson, *When the Man Comes Around*, Kindle Location 1843.
48   See Josephus, *Wars*, 6.3.3–4.
49   See Josephus, *Wars*, 5.11.1.

The Sixth Vision (15:1–16:21)

A Prelude

Chapter 15, verse 1: "Then I saw another sign in heaven, great and amazing, seven angels with seven plagues, which are the last, for with them the wrath of God is finished." This is the introduction to the final set of judgments depicted in the Apocalypse—that is, the seven bowls filled with the wrath of God described in chapter 16. Once again, these acts of vengeance are a part of what was written in the scroll, which only Jesus could open as the Lion of Judah since it was He alone who accomplished them in His death as the Lamb slain (5:5–7). They are the final buildup in intensity in Christ's judgments against the covenant-breakers of Israel before the actual destruction of the temple.

Verses 2–4 provide a small interlude. Those saints who have endured to the end and have kept "the commandments of God and their faith in Jesus" (14:12), now respond to the faithfulness of the Lamb with a song of praise.

Verse 2: "And I saw what appeared to be a sea of glass mingled with fire—and also those who had conquered the beast and its image and the number of its name, standing beside the sea of glass with harps of God in their hands." This image was first mentioned in 4:6, where it symbolized God's power to conquer His enemies and stood as a heavenly version of the sea in Solomon's temple. These saints are now standing beside it because they have conquered even unto death and have been faithful to their Messiah to the end of their lives. Truly, they have not caved to the social pressures of the day, which demanded they worship the beast through offering a pinch of incense on the altar unto Caesar. Not only that, but they have kept their eyes fixed on their Lord and Savior, even while being publicly tormented at the hands of Nero. Now they stand victorious with Him and worship Him wholeheartedly.

What tremendous comfort this picture gives us—what often seems like the end is really not the end! God's promises to His people in chapters 2–3 are "yes and amen!" in Christ Jesus, and we must remind ourselves of them when the fiery storms of tribulation crash in upon our shore. Even though it seems like all is lost in the midst of the gale, and continuing to persevere therethrough is nothing short of exhausting, in the end a place has been reserved for us on the strand of the glassy sea. Why? Because all along, it has been the Lord Almighty who has seen fit to bring us thereto in His infinite kindness. All praise be to His name alone!

Verse 3a: "And they sing the song of Moses, the servant of God, and the song of the Lamb." A parallel betwixt Moses and Christ is here presented. Moses delivered God's people out of the miseries of Egypt, and he did so by leading them to safety through the Red Sea. The response of the people was corporate worship to Yahweh through song (see Ex. 15). In the same way, Christ Jesus has delivered these saints out of their life of misery under the boot of Rome and its loyal accomplice, national Israel. The Lord has done this by bringing them safely into His immediate presence as He is currently enacting in His resurrection everything that He fully accomplished in His death.

Verses 3b–4: "saying, 'Great and amazing are your deeds, O Lord God the Almighty! Just and true are your ways, O King of the nations! Who will not fear, O Lord, and glorify your name? For you alone are holy. All nations will come and worship you, for your righteous acts have been revealed.'" The first two phrases are parallel to each other, in keeping with the style of Hebraic poetry. The deeds of the Lord God Almighty are great and amazing because He alone has the power to deliver His people out of the bondage of their miseries. Likewise, the ways of the King of the nations are just and true since He always does in His might what is right and fitting in accordance with His own character, for He cannot possibly do otherwise (see 2 Tim. 2:13). Therefore, the only proper response to such a pure and set-apart God is to fear and glorify Him for who He is and for the great things He's done. Not only is this what *ought* to happen, but the song proclaims that this is in fact what *will* happen—"All nations *will* come and worship you, for your righteous acts have been revealed" (v. 4, author's emphasis)! What a great and glorious promise to be cherished, rejoiced in, and lived in light of!

Many a Christian in our day has a dark and dreary view of history. They see the situation getting progressively worse over time until Jesus finally returns to obliterate this present sin-corrupted creation and start over with a fresh new slate. This view keeps us from really, truly obeying Jesus's command to be salt and light in the earth and thus fulfilling the dominion mandate as image bearers in His world in light of His universal lordship. It creates a mindset of cultural retreat in the name of piety since, as it is often touted, "the world's going to hell in a handbasket"; "Jesus is about building His church, *not* transforming the world"; "they won't listen anyway"; therefore, "why polish brass on a sinking ship?" If every believer was consistent with this pessimism, it would mean the end of all evangelistic and missionary endeavors! We must repent of such an unbiblical, unbelieving ideology and heart attitude and return to the message of this song!

Verses 5–6: "After this I looked, and the sanctuary of the tent of witness in heaven was opened, and out of the sanctuary came the seven angels with the seven plagues, clothed in pure, bright linen, with golden sashes around their chests." Seven heavenly messengers come out of the "sanctuary of the tent of witness in heaven." This is the Most Holy Place in the heavenly tabernacle into which Hebrews 9 says that Jesus entered with the blood of His own sacrifice. Instead of mercy coming forth from the mercy seat, merciless judgment pours forth from the inner sanctum wherein Yahweh's most glorious presence dwells.[1] These judgment messengers are dressed in "pure, bright linen, with golden sashes around their chests," indicating they are carrying out official business on behalf of their King since they are dressed in the garments of the high priest.[2]

Verses 7–8: "And one of the four living creatures gave to the seven angels seven golden bowls full of the wrath of God who lives forever and ever, and the sanctuary was filled with smoke from the glory of God and from his power, and no one could enter the sanctuary until the seven plagues of the seven angels were finished." Yahweh's glory manifests itself in overwhelming, all-consuming, holy wrath against the wicked, just as much as

---

1 See Wilson, *When the Man Comes Around*, Kindle Location 1892.
2 See Henry, *Commentary*, Revelation 15:5–8.

it does so in overwhelming fatherly love toward His children. The picture here shows God's wrath to be so overpowering that no one can enter into His presence until it has completely consumed His enemies. This is the answer to the pleading prayer of the saints under the altar back in 6:10 who asked, "O Sovereign Lord, holy and true, how long before you will judge and avenge our blood on those who dwell [in the land]?" Here lays before us the last round of seven acts of vengeance upon apostate Israel.

THE FIRST BOWL

Chapter 16, verse 1: "Then I heard a loud voice from the temple telling the seven angels, 'Go and pour out on the earth the seven bowls of the wrath of God.'" The loud voice evidently belongs to Yahweh Himself since it proceeds from inside the temple. He commands His seven messengers of vengeance to begin pouring out the bowls of wrath given them on those inhabitants of the earth for whom they are intended.

Verse 2: "So the first angel went and poured out his bowl on the earth, and harmful and painful sores came upon the people who bore the mark of the beast and worshiped its image." This first judgment is specifically against those who have pledged allegiance to the beast, particularly apostate Israel living as a nation within the Roman Empire. This historically involved offering a pinch of incense on the altar to honor Caesar as the ultimate lord over all and then carrying a *libellus* (official certificate) to prove that allegiance in the public square. The plague delivered seems to be very much in the same vein as the first four trumpet judgments in that it mimics the plagues against Egypt. Moses recorded that the sixth plague was boils that broke out in sores on man and beast alike, through which Yahweh hardened the heart of Pharaoh further, ensuring his imminent destruction (Ex. 9:8–12).[3] This is what Yahweh is also doing with apostate Israel, who openly called down His judgment when they cried out at Jesus's trial, "His blood be on us and on our children!" (Matt. 27:25), as well as pledging their allegiance to Caesar—they would rather have Caesar as Lord than God's Anointed One (cf. John 19:12–16)!

How about for us as twenty-first-century Christians in the West? When the civil government insists that it is the head of the local church in

---

3   See Gill, *Exposition*, Kindle Location 359650. Although there is disagreement with Gill's interpretation of this plague being designed for "professors of the Popish religion," his exegetical connection to the plagues of Egypt is noteworthy. See also Beale and McDonough, "Revelation," 1135.

the place of Christ, as if He is somehow subservient to the state, will we "go along to get along" and make Scripture stand on its head in order to do so? Or will we acknowledge the truth that the God-ordained governments of family, church, *and* state all operate under the ultimate authority of King Jesus and His good law and are, in fact, accountable to one another? Although distinct spheres of authority, we know that the local congregation has the responsibility to speak prophetically into a family situation when there is a clear twisting of roles therein. Likewise, the family and the local church have a responsibility to speak prophetically to the civil government when it is clearly violating its God-given role, even attempting to swallow up the other two spheres as if Jesus doesn't exist and it has become all in all (e.g., Ps. 2:10–12; Isa. 1:12–17). Case in point of what happens when Christians abdicate this responsibility would be the progressively unfettered slaughter in the West of our preborn neighbors while in the womb—the holy sacrament of the "culture of death" continues on because we will not go into the public square ourselves and assert the crown rights of King Jesus in this area, and so fight against it with the law and gospel![4] When the civil magistrate rebels against the living God in this way, will we find ourselves aligning more with national Israel's response or with that of the early church throughout the book of Acts? May the Lord be pleased to give us the courage to stand squarely on this truth and, when His Word requires, be willing to call the governing authorities of the land to repentance with humility, respect, and boldness, being motivated by love for the true Lord over all and love for our fellow man. May He so work in us unto greater faithfulness to Jesus Christ our King!

THE SECOND AND THIRD BOWLS

Verses 3–4: "The second angel poured out his bowl into the sea, and it became like the blood of a corpse, and every living thing died that was in the sea. The third angel poured out his bowl into the rivers and the springs of water, and they became blood." These two bowls are akin to the first trumpet judgment in that they recapitulate the first plague against Egypt (cf. Ex. 7:14–24), but these are much more severe. The text here tells us that these judgments involve the whole sea and every creature therein, not

---

4   See End Abortion Now to see what faithfulness and consistency can look like: https://endabortionnow.com. EAN is an umbrella ministry started by Apologia Church in Mesa, Arizona.

merely one third. Furthermore, they involve the putrid stench of rotting corpses, those slaughtered under the Lamb's wrath, not merely some ships and sea creatures. Truly, apostate Israel's complete destruction is right at the doorstep, along with all of her old covenant vestments!

Verses 5–6: "And I heard the angel in charge of the waters say, 'Just are you, O Holy One, who is and who was, for you brought these judgments. For they have shed the blood of saints and prophets, and you have given them blood to drink. It is what they deserve!'" The text tells us that the angel who held the third bowl and poured out its judgment called out this declaration of praise. He honors the Lord for bringing judgments to avenge the blood of the martyrs. Indeed, Yahweh must be praised for all His great and marvelous deeds! The martyrs in view here are those saints who cried out from beneath the altar and were assured that they must wait only a short time until their blood would be avenged (cf. 6:10–11). This is textual confirmation that all three sets of judgments are being poured out on the same group in progressively greater severity. This means that the object of these bowl judgments is most certainly apostate Israel, which shed the blood of the prophets and apostles, of which Jesus righteously accused them (cf. Matt. 23:34–36).

Why is this "what they deserve"? Because Yahweh is infinitely holy, He can only deliver judgments that are most just in keeping with that holiness. Therefore, these deserve every ounce of this divine justice since they have rebelled against His most holy character. "God's acts of judgment are never arbitrary or spiteful, but just payment for evil deeds."[5] They have rebelled by pledging allegiance to Caesar as their ultimate authority over against Yahweh and His Anointed King.

Verse 7: "And I heard the altar saying, 'Yes, Lord God the Almighty, true and just are your judgments!'" Even the very instruments of worship in heaven cry out in hearty agreement!

THE FOURTH BOWL

Verses 8–9, "The fourth angel poured out his bowl on the sun, and it was allowed to scorch people with fire. They were scorched by the fierce heat, and they cursed the name of God who had power over these plagues. They did not repent and give him glory." This plague is the exact opposite of

---

5 Reformation Study Bible notes, Revelation 15:3.

the fourth trumpet in that instead of partial darkness falling on the land, here the sun scorches the land with fiery heat, no doubt leaving great and terrible burns on all it touches, whether man, animal, or crop. Yet the response of those under God's judgment is to curse "the name of God who had power over these plagues." Instead of the plague driving them to repentance and giving Him glory, it drives them unto further hardness of heart and rebellion. Their response is identical to that of Pharaoh, which was the intended purpose of Yahweh's judgments against him and all Egypt (Ex. 4:21; 7:1–4; Rom. 9:17–18).

Is this not what the faithful preaching of the gospel of Christ's kingdom does—namely, "to one a fragrance from death to death, to the other a fragrance from life to life" (2 Cor. 2:16)? It is through the faithful efforts of God's people in delivering His terms of surrender to His enemies as His ambassadors that the Messianic King is gradually conquering the whole world and putting all of His enemies under His feet. Indeed, the war has already been won since Jesus has crushed the head of the serpent through His death and resurrection (cf. Gen. 3:15)! To those appointed unto eternal life, the gospel comes as a sweet-smelling savor as the Spirit of God conquers their rebellious hearts, replacing them with soft hearts that love Him and His law. Yet simultaneously, to those passed over, the good news comes as the stench of death as the Spirit drives them deeper in their stiff-necked rebellion against their Creator and Judge.

Many have followed the example set by Charles Finney in tinkering with the message, as well as the environs in which it is presented, in order to achieve desired results. This kind of mindset ignores the plain truth that while the faithful delivering of the message is our responsibility, the results are wholly the work of the Holy Spirit since only *He* can change the heart of a sinner, creating in him saving faith and repentance. The Spirit alone has the power to glorify the Lord Jesus in converting the sinner on the one hand, or in further hardening his heart on the other. This is how our great Messiah is putting all of His enemies under His feet and receiving all the nations as His heritage!

THE FIFTH BOWL

Verses 10–11: "The fifth angel poured out his bowl on the throne of the beast, and its kingdom was plunged into darkness. People gnawed their tongues in anguish and cursed the God of heaven for their pain and sores.

They did not repent of their deeds." "The throne of the beast" represents the heart of the beast—that is, Rome itself. Indeed, the Greek term used here for throne is *thronos*, denoting the seat of power and authority,[6] which points to the empire's capital city. Although Jerusalem is "ground zero" and the recipient of the majority of the prescribed judgments flowing from the scroll, Rome also experiences the Lord's wrath for its own hardness of heart toward Him.[7] As was discussed at 13:3, Nero is forced to commit suicide in AD 68, resulting in a local civil war and the assassination of the next three emperors, all within the year 69. In the midst of the beast acting under the influence of the great dragon, Yahweh is still very much in control of the situation and accomplishing His good, eternal purposes through those circumstances, even bringing judgment on Rome itself.

This plague is a ramped-up version of the fourth trumpet, an allusion to the plague of darkness against Egypt (cf. Ex. 10:21–29). Here it is so severe that it drives those being judged to experience extreme psychological pain, denoted by "gnaw[ing] their tongues in anguish" and inflicting "pain and sores" on themselves.[8] Its purpose is one and the same as the previous bowl: to further harden the hearts of its recipients so they would continue on in unrepentance. These tumultuous events at the Empire's capital are directly related to those in Judea. How so? Wilson points out the historic fact that since Vitellius had met the same fate as Galba and Otho, Vespasian was forced to leave his son Titus to lead the Roman forces through the remainder of the war in order to return to Rome to help restore order.[9] In this way, Vespasian became the succeeding Caesar while Jerusalem was successfully captured and leveled.

THE SIXTH BOWL

Verse 12: "The sixth angel poured out his bowl on the great river Euphrates, and its water was dried up, to prepare the way for the kings from the east." The Euphrates acted as the northeast border of the tract of land originally called Eden (Gen. 2:14) and then later promised to Abraham and his descendants (Gen. 15:18), the extent of which was gained during the time of

---

6   *Thronos*, The NAS New Testament Greek Lexicon, https://www.biblestudytools.com/lexicons/greek/nas/thronos.html.
7   See Wilson, *When the Man Comes Around*, Kindle Location 1982.
8   See Gill, *Exposition*, Kindle Location 359766.
9   See Wilson, *When the Man Comes Around*, Kindle Location 1990.

Solomon, son of David (2 Chron. 9:26). In the first century, the Euphrates served as a border between Roman and Parthian territory.[10] The phrase "its water was dried up" indicates something miraculous. Just as Yahweh extraordinarily created a way for Israel to escape Egypt's clutches through the Red Sea, so now He is extraordinarily creating a way for Roman military forces to cross the Euphrates so as to come upon Judea and Jerusalem from the east. In addition, by mentioning the "kings from the east," this may be a reference to how Titus increased his troops with the help of local rulers lending soldiers. Wilson notes, "Josephus tells us that the general Titus brought additional reinforcements to the siege of Jerusalem from the region of the Euphrates."[11] Whether this means God literally parted the Euphrates in the same way He did the Red Sea or that He created some other miraculous way for the Tenth Legion to cross, the point is still the same: the whole of it was entirely *His* design!

Verses 13–14: "And I saw, coming out of the mouth of the dragon and out of the mouth of the beast and out of the mouth of the false prophet, three unclean spirits like frogs. For they are demonic spirits, performing signs, who go abroad to the kings of the whole world, to assemble them for battle on the great day of God the Almighty." Chapter 13 introduced the dragon working through his two servants, the beast of the sea and the beast of the land, which is now called the "false prophet." Where the dragon in the Apocalypse represents Satan, and the beast of the sea symbolizes the Roman Empire in general and Caesar Nero specifically, the false prophet is given to generically picture the Jewish high priesthood of the day, and Hanan ben Hanan specifically, who had great sway over his closest priestly assistants so as to accomplish his devices.[12]

Just as there is an unholy trinity formed in these three, so also they send forth "three unclean spirits like frogs." Beale points out that this harkens back to the second plague against Egypt, when masses of frogs invaded the land and polluted it (cf. Ex. 8:1–7).[13] These are described here as demonic spirits that perform many signs and wonders in order to convince the whole known world (the Roman Empire,) to come together to wage war at

---

10 See Wilson, *When the Man Comes Around*, Kindle Location 2004.
11 See Wilson, *When the Man Comes Around*, Location 2005 in reference to Josephus, *Wars*, 3.4.2.
12 See notes at 13:11.
13 See Beale and McDonough, "Revelation," 1135.

the time appointed by God. According to verse 16, the place of convening for battle is called in Hebrew, *Har-Megiddo*—"And they assembled them at the place that in Hebrew is called [*Har-Megiddo*]" (16:16). The meaning is "Mountain of Megiddo" and likely refers to Mount Carmel, which forms the northwest border of the Valley of Megiddo.[14] Along this valley runs the Kishon River southeast toward the Jordan River, topographically connecting to another valley that leads as far south as Mount Ebal and Gerizim and on to the Jordan itself. This valley is also known as the Jezreel Valley. It is likely that this entire valley is in view here, from Mount Carmel southeast to the Jordan River east of Mount Gerizim. It is through this valley that the Tenth Legion of the Roman army would have had to pass while en route to Jerusalem. Seeing as numerous historic battles were fought near Megiddo—including those of Egyptian Pharaoh Thutmose III during the fifteenth century BC and Pharaoh Necho II's defeat of King Josiah during the sixth century BC—due to its strategic location overlooking several important trade routes[15]—it would have been crucial in the minds of Zealot leaders to protect this geographical area. Thus, it is not beyond reason to suppose that the Tenth Roman Legion engaged in battle with Zealot defenders while en route to Jerusalem, which is what the text here indicates. Indeed, seeing as both history and Scripture record for us that Titus's legion made it to Jerusalem and eventually decimated it with fire, this means they defeated the Zealot rebel forces at the Jezreel Valley as under satanic influence, according to the eternal counsel of Yahweh's will.

Verse 15: "('Behold, I am coming like a thief! Blessed is the one who stays awake, keeping his garments on, that he may not go about naked and be seen exposed!')" This verse gives us yet another brief interlude of encouragement. The phrase "Behold, I am coming like a thief!" brings us once again back to Matthew 24, this time to verses 36–44. The comparison Jesus makes is between the masses of unrepentant men who were suddenly taken away in the floods of judgment, while Noah and his family were kept safe, and the believers who live in anticipation of His coming. The context of verses 36–44 as part of the Olivet Discourse concerns Jesus's metaphorical coming in judgment on the covenant-breakers of Israel, which language John picks up here also.[16]

14　See Wilson, *When the Man Comes Around*, Kindle Location 2016.
15　See Owen Jarus, "Welcome to Armageddon: Meet the city behind the biblical story," LiveScience, May 5, 2020, https://www.livescience.com/megiddo-armageddon.html.
16　See notes at 1:7 for a brief exposition of the Olivet Discourse.

Therefore, Jesus reminds His saints, "Blessed is the one who stays awake, keeping his garments on, that he may not go about naked and be seen exposed!" This is very much in tune with what Jesus has been reminding the first-century suffering believers—those saints of the seven assemblies in Asia—throughout this letter. These exhortations have been to faithfully persevere in following their conquering Lamb because it is *He* who is being victorious over all evil in the world![17] Jesus specifically instructs His people to do two things. First, they must "stay awake," meaning they must remain alert, watchful, and ready in order to actively keep their eyes fixed on Him and serve Him in His world effectively. Why? He will shortly be coming suddenly like a thief in the night! Secondly, they must keep their "garments" on, meaning they must continue living in light of their peace with God, which is eternally and securely theirs only because of the Messiah's pure and spotless righteousness in their place. Again, why? His coming is imminent and they must be ready![18] Hendriksen observes, "Now, at this moment of tribulation and anguish, of oppression and persecution, Christ suddenly appears (verse 15). He comes as a thief, suddenly, unexpectedly.[19] Therefore the believer must be vigilant. Let him keep his garments of righteousness unspotted, lest men see his sins (cf. Rev. 3:18; 7:14)."[20]

There is a similar command for us as twenty-first-century believers to do the same in relation to Messiah's bodily second coming on the Last Day. Though the notion of imminency cannot be transferred from those to whom John wrote prior to AD 70, the idea of living vigilantly and expectantly can. Directly following Matthew's record of Jesus's sermon on the Mount of Olives, his Master shifts to begin focusing on His second advent with what has been called "The Parable of the Ten Virgins" (Matt. 25:1–13). Here, Jesus explicitly teaches that when He comes in His role as Bridegroom, only those who have been "about my Father's business" (Luke

---

17 1:9; 2:7, 11, 17, 26–28; 3:5–6, 12–13, 21–22; 13:9–10; 14:12 contain this exhortation thus far in the Revelation.
18 See Wilmshurst, *Revelation: The Final Word*, Kindle Location 2373. While Wilmshurst wants to interpret this in reference to Christ's second advent instead of His coming in AD 70, his observation that the saints need to be ready is noteworthy.
19 See Matt. 24:29ff; 1 Thess. 5:2–4; 2 Peter 3:10.
20 Hendriksen, *More Than Conquerors*, Kindle Location 2867. Although there is disagreement with Hendriksen's use of 1 Thessalonians 5:4 and 2 Peter 3:10 at this point—since the context here concerns Jesus's metaphorical coming in AD 70 rather than His second advent on the Last Day—he unambiguously explains the essence of verse 15.

2:49 KJV), just as their Master has been, will be prepared and ready to be received as His bride. However, all those who claim to belong to Him and claim to be "therefore watching" through their spiritual apathy, lack of saltiness, and shining His light out into the world will be met with rejection and the words, "I do not know you." Due to the widespread influence in the West, and beyond, of that dualistic system of reading Scripture created in the 1820s and '30s by an Irish clergyman named John Nelson Darby, many a well-meaning Christian has been led to take the exact opposite approach to preparing for Christ's return. According to Jesus's own words, both in Matthew 25 in teaching and here in Revelation 16:15 in application, those who take a retreatist/escapist mindset toward the world and the cultural context in which they live to prepare for "the end" will be met with the words "I do not know you" at His coming. Therefore, let us be fully engaged in bringing the crown rights of King Jesus to bear in all of life, in both the private and public sectors, so that we may be found faithful whenever He has been appointed from all eternity to return.

Verse 16: "And they assembled them at the place that in Hebrew is called [Har-Megiddo]." It is important to flesh out the importance of John's specific mention of this place name in *Hebrew*. The apostle penned the Apocalypse in Koine Greek on the Isle of Patmos since his recipients on the mainland spoke this ancient language. The word rendered in Greek as *Harmagedon* is the Hebrew designation *Har-Megiddo*, meaning "Mount Megiddo." John purposely brings this up in the text in order to direct his readership to the geographical region wherein Christ's acts of vengeance are focused—namely, Judea in Roman-occupied Palestine. As was noted above in verse 14, this refers to the valley system running between Mount Carmel and the Jordan River, wherein the Tenth Legion of Rome's military forces met, battled, and defeated the Jewish Zealots.[21]

THE SEVENTH BOWL

Verse 17: "The seventh angel poured out his bowl into the air, and a loud voice came out of the temple, from the throne, saying, 'It is done!'" The object of this judgment is "the air." This is the kingdom of the devil, as seems to be indicated in Ephesians 2:2, through which he has been striving to destroy the Messianic community found in Jerusalem and its surrounding

---

21 See notes at 16:14 for further explanation.

constituencies (cf. 12:13–17).²² Henry notes, "His powers were restrained, his policies confounded; he was bound in God's chain: the sword of God was upon his eye and upon his arm; for he, as well as the powers of the earth, is subject to the almighty power of God. He had used all possible means to preserve the anti-Christian interest, and to prevent the fall of Babylon—all the influence that he has upon the minds of men, blinding their judgments and perverting them, hardening their hearts, raising their enmity to the gospel as high as could be. But now here is a vial poured out upon his kingdom, and he is not able to support his tottering cause and interest any longer."²³ Furthermore, the loud voice belongs to Yahweh Himself as His presence rushes out of the temple, just as His glory departed the first temple right before it was destroyed at the hands of the Babylonians (cf. Ezek. 10). The words Yahweh cries out are, "It is done!" which are in fulfillment of Jesus's lament, "See, your house is left to you desolate" (Matt. 23:38). This signals that vengeance has come upon the covenant-breakers and the old covenant system is now over, just as Jesus predicted. The Lord God *always* keeps His promises because that is who He is—to act in any other way would violate His Godness.

Verse 18: "And there were flashes of lightning, rumblings, peals of thunder, and a great earthquake such as there had never been since man was on the earth, so great was that earthquake." This kind of cosmic deconstruction language has already appeared in the sixth seal judgment (6:12–14), the introduction to the trumpets (8:5), and the seventh trumpet plague (11:19). The Lord used this language to speak of Israel's judgment at the hands of the Babylonians (Isa. 13:10; 29:5–6). Jesus quoted Isaiah 13:10 in speaking of the destruction of Jerusalem and her temple (Matt. 24:29). This description is an indication of catastrophic judgment, not necessarily the end of the current physical cosmos. Verse 20 also reflects this same idea. Wilson points out that this is the event to which Hebrews 12:26–27 was referring in order that the old covenant age should be removed, leaving the newly established new covenant aeon in its place. Thus, just as Jesus predicted in Matthew 21:43–44, the kingdom would be taken away from national Israel and given to those who bear fruit in keeping with repentance.²⁴

---

22 See Gill, *Exposition*, Kindle Location 359907.
23 Henry, *Commentary*, Revelation 16:17–21.
24 See Wilson, *When the Man Comes Around*, Kindle Location 2038.

Verse 19: "The great city was split into three parts, and the cities of the nations fell, and God remembered Babylon the great, to make her drain the cup of the wine of the fury of his wrath." We learn in 17:6 and 18 that Babylon the Whore is one and the same as the great city, which has martyred many saints—that is, Jerusalem.[25] This verse harkens back to Jesus's words "Every kingdom divided against itself is laid waste, and no city or house divided against itself will stand" (Matt. 12:25).

There were three major political factions present in Jerusalem during the time of Nero's reign, and then also when Titus attacked her. There were those Zealots under the leadership of John of Gischala, those under Eleazar ben Simon, and those under Simon bar Giora.[26] Furthermore, Jerusalem was not the only fortified community that fell at the hands of the Romans during the war, but also Herodium, Machaerus, and Masada, denoted here by "the cities of the nations." At the height of the conflict, not only was every last stone of the temple knocked down and the fire from the temple spread ferociously throughout the entire city, but the confused fighting resulted in horrific bloodshed. Josephus records:

> But as for the legions that came running thither, neither any persuasions nor any threatenings could restrain their violence, but each one's own passion was his commander at this time; and as they were crowding into the temple together, many of them were trampled on by one another, while a great number fell among the ruins of the cloisters, which were still hot and smoking, and were destroyed in the same miserable way with those whom they had conquered: and when they were come near the holy house, they made as if they did not so much as hear Caesar's orders to the contrary; but they encouraged those that were before them to set it on fire. As for the seditious they were in too great distress already to afford their assistance [toward quenching the fire], they were everywhere slain, and everywhere beaten; and as for a great part of the people, they were weak and without arms, and had their throats cut wherever they were caught. Now round about the altar lay dead bodies heaped one upon another; as at the steps going up to it ran a great quantity of their blood, whither also the dead bodies that were slain above [on the altar] fell down.[27]

---

25 See notes at 17:6 and 17:18.
26 See Peter Schäfer, *The History of the Jews in the Greco-Roman World: The Jews of Palestine from Alexander the Great to the Arab Conquest*, (London: Routledge, 2003), 129.
27 Josephus, *Wars*, 6.4.6.

Verse 20: "And every island fled away, and no mountains were to be found." As was noted above at verse 18, this cosmic deconstruction language is typical of the prophets in describing catastrophic judgment. Thus, given the already established context, this verse must be understood metaphorically in relation to the judgments surrounding the fall of Jerusalem in AD 70 rather than the end of the world as spoken of in 20:11.

Verse 21: "And great hailstones, about one hundred pounds each, fell from heaven on people; and they cursed God for the plague of the hail, because the plague was so severe." The text indicates that each hailstone weighs a *talantiaya* ("talent"), translating to approximately one hundred pounds in modern-day weights and measures.[28] From the standpoint of those in the city, the Tenth Legion's massive white stones, which did in fact weigh one talent each, would have looked like hailstones falling on them.[29] This is most likely what is being described here. The result is that the hearts of those apostate Jews within the city's walls are hardened even further, so they curse God in response to this most severe plague.

---

[28] See ESV's note at 16:21.
[29] See Josephus, *Wars*, 5.6.3.

The Seventh Vision (17:1–19:10)

Here we come to the bowl judgments, the last round of plagues flowing from the scroll in preparation for the final judgment upon the covenant-breakers. In this new vision, one of the seven heavenly messengers who delivered the bowls will now show John that final act of vengeance that destroys Jerusalem and apostate Israel as a nation.

Babylon Rides the Beast

Chapter 17, verses 1–2: "Then one of the seven angels who had the seven bowls came and said to me, 'Come, I will show you the judgment of the great prostitute who is seated on many waters, with whom the kings of the earth have committed sexual immorality, and with the wine of whose sexual immorality the dwellers on earth have become drunk.'" Jerusalem is described as the "great prostitute," which is not the first time such a comparison has been made to describe Israel's dubious character. In Ezekiel 16, Yahweh described Israel as a whore who was so wicked that she clad herself with great beauty and then went out bribing her lovers to come into her. This is exactly what she has done here in her relationship with Rome by rejecting her rightful Lord in favor of Caesar (see John 19:15). Toward the end of Ezekiel 16, God promised Israel the new covenant through the atoning blood of a once-for-all-time sacrifice (cf. Ezek. 16:59–63). It is this new covenant she has rejected via rejecting Yahweh's Servant who established it with the elect in His death. In this way, she has committed spiritual adultery against her covenant God for the last time! Furthermore, the "kings of the earth" have become intoxicated with her whorings because they are the various Roman officials in service to their emperor, and they thrive on loyalty and worship being offered unto him. May the Lord protect His congregations from emulating national Israel's spiritual adultery in any way! May we take seriously the many promises and warnings given to the seven churches in chapters 2 and 3!

Verse 3: "And he carried me away in the Spirit into a wilderness, and I saw a woman sitting on a scarlet beast that was full of blasphemous names, and it had seven heads and ten horns." The wilderness is the place to which the Messianic community has fled for the duration of 1,260 days (Rev. 12:6). Now this vision depicts Babylon the Whore in the wilderness gloating over the corpses of those saints she has been successful in putting to death for their faithfulness to Jesus. Babylon the Whore is riding on the beast of the sea (13:1) because she's dependent on the beast for her continued existence. There is no difference in description of the beast between chapter 13 and here, save that at this juncture it is described as "scarlet." This shows the immense royal prestige and power that Rome had over its subjects, including Jerusalem. It is meant to emphasize how much Jerusalem is dependent on Rome for her continued survival. Thus, as Wilson points out, "Jerusalem [is] riding upon, dependent upon, the imperial city."[1]

Verse 4: "The woman was arrayed in purple and scarlet, and adorned with gold and jewels and pearls, holding in her hand a golden cup full of abominations and the impurities of her sexual immorality." Various and sundry commentators agree that both the colors mentioned and the precious stones which adorn her indicate the whore's decadent and lavish lifestyle, likened unto that of royalty.[2] Furthermore, Exodus 28 describes the priestly garments that were made "for glory and for beauty" (28:2). Repeatedly, different aspects of the garments are required to be made with "gold, blue and purple and scarlet yarns, and fine twined linen."[3] As well, repeatedly, various components are required to be made of gold.[4] The high

---

[1] Wilson, *When the Man Comes Around*, Kindle Location 2070. For a fuller explanation as to the complex relations betwixt Jerusalem and Rome, see notes at 13:11.

[2] See Wilmshurst, *Revelation: The Final Word*, Kindle Location 2423; Wilson, *When the Man Comes Around*, Kindle Location 2083; Henry, *Commentary*, Revelation 17:1–6.

[3] See Ex. 28:5, 6, 8, 15, 33. See also Beale and McDonough, "Revelation," 1137–1138.

[4] See Ex. 28:11, 13–14, 22, 23–24, 26–27, 33–34, 36.

priest, originally Aaron the brother of Moses, was required to wear a gold plate engraved with the words "Holy to [Yahweh]," upon his turban (Ex. 28:36). The parallels between the priestly garments and the manner of the harlot's attire are striking![5] Indeed, her great wealth lies in the temple, which is where the high priest served.[6] It is as though she wishes to be publicly recognized as one serving Yahweh and speaking to the people on His behalf, but at the same time, killing off all those who are actually doing so! In addition, the "golden cup full of abominations and the impurities of her sexual immorality" only serve to accentuate her utter hypocrisy all the more.

We can become two-faced like apostate Israel, can we not? It is easy to put on a nice, religious front when around other believers when gathered for public worship, especially while in the presence of elder-pastors. Meanwhile, we may be harboring great bitterness against another in our heart, suffering from an overinflated ego, feeding our lust with pornographic images, or binge eating to satisfy that insatiable craving for more. It is more than evident that King Jesus detests such corruption and commands each of us to fall on our faces before our heavenly Father, who is a most holy, all-consuming fire, in genuine godly sorrow and repentance. May the Spirit of the living God so work in each and every one of us to this end!

Verse 5: "And on her forehead was written a name of mystery: 'Babylon the great, mother of prostitutes and of earth's abominations.'" In direct contrast to the high priestly role she is trying to usurp, the name upon the whore's forehead reveals her true identity. While the high priest wore a plate on his forehead reading "Holy to Yahweh" (Ex. 28:36), the harlot riding the beast bears these words instead: "Babylon the great, mother of prostitutes and of earth's abominations."

As to the first part of her name, "Babylon the great," it has been established since the pages of Genesis that Babylon consistently depicts the easterly destination of God's judgment. While the title "Babylon the great" begins its usage at Daniel 4:30, the city title "Babylon," *Babel* in Hebrew,[7]

---

5   See Gentry, *He Shall Have Dominion*, 424.
6   See notes at 18:3 and 18:19–20 concerning the wealth of Jerusalem and her temple.
7   See "Bereshit, Genesis—Chapter 11," Chabad, https://www.chabad.org/library/bible_cdo/aid/8175/jewish/Chapter-11.htm; and "Melachim II, II Kings, Chapter 25," https://www.chabad.org/library/bible_cdo/aid/15931. At both Gen. 11:9 and 2 Kings 25:22, the Hebrew Tanakh uses the term *Babel* in reference to the same city—namely, Babylonia.

extends back to Genesis 11. Adam was excommunicated from Eden and its garden to the east (Gen. 3:24), and eventually his descendants reached Shinar, where they built Babylon in unified rebellion against God (Gen. 11:1–9). Later, national Israel repeated their forefathers' rebellion and covenant unfaithfulness, being taken captive for seventy years in Babylon (2 Kings 25; 2 Chron. 36:17–21; Hos. 6:7). Now blinded once again by great pride, national Israel cannot see that it has become the object of Yahweh's vengeance for the last time.

She is also titled "mother of prostitutes." Just as in Ezekiel 16, Israel again is shown to be worst of all whores since, unlike the average prostitute, she has freely bribed her lovers to come into her! She prefers idolatry, which here is the worship of Caesar, rather than covenant faithfulness to her rightful Lord and God.

Finally, the woman bears the name "mother ... of earth's abominations." Not only does she raise up her children to love false worship, but also to love all that is abominable in the sight of Yahweh.[8] What an odious, vile, deplorable wife Jerusalem has become! Far be it from any of Christ's beloved sheep to emulate her!

As a last word to the whore's name, John says her name is a "name of mystery." Wilson comments on why her name is so mysterious. He asks most pertinently, "How was it that the people of Israel, delivered by Jehovah so many times, had now come to this?"[9] One would have thought that God's covenant people would be the ones to understand the ways and promises of Yahweh by now. One would have thought that *they*, amongst all the peoples of the earth, should be the ones to fully embrace and celebrate the arrival of their Anointed King rather than to reject and crucify Him. This deep and abiding hardness of heart is a great and terrible thing, something that must cause great sorrow in the hearts of all God's elect who read these words. May we guard against, with the help of the Spirit, any sign of this same hardness of heart developing in us!

Verse 6a: "And I saw the woman, drunk with the blood of the saints, the blood of the martyrs of Jesus." These are the very same saints who were calling out from beneath the heavenly altar in 6:9–11. They were promised that after a short time, when the full number of those appointed unto

---

8   See Henry, *Commentary*, Revelation 17:1–6.

9   Wilson, *When the Man Comes Around*, Kindle Location 2085.

martyrdom had received their deaths, their blood would be avenged. The one gleefully shedding their blood is Jerusalem, and the day of reckoning has now arrived! This is precisely how Jesus described Jerusalem in Matthew 23:37–38: "O Jerusalem, Jerusalem, the city that kills the prophets and stones those who are sent to it! How often would I have gathered your children together as a hen gathers her brood under her wings, and you were not willing! See, your house is left to you desolate!" This is exactly what Jesus indicated would happen as He spoke with the women on the road to Golgotha, "Daughters of Jerusalem, do not weep for me, but weep for yourselves and for your children. For behold, the days are coming when they will say, 'Blessed are the barren and the wombs that never bore and the breasts that never nursed!'" (Luke 23:28–29). How faithful and true is the just arm of our Messianic King! May He be praised forever!

Verses 6b–7: "When I saw her, I marveled greatly. But the angel said to me, 'Why do you marvel? I will tell you the mystery of the woman, and of the beast with seven heads and ten horns that carries her.'" John's response is pure shock and amazement, but the heavenly messenger draws his attention back to the significance of these visionary figures. The angel is about to explain the mystery of both the harlot and the beast.

Verse 8a: "The beast that you saw was, and is not, and is about to rise from the bottomless pit and go to destruction." The time has come for Nero to commit suicide and the Empire to descend into utter chaos. This explains the outcome of 13:3.[10]

Verse 8b: "And the dwellers on earth whose names have not been written in the book of life from the foundation of the world will marvel to see the beast, because it was and is not and is to come." These "dwellers on earth" or, more to the point, "dwellers in the land," are those reprobate members of national Israel. They have apostatized for the last time by rejecting their Messiah. They are those who were not chosen by God to be His holy and blameless adopted sons (cf. Eph. 1:3–6)—their salvation was never a part of the immutable counsel of His will. These marvel with great reverence and awe at the beast, Rome, as it recovers from its near utter destruction, a reverence and awe that belongs exclusively to Yahweh because He alone is an all-consuming fire (Heb. 12:28–29). May we, His saints, always be careful to honor Him as He rightly deserves.

---

10   See notes at 13:3.

Verse 9a:, "This calls for a mind with wisdom." The angel calls John to carefully discern the true meaning of the aforementioned mysteries, in verse 7, which concern both the whore and the beast. However, just as the apostle encouraged his readers in 13:18, the angel expects John to be able to come up with the answer.[11]

Verse 9b: "the seven heads are seven mountains on which the woman is seated." In the first century, Rome was known as the "City on Seven Hills" since it was surrounded by seven large hills. Thus, the beast represents Rome and her Empire. Gentry notes, "It is the assured conviction of the great majority of Revelation scholars. . . . Ironically, I agree with dispensationalist Ryrie at this point: 'No reasonable doubt can be entertained as to the meaning of these words. The seven hills of Rome were a commonplace with the Latin poets. In other words, the center of the beast's power is Rome.' Pentecost concurs [with Ryrie]."[12] He also says, "Perhaps nothing is more obvious in Revelation than this: the seven mountains symbolize Rome. After all, Rome is the one city in history distinguished by and recognized for its seven mountains. The referent is virtually beyond doubt: the very Rome existing in the day of John's seven churches (Rev. 1:4, 11; 2:1–3:22)—not a 'revived Roman Empire,' as per dispensationalism."[13] At the same time, this specifically signifies its emperor, Caesar Nero (cf. Rev. 13).

The text indicates the woman is seated on the beast, thus riding it willingly. This symbolizes Jerusalem's decided dependence upon Rome since she has pledged allegiance and worship to the crown (cf. John 19:14–16). This is a perilous alliance since Rome only means to use Jerusalem for its own self-serving gain, just as it has done with every other region and people it has conquered.

Indeed, it is a most dangerous thing for any people to unquestioningly trust and/or follow governmental leaders who seek to procure more and more power for themselves! Why? Although they are made in the image of God, they are sinners like the rest of us. Given the opportunity, they will take great advantage of others in the process of taking total control over all areas of society, as if they themselves are divine. Just as with all other image bearers in hot rebellion against their Creator, the kings of the earth must "be wise, be warned . . . serve [Yahweh] with fear, and rejoice with

---

11   See notes at 13:18.
12   Gentry, *Before Jerusalem Fell*, Kindle Location 371.
13   Gentry, *He Shall Have Dominion*, 420.

trembling." They must "kiss the Son, lest He be angry, and [they] perish in the way, for his wrath is quickly kindled." Yet they are promised, "Blessed are all who take refuge in him" (Ps. 2:10–12). Even the rulers of nations must willingly love and obey Jesus, God's Messianic King, ruling justly according to *His* law, *not* what suits them in the moment! May His fame fill the earth and His name be hallowed in all four of its corners!

Verse 10,:"they are also seven kings, five of whom have fallen, one is, the other has not yet come, and when he does come he must remain only a little while." The "five of whom have fallen" are chronologically Julius, Augustus, Tiberius, Caligula, and Claudius. The one who "is" is Nero. The other "not yet come" who "must remain only a little while" is Galba.[14] Some will dispute Julius as the first, yet ancient records listing the great Caesars of Rome almost always begin with Julius rather than Augustus, and claim an *uninterrupted* line of succession. Not only did Julius use the title "Imperator" for himself and his successors used his name "Caesar" for themselves, but more significantly, two relatively contemporary Roman historians to the apostle John, Suetonius (ca. AD 70–160) and Dio Cassius (ca. AD 150–235), both number Julius as the first of the emperors.[15] However, most significantly to this point is that Flavius Josephus (AD 37–101), a true contemporary of the apostle and historian writing for Roman and Jewish benefit, explicitly recognizes Julius Caesar as the first emperor of Rome at several junctures in his *Antiquities*.[16] For this reason, it is entirely natural for John, under the inspiration of the Holy Spirit, to view Nero as the sixth Roman emperor, instead of the fifth, in his listing of kings in 17:10.

Verse 11: "As for the beast that was and is not, it is an eighth but it belongs to the seven, and it goes to destruction." This confirms that there is at least one more king after Galba, whose end is the same as his. Historically, Galba, Otho, and Vitellius, collectively, only last the year of AD 69, all three of whom were brutally assassinated. These were followed directly by Vespasian toward the end of that year. Gentry, in quoting Greek grammarians Dana and Mantey, explains, "'The articular construction emphasizes *identity*; the anarthrous construction emphasizes *character*.' The absence of the article, as here in 17:11, 'places stress upon the qualitative aspect of the noun rather than its mere identity.' This is precisely my point: Vespasian is

---

14   See notes at 12:3 for a more complete explanation.
15   Gentry, *Before Jerusalem Fell*, Kindle Location 3856.
16   Gentry, *Before Jerusalem Fell*, Kindle Location 3861.

not *the* eighth, but *an* eighth; that is, he is not in the specified enumeration, but possesses the quality of an eighth, a resurrection."[17] Thus, the function of "an eighth" at this juncture is qualitative, *not* strictly numerical.

Verse 12: "And the ten horns that you saw are ten kings who have not yet received royal power, but they are to receive authority as kings for one hour, together with the beast." These most likely are the ten governors of the ten imperial provinces of Rome, who are subordinate to the emperor himself.[18] At this point in Roman history, the provinces were divided into "imperial provinces, senatorial provinces, and client states." The provinces referred to here are *imperial*. These rulers are said to rule with Nero for the same length he does, which is signified to be a short time by the phrase "one hour."

Verse 13: "These are of one mind, and they hand over their power and authority to the beast.'" These provincial governors are in glad subjection to Rome and its emperor.

Verse 14: "They will make war on the Lamb, and the Lamb will conquer them, for he is Lord of lords and King of kings, and those with him are called and chosen and faithful." This verse brings us all the way back to chapters 1–3 with its images of the ruling and conquering King and their call for His bride to be faithful unto death as they conquer with Him. This also harkens back to the mission of the enthroned Messiah given in 1 Corinthians 15:25–26, which declares, "For he must reign until he has put all his enemies under his feet. The last enemy to be destroyed is death." Though Caesar Nero and his vast empire seem unstoppably mighty as they oppose Christ, and though Jerusalem and the rest of apostate Israel thus seem invincible in their hatred of His church, they are in fact as children's toys to the smallest toe of Christ's foot![19] Thus, all those saints conquering with Him end up victorious as well, making all the trials and suffering they have experienced along the way pale in comparison to the thankful relief now enjoyed. Though it was difficult along the journey to recognize their faithful perseverance through suffering for His name's sake as actually conquering with their beloved King, now in hindsight all is made clear. The very same lesson is true for us today as we follow our beloved King in His narrow way with the eyes of faith.

---

17 Gentry, *Before Jerusalem Fell*, Kindle Location 427.
18 Wilson, *When the Man Comes Around*, Kindle Location 2136.
19 To understand the relationship between Rome and apostate Israel, see notes at 13:11.

Verse 15: "And the angel said to me, 'The waters that you saw, where the prostitute is seated, are peoples and multitudes and nations and languages.'" This relates back to verse 1 where John saw the woman "seated on many waters." Here the angel explains that she sits on "peoples and multitudes and nations and languages." Where her sitting "on a scarlet beast" in verse 3 refers to her dependency on Rome, in verse 1 her "sitting on many waters" indicates her rule over many peoples, nations, and languages "by means of her dalliance with the beast."[20] Such is the nature of this unholy alliance.

Verse 16, "And the ten horns that you saw, they and the beast will hate the prostitute. They will make her desolate and naked, and devour her flesh and burn her up with fire.'" Rome and her legions would make Jerusalem a heap of smoldering rubble! The angel picks up on the same language Jesus used when speaking about Jerusalem, "See, your house is left to you desolate" (Matt. 23:38). After successfully sieging the city, history records that that Roman army set the temple ablaze and the fire spread uncontrollably throughout the city, just as the heavenly messenger here predicts. "The Temple was captured and destroyed in 9/10 Tisha B'Av, sometime in August 70 CE, and the flames spread into the residential sections of the city."[21] What a wonderful attestation to Jesus's Messiahship, since His word came to pass exactly on time and in the manner predicted!

Verse 17: "for God has put it into their hearts to carry out his purpose by being of one mind and handing over their royal power to the beast, until the words of God are fulfilled." Just as Yahweh hardened the already hard heart of Pharaoh in order to show His power in delivering Israel (Ex. 4:21; Rom. 9:17–18), and just as He put it in the heart of the Assyrian king to attack Israel's northern kingdom in order to bring judgment upon her (Isa. 10:12ff), He has done the same with all ten provincial governors. To what end? In order to be completely aligned with Nero and his desire to obliterate the city of Jerusalem so that God's decree would be fulfilled. Truly, His hand cannot be stayed nor can His purposes be thwarted! He will not allow His glory to be given to any other, and for this He ought to be praised!

---

20 Wilson, *When the Man Comes Around*, Kindle Location 2141.
21 "Siege of Jerusalem (70 CE)," Wikipedia, https://en.wikipedia.org/wiki/Siege_of_Jerusalem_(70_CE); in reference to Peter Schäfer, *The History of the Jews in the Greco-Roman World*, 129–130 and Barbara Levick, *Vespasian*, 116–119.

Verse 18: "And the woman that you saw is the great city that has dominion over the kings of the earth." This woman is Jerusalem, the harlot who has committed covenantal infidelity against her Lord. Her dominion is over the rulers of the known world, which comprises the many territories procured by Rome. As we have noted, the word translated here as "earth" is *ge* and normally refers to a specific tract of land or country. However, it can also mean "the inhabited earth,"[22] which here seems to be the case. Given the context in this passage, the "inhabited earth" in question is the world known by Rome. In verse 15, we learned that, via her dalliance with Rome, Jerusalem rules over "peoples and multitudes and nations and languages." This final statement of chapter 17 serves to underscore the same point.

THE JUDGMENT OF BABYLON

Chapter 18, verse 1: "After this I saw another angel coming down from heaven, having great authority, and the earth was made bright with his glory." Similar to the angel in 10:1, this heavenly messenger also emanates the very glory of God since he has spent the majority of his time very close to the throne and to the one who ever sits upon it.[23]

Verse 2: "And he called out with a mighty voice, 'Fallen, fallen is Babylon the great!'" Where 17:14–18 describes the Messiah bringing judgment on the great city through the powerful beast on which she rides, now the various and sundry responses to her destruction begin to come forth.

Verse 2: "She has become a dwelling place for demons, a haunt for every unclean spirit, a haunt for every unclean bird, a haunt for every unclean and detestable beast." What a menacing description! Everything that represents life and righteousness has been driven out. All that's left are evidences of destruction and death, a place in which only evil spirits can reside.[24]

Verse 3: "For all nations have drunk the wine of the passion of her sexual immorality, and the kings of the earth have committed immorality with her, and the merchants of the earth have grown rich from the power of her luxurious living." Here is given the reason for Jerusalem's desolation: her covenantal adultery against Yahweh through aiming to please Rome.

---

22   See NAS New Testament Greek Lexicon, Genesis, https://www.biblestudytools.com/lexicons/greek/nas/genesis-5.html.
23   See Reformation Study Bible notes, Revelation 18:1.
24   See Wilson, *When the Man Comes Around*, Kindle Location 2194.

As for her immense wealth, "even Tacitus, Rome's greatest hater of Israel, wrote of the Temple in glowing terms: 'Jerusalem is the capital of the Jews. In it was the Temple possessing enormous riches' (*Historiae*, V, 8, 1); and 'The Temple was built like a citadel, with walls of its own, which were constructed with more care and effort than any of the rest; the very colonnade about the temple made a splendid defence' (ibid, 12, 1, translation C. H. Moore)."[25] During his thirty-three-year reign (37–4 BC), Herod worked hard to transform Jerusalem into a city that would greatly impress the leaders of Rome. The greatest of these architectural feats was the refurbishing of the temple, which from the Mount of Olives was made to look as though it was glowing with absolute brilliance in the sunlight. Furthermore, the Upper City was especially grand and exhibited luxury.[26] The holy city's extravagance continued right up until the time that Titus and his legions ended it. Indeed, by rejecting Yahweh's Anointed King, Israel also rejected the command to bend everything in their lives to please Him. Instead, they sought to please Rome in everything and thus improve their position in the emperor's good graces. This was Jerusalem's purpose in taking such great measures to beautify herself. It was from the power gained through the accumulation of this wealth that various and sundry merchants throughout the land of Israel did significantly benefit.

This can be a lesson for us today. The more attention that is given to a particular endeavor, whatever the project may be, the more it is evident what the heart of the one endeavoring truly values—this treasure is the deity he *actually* serves. Even when attempts are made to distract from the true intent, the heart's true motivations will eventually shine through as more and more time and resources are utilized toward the project's accomplishment. We must be very careful to examine the intentions of the heart prior to embarking on such a commitment lest we find ourselves led astray by the trickery of our own heart and fall headlong into the ditch of seeking to justify our idolatry, both to ourselves and to others. Instead, may such an endeavor be offered from the heart as a sweet-smelling aroma to the one true and living God of Holy Writ.

Verse 4: "Then I heard another voice from heaven saying, 'Come out of her, my people, lest you take part in her sins, lest you share in her plagues.'"

---

25 Aryeh Kasher and Eliezer Witztum, *King Herod: A Persecuted Persecutor: A Case Study in Psychohistory and Psychobiography*, trans. Karen Gold (Berlin: Walter de Gruyter, 2007), 229.
26 See "Maps, Images, Archaeology, First Century Jerusalem," Bible History, https://www.bible-history.com/jerusalem/firstcenturyjerusalem_overview.html.

That this heavenly personality refers to His audience as "*my* people" seems to indicate that Jesus Himself is now speaking. He urges His people to flee Jerusalem. Why? He provides two reasons. Firstly, so that the saints will not "take part in her sins" of worshiping Caesar. Secondly, in order that they might not "share in her plagues," which plagues she rightly deserves. This call fits well with the previous calls throughout the Apocalypse for the first-century believers to endure and conquer by keeping their eyes fixed on their Messianic King. It is He who is in the process of conquering all His enemies. It is also consistent with Jesus's exhortation in the Olivet Discourse: "But when you see Jerusalem surrounded by armies, then know that its desolation has come near. Then let those who are in Judea flee to the mountains, and let those who are inside the city depart, and let not those who are out in the country enter it, for these are days of vengeance, to fulfill all that is written" (Luke 21:20–22). History records that, indeed, these words did not fall on deaf ears.

Furthermore, there may be an allusion here to the angels' words to Lot and his family at Genesis 19, as Gill suggests.[27] Starting at verse 12, the two angels beseeched them to immediately leave the city of Sodom. Why? They explain their reason: "For we are about to destroy this place, because the outcry against its people has become great before [Yahweh,] and [Yahweh] has sent us to destroy it" (Gen. 19:13). Just as it was due to the five cities' wickedness having reached its fullness that the heavenly messengers urged Lot to flee, so also Jerusalem's iniquity has reached completion, and therefore Jesus now urges His people to flee the vengeance He is about to bring.

Verse 5: "for her sins are heaped high as heaven, and God has remembered her iniquities." The purpose for these two reasons is now laid bare. Christ does not want His bride to become entangled with the city's wickedness because it is immense in the sight of Almighty God. He has not forgotten or overlooked it, and His wrath is about to boil over against the covenant-breakers.

The language here is very similar to that utilized in Yahweh's promise to Abraham concerning the Amorites. In speaking of Abraham's descendants returning to take possession of the land, He promises, "And they shall come back here in the fourth generation, for the iniquity of the Amorites is not yet complete" (Gen. 15:16; cf. Gen. 18:20 and 19:13 in reference

---

27   Gill, *Exposition*, Kindle Location 360507.

to the cities of the Jordan Valley).²⁸ Now, after approximately twenty-two hundred years, apostate Israel is experiencing the same dispossession from their own inheritance, since their own wickedness has reached its full measure! The irony is unmistakable!

Verses 6–7a: "Pay her back as she herself has paid back others, and repay her double for her deeds; mix a double portion for her in the cup she mixed. As she glorified herself and lived in luxury, so give her a like measure of torment and mourning." This is in keeping with what Jesus has already taught: "Judge not, that you be not judged. For with the judgment you pronounce you will be judged, and with the measure you use it will be measured to you" (Matt. 7:1–2). Jesus's words are not new, but are in fact repeating the oft-mentioned rule of *lex talionis* in the law—that is, exact retributive justice.²⁹ His apostles also teach the continuing validity of *lex talionis* both for the civil magistrate and on the cosmic scale. Paul teaches that the state is God's deacon to uphold *His* law in society and to be *His* means of bringing *His* judicial wrath to bear on those who externally violate that law (see Rom. 13:1–4). James instructs believers to "speak and so act as those who are to be judged under the law of liberty." The reason he gives is thus: "For judgment is without mercy to one who has shown no mercy" (James 2:12–13). He also teaches that "not many of you should become teachers, my brothers, for you know that we who teach will be judged with greater strictness" (James 3:1). It is clear that *lex talionis* is Yahweh's definition of true justice and is what His law demands in upholding the image of God in the victim of a crime. By *this* standard, Jesus has planned Jerusalem's downfall.

Verse 7b: "since in her heart she says, 'I sit as a queen, I am no widow, and mourning I shall never see.'" Jerusalem's arrogance is akin to that of her ancient cousin and enemy, Edom, the descendants of Esau. The Edomites thought they were untouchable and would never be defeated because they had built their homes high in the cliffs of Petra. Yet Yahweh swore to completely destroy them (cf. Obad. 1:1–4), which word He kept to the point that Edom as a nation has never recovered, even to this day. After helping Babylon round up Jews in the southern kingdom, Edom fell into decline and was conquered by the Babylonians in the

---

28 See Beale and McDonough, "Revelation," 1140.
29 E.g., Gen. 9:5–6; Ex. 21:22–25; Ex. 22:1–9; Deut. 19:14, 16–21; Deut. 22:22.

sixth century BC.[30] Some Edomites moved west and intermarried with remaining Jews in Judea, becoming known as Idumeans and eventually becoming Jewish proselytes.[31]

Now, in true irony, national Israel is receiving the same end for the same reason! They thought they could reject God's Messiah without being rejected from the covenant since they were blood descendants of Abraham (see John 8:31ff). To further the irony, Herod Agrippa, king of Judea, is himself of Idumean blood! Likewise, the great city's words here echo those of Babylon in Isaiah 47:7–8 in prophesying her destruction: "You said, 'I shall be mistress forever,' so that you did not lay these things to heart or remember their end." Beale brings out the direct parallel between that passage and this, thus establishing the Old Testament background for the wording at this point in the Apocalypse. He points out that "the prediction of historical judgment in Isa. 47 . . . portends eschatological Babylon's sinful arrogance."[32] Israel truly has become like its ancient enemies to its utter disgrace!

Verse 8: "For this reason her plagues will come in a single day, death and mourning and famine, and she will be burned up with fire; for mighty is the Lord God who has judged her." Just as Jerusalem brought "death and mourning and famine" to Jesus's followers and their families, now the Lord God is bringing the same upon her all in one swift blow. The final element of this judgment is fire burning her up, which is exactly what happened in AD 70 when the Roman soldiers set the temple on fire and it spread uncontrollably throughout the city!

This message would have been a great encouragement to the suffering saints for two reasons. In the first place, the number of elect martyrs was finally full and their blood was finally being avenged as was promised them (see 6:9–11). In the second, Hebrews 12:27 was now being fulfilled—namely, "the removal of things that are shaken . . . in order that the things that cannot be shaken may remain."[33] The new covenant and the rule of the Messiah over all things had finally been established in His death and resurrection, meaning that the old covenant and the kingdom of Israel must

---

30   See Avraham Negev and Shimon Gibson, *Archaeological Encyclopedia of the Holy Land: Edom, Edomites*,(New York: Continuum, 2001), 149–150.
31   See Josephus, *Antiquities of the Jews*, 13.9, 14.4.
32   See Beale and McDonough, "Revelation," 1141.
33   See Wilson, *When the Man Comes Around*, Kindle Location 2245.

be done away with. This historically took place at the zenith of the First Jewish-Roman War.

This is how the Lord Jesus tends to operate throughout history, isn't it? He shakes those ideologies, kingdoms, and systems that set themselves up against His holy rule in order to remove them, leaving behind His dominion, which cannot be shaken or removed from the earth. For example, during the second world conflagration (1939–1945), the Lord worked through the Allied forces to systematically obliterate the Third Reich and turn Nazi ideology into something with which the world would never again want to be associated. In addition to putting this great enemy under His feet, through these events King Jesus also created a massive missionary movement. Through Christian soldiers being exposed to many parts of the world during the war, their hearts were moved for those people, and in the aftermath, returned thereto with the gospel, resulting in the conversion of many, many sinners! Such is the counterintuitive methodology of our great God and King!

Verse 9: "And the kings of the earth, who committed sexual immorality and lived in luxury with her, will weep and wail over her when they see the smoke of her burning." The "kings of the earth" in this verse are the same as those in 17:18—that is, the various rulers throughout the land of Israel. They became prosperous due to participating in their great city's infidelity to Yahweh, and now they "weep and wail over her when they see the smoke of her burning." Why? Their prosperity has come to a sudden end. Not only this, but the splendor of their beloved city has been turned to ashes and ruin.

Verse 10: "They will stand far off, in fear of her torment, and say, 'Alas! Alas! You great city, you mighty city, Babylon! For in a single hour your judgment has come.'" This is not the cry of repentant hearts throughout the land, but rather the cry of those who are indignant that Babylon was foolish enough to get caught and so lose everything from which they were previously benefiting. Although they recognize the destruction by fire as an act of divine judgment, they refuse to admit their own guilt and blame in participating with her in her whorings. Thus, the rulers distance themselves from what they also deserve, as coming from the hand of Yahweh and His Anointed One (cf. Ps. 2:1–3; Acts 4:23–28).

The apostle Jacob—commonly called James—makes it clear in quoting Proverbs 3:34 that "God opposes the proud but gives grace to the humble" (James 4:6). Hubris seeks to advance self rather than Christ. It's a multi-headed monster that has a way of reappearing under a different guise in our lives when we least expect it. Thus, we must always be on the lookout for ways in which arrogance would manifest itself in our hearts and minds, slaying it in the power of the indwelling Spirit of Christ through repentance and trust in the forgiveness found in the gospel, *before* it grows like a weed to full maturity.

Verses 11–13: "And the merchants of the earth weep and mourn for her, since no one buys their cargo anymore, cargo of gold, silver, jewels, pearls, fine linen, purple cloth, silk, scarlet cloth, all kinds of scented wood, all kinds of articles of ivory, all kinds of articles of costly wood, bronze, iron and marble, cinnamon, spice, incense, myrrh, frankincense, wine, oil, fine flour, wheat, cattle and sheep, horses and chariots, and slaves—that is, human souls." Not only are regional leaders upset, but so also are the merchants who traded with Jerusalem for all kinds of luxurious goods, the kind that royalty would buy. Like the rulers who hired them, they mourn for the trade they've lost, *not* for their rebellion against Yahweh in gladly breaking covenant with Him. Henry notes, "All those who rejoice in the success of the church's enemies will share with them in their downfall; and those who have most indulged themselves in pride and pleasure are the least able to bear calamities; their sorrows will be as excessive as their pleasure and jollity were before."[34]

Verse 14: "The fruit for which your soul longed has gone from you, and all your delicacies and your splendors are lost to you, never to be found again!" This is the response of the merchants to having lost all their commerce due to Jerusalem's catastrophic downfall.

Verse 15: "The merchants of these wares, who gained wealth from her, will stand far off, in fear of her torment, weeping and mourning aloud." The wording here is identical to that at verse 10—namely, "[they] will stand far off, in fear of her torment." The merchants respond in the same way as the regional rulers of Israel by distancing themselves from the judgment they also deserve.

---

34 Henry, *Commentary*, Revelation 18:9–24.

Verses 16–17a: "Alas, alas, for the great city that was clothed in fine linen, in purple and scarlet, adorned with gold, with jewels, and with pearls! For in a single hour all this wealth has been laid waste." The words of their fearful wailing communicates the same sentiment as those of their regional leaders (see v. 10). Here, the merchants mention the whore's clothing in connection with her wealth and destruction.[35] Although Babylon may have been able to fool others with her charade of religious piety, all her whorings have been plain to Yahweh all along, and now she has received her due reward.

Verses 17b–18: "And all shipmasters and seafaring men, sailors and all whose trade is on the sea, stood far off and cried out as they saw the smoke of her burning, 'What city was like the great city?'" Just like the kings of the land and the merchants, the seafaring traders respond to Babylon's destruction by distancing themselves and mourning the loss of the prosperity they gained through her harlotry.[36] Noteworthy is the repetition from verse 8 of the way in which she's judged, which is by fire—"they saw the smoke of her burning." This is another textual indication that the "great city" throughout the Apocalypse is referring to Jerusalem since she was indeed destroyed by fire at the hands of the Romans. While there have been several cities throughout history that have met such destruction, the events here are precisely what the apostle Peter predicted would happen—namely, that the old covenant economy would come to a sudden and violent end by means of fire (see 2 Peter 3:8–13).[37]

Verse 19a: "And they threw dust on their heads as they wept and mourned." This was an ancient Jewish practice to demonstrate one's immense grief.[38] This shows that these seafaring traders, as well as the crews that manned their ships, were most likely ethnically Jewish, though just as likely from the Diaspora.

Verses 19b–20: "crying out, 'Alas, alas, for the great city where all who had ships at sea grew rich by her wealth! For in a single hour she has been laid waste. Rejoice over her, O heaven, and you saints and apostles and prophets, for God has given judgment for you against her!'" The question may be asked, "How does Jerusalem have such great wealth, seeing as other

---

35 See notes at 17:4.
36 See Wilmshurst, *Revelation: The Final Word*, Kindle Location 2622.
37 See notes at 20:9.
38 See, e.g., Est. 4:1–3; Job 2:8; Jer. 6:26; Lam. 2:10; Dan. 9:3; Matt.11:21.

first-century cities in the same region had a similar amount—for example, Alexandria?" Israel's capital city had a posit of wealth that no other ancient city possessed—namely, the temple. Indeed, the temple tax was a tremendous source of revenue. Josephus records that when Pompey unlawfully entered the temple, "he saw what was reposited therein, the candlestick with its lamps, and the table, and the pouring vessels, and the censers, all made entirely of gold, as also a great quantity of spices heaped together, with two thousand talents of sacred money."[39] Not only was it extremely expensive to form several large items entirely from gold, as well as to possess a huge amount of costly spices, but also of significance was their possession of two thousand talents worth of sacred coin, which translates to approximately two hundred thousand pounds in modern weights and measures! The temple treasury by itself made Jerusalem tremendously wealthy for their time—wealthy on the level of highly successful empires and kings! Not only this, but Herod the Great had also infused the city with many Hellenistic cultural expressions that, in attracting people from various and sundry sectors of the Empire, had greatly increased her wealth. Caesarea had been built as a coastal port for just such a purpose, and via the city's maritime economy, both Jerusalem and her offshore trading partners prospered. All this made Jerusalem a prize worth taking. In the end, seeing as Yahweh's judgments upon Jerusalem concerned her adultery against the covenant, most notably by rejecting His Messiah and then by persecuting His followers, her wealth vanished the moment the temple was destroyed and her city burned to the ground at the hands of the Romans.

As the text indicates, these seamen recognize that the ancient city of Jerusalem is being judged as an act of divine retribution to avenge the blood of the saints she so ruthlessly put to death for their loyalty to the Lamb. This is precisely what Jesus told the apostate Jewish leaders would happen to them: "Therefore I send you prophets and wise men and scribes, some of whom you will kill and crucify, and some you will flog in your synagogues and persecute from town to town, so that on you may come all the righteous blood shed on earth, from the blood of righteous Abel to the blood of Zechariah the son of Barachiah, whom you murdered between the sanctuary and the altar. Truly, I say to you, all these things will come upon this generation" (Matt. 23:34–36). The call is for the "saints and apostles and prophets" to "rejoice over her" because the Almighty has avenged their

---

39 Josephus, *Wars of the Jews*, 1.7.6.

blood and given them the justice for which they were anxiously longing. John spoke of this back in 6:9–11.

Most often the songs we sing when gathered for public worship focus primarily on God's love and mercy toward us in Christ. When we as evangelicals think about how to treat one another, many times we speak in terms of gentleness, kindness, and compassion. While these are all very true and biblical, it seems that we find it very difficult to fathom responding to the other side of the gospel—namely, the Lord's holiness, justice, and wrath, with equally enthusiastic praise. A significant contributor to this massive imbalance would be a great neglect in singing the psalms as we have been commanded (see Eph. 5:19; Col. 3:16). Another contributor would be the antinomian spirit that pervades many of our congregations, whereby we have neglected to teach the Old Testament ethical imperatives in their fullness, how later revelation utilizes them, and how they rightly apply to our context today. We desperately need to repent as the church in the West for allowing this grave imbalance to come into our midst! Then, and only then, will our hearts be able to respond with a shout, "Hallelujah!" with all the saints and apostles and prophets!

Verse 21: "Then a mighty angel took up a stone like a great millstone and threw it into the sea, saying, 'So will Babylon the great city be thrown down with violence, and will be found no more.'" This harkens back to Jesus's words in Matthew 18:5–6: "Whoever receives one such child in my name receives me, but whoever causes one of these little ones who believe in me to sin, it would be better for him to have a great millstone fastened around his neck and to be drowned in the depth of the sea." The mighty angel announces that this is Jerusalem's due for persecuting and murdering the faithful saints of Christ. Several commentators observe that this image represents an irreversible act and is much akin to the image found in Jeremiah 51:63–64.[40] In fulfillment of Jeremiah's prophecy, Babylon became "desolate forever" as the capital of a great empire, yet still existed under Persian rule up until the Islamification of the Middle East in the sixth century. In the same way, Jerusalem as the focal point of Israel, a nation in covenant with God, was obliterated, yet later that city was rebuilt by the Romans

---

40 See Reformation Study Bible notes, Revelation 18:21; Henry, *Commentary*, Revelation 18:9–24; Wilmshurst, *Revelation: The Final Word*, Kindle Location 2627; Hendriksen, *More Than Conquerors*, Kindle Location 3076; Wilson, *When the Man Comes Around*, Kindle Location 2298; Beale and McDonough, "Revelation," 1142.

and continues in such form to this day. John's words here are meant to be taken in just such a prophetic way. Furthermore, the prophetic image of Mount Zion being cast into the sea appears in Matthew 21:20–22 and Mark 11:20–23 and is fulfilled in this most horrific of events.[41]

Verses 22–23a: "and the sound of harpists and musicians, of flute players and trumpeters, will be heard in you no more, and a craftsman of any craft will be found in you no more, and the sound of the mill will be heard in you no more, and the light of a lamp will shine in you no more, and the voice of bridegroom and bride will be heard in you no more." The musicians and their instruments represent the cultural endeavors of apostate Israel and her capital city. The craftsmen likewise represent her commercial and economic ventures. The mill symbolizes her ability to feed her own people, while the shining light symbolizes the presence of life and activity. The voice of the bride and her bridegroom stands for the continuance of Jerusalem's families and thus, society as a whole. The mighty angel announces that all these things have come to a sudden end as the great city has been violently and swiftly thrown down in utter destruction.

Verses 23b–24: "for your merchants were the great ones of the earth, and all nations were deceived by your sorcery. And in her was found the blood of prophets and of saints, and of all who have been slain on earth." The heavenly messenger gives two reasons for Jerusalem's cataclysmic end. Firstly, she bewitched the nations with her great wealth and prosperity so that they sent their merchants to trade with her. Secondly, she put to death those faithful to Messiah. The reason for doing so, as explained above, is her covenant adultery through rejecting Yahweh's Anointed King in favor of Caesar.[42] May the Lord keep us far away from the evils for which she's been judged!

Revelation 19:1–6 presents four songs of praise in response to Messiah putting His first enemy since His death and resurrection, apostate Israel, under His feet. Most significantly, these contain the only four occurrences of "hallelujah" in the entire New Testament.[43] The significance is found in that *hallelujah* is a Hebrew exclamation of praise, meaning "praise to Yahweh," and is used throughout the Old Testament in worship unto Yahweh, most notably at the first and last stanzas of the last five psalms (i.e. Pss.

---

41 Wilson, *When the Man Comes Around*, Kindle Location 2304.
42 See notes at 17:1–5.
43 Wilson, *When the Man Comes Around*, Kindle Location 2336.

146–150). John transliterates this expression in Greek in this section. Thus, the saints respond in praise.

Chapter 19, verses 1–2: "After this I heard what seemed to be the loud voice of a great multitude in heaven, crying out, 'Hallelujah! Salvation and glory and power belong to our God, for his judgments are true and just; for he has judged the great prostitute who corrupted the earth with her immorality, and has avenged on her the blood of his servants.'" This is the same "great multitude" that sang in 7:9–10 that "no one could number [them], from every nation, from all tribes and peoples and languages"—it was likewise sung of them previously in 5:9–10. In chapter 7, they sang, "Salvation belongs to our God who sits on the throne, and to the Lamb!" (7:10). Now the Father and the Son are praised for Their judgments against the great prostitute. Earlier in chapter 5, the Lamb is ascribed "blessing and honor and glory and might forever and ever" (5:13) for His ability to save the world to Himself and to open the scroll. Now He is ascribed "salvation and glory and power" for bringing final judgment on the whore and, in so doing, avenging the deaths of His saints.

Verse 3: "Once more they cried out, 'Hallelujah! The smoke from her goes up forever and ever.'" The great multitude sings again, this time praising Yahweh for the smoke of her torment, which ascends without end before them and the Lamb. Where the angel in 14:9–11 describes their eternal torment for worshiping the beast and its image, the saints in heaven now rejoice over it.

According to our modern Christian sensibilities, this would count as an extremely ungodly, insensitive response. Yet here it is in Holy Writ. This ought to bring us to our knees in heartfelt repentance, flooding the floors of our homes and church buildings with tears for neglecting to truly love Yahweh's holiness, righteousness, and justice. It is for these attributes of our great God that the innumerable multitude praise Him. Their joy is our indictment!

Verse 4: "And the twenty-four elders and the four living creatures fell down and worshiped God who was seated on the throne, saying, 'Amen. Hallelujah!'" In chapter 4, the twenty-four elders and the four living creatures worship the Lord God in His presence day and night. Again, in chapter 5, they worship the Lamb for ransoming the world from sin, as well as for opening the scroll. Now they join the great multitude in heaven in singing praises to Yahweh and the Lamb. They emphatically desire Him to be glorified, which is denoted here by the Greek transliteration of the Hebrew exclamation, *Amen*. For what do they worship? First, for bringing the full measure of the judgments written in the scroll down upon the head of Israel, just as He had promised. And second, for keeping His word to the martyrs under the altar in heaven through avenging their blood now that their full number has come to completion.

How exceedingly faithful is our God! How far above our comprehension is His immaculately just and merciful promise-keeping nature! All praise, honor, and laud be to His name alone from this day forth and forevermore!

Verse 5: "And from the throne came a voice saying, 'Praise our God, all you His servants, you who fear him, small and great.'" The Messianic King urges all his people on to greater worship, no matter what social status they may have been given by men. This command makes celebrating Yahweh for the exercise of *all* His attributes, not just the loving and gracious ones, obligatory for *all* God's people. That is to say, followers of the Lord Jesus are not allowed to "cherry pick" certain of His attributes for which to praise Him and then pretend that others are of little to no concern. We must love the Triune God for *all* of Him! Being a Christian necessarily means wanting from the heart "all of Christ, for all of life!"

THE MARRIAGE SUPPER OF THE LAMB

Verse 6: "Then I heard what seemed to be the voice of a great multitude, like the roar of many waters and like the sound of mighty peals of thunder, crying out, 'Hallelujah! For the Lord our God the Almighty reigns.'" Once more the great multitude sings their praises, yet this time with such gusto, resonance, and volume that it is as though the loudest, most violent parts of creation are themselves crying out. They worship Yahweh for His absolute, meticulous governance over all things, whether great or small. They refer to Him as "the Almighty," which is what the Hebrew title *Shaddai* means. This title denotes absolute control and authority over all aspects of creation. All of heaven cries out, "Hallelujah"—that is, "Praise to Yahweh!" Thus, the great tribulation of Matthew 24 and Revelation 7 is something ultimately for which the Triune God must be abundantly praised! This is quite the opposite of what we hear in many Western Christian circles on this subject. Therefore, let our thoughts and expectations be formed by God's holy Word in all its fullness rather than by the opinions and traditions of men.

Verse 7: "Let us rejoice and exult and give him the glory, for the marriage of the Lamb has come, and his Bride has made herself ready." At this point, the vision skips ahead to the very end of history. The author of this commentary sides with the NASB's division of the text over against the ESV's, as the subject seems to shift at this point. The great multitude of saints calls all of heaven to worship and adore the Lord their God. Why? "For the marriage of the Lamb has come"! Beale notes, "The language of the marriage supper echoes the prophecy of Isa. 61:10, 'I will rejoice in the LORD, my soul will exult in my God; for he has clothed me with garments of salvation, he has wrapped me with a robe of righteousness; as a bridegroom decks himself with a garland, and as a bride adorns herself with jewels.'"[44] Even though the dragon, the beast, the false prophet, and the whore have all sought to destroy the Lamb and His people, those who are part of the redeemed multitude have, in fact, gained the eternal victory with Him. They've done so in such a way that they're now united to Him in every way, just as it was promised them, along with every other saint—"When Christ who is your life appears, then you also will appear with him in glory" (Col. 3:4), and "We know that when he appears we shall be like him, because we shall see him as he is" (1 John 3:2). As Michael Horton has said, "Christ has so united us to Himself that He will not be glorified without us."[45] The marriage supper of the Lamb is the antitype to which the Lord's Supper has been pointing all along—that is, perfect and uninterrupted union and communion with our Lord and Savior! Furthermore, "The wedding imagery expresses the intimacy, love and joy between Christ and His people. It fulfills the commitments expressed earlier in Scripture," most notably that found in Ephesians 5:22–33.[46] Why? The text tells us that "his Bride has made herself ready" for that wedding celebration. The obvious question is "How? In what way?" Verse 8 answers this question.

Verse 8: "'it was granted her to clothe herself with fine linen, bright and pure'—for the fine linen is the righteous deeds of the saints." These "righteous deeds" are those of the saints who heeded the call of 13:10 and 14:12 to persevere through their sufferings, keeping "the commandments of God and their faith in Jesus." In this way, they have conquered with

---

44 Beale and McDonough, "Revelation," 1142.
45 Michael Horton, "Calvin on Union with Christ," YouTube Video, 51:50, https://www.youtube.com/watch?v=ZamfcD9g_Qo.
46 Reformation Study Bible notes, Revelation 19:7.

their conquering Messianic King. They are clothed with white robes, just as Jesus promised to all those who conquer (3:5). Jesus told two parables that point to this reality. Firstly, only those who are wearing the wedding garments will be allowed therein (Matt. 22:1–14). Likewise, only those with their lamps full of oil will be permitted to enter (Matt. 25:1–12).

Verse 9: "And the angel said to me, 'Write this: Blessed are those who are invited to the marriage supper of the Lamb.' And he said to me, 'These are the true words of God.'" "Those who are invited to the marriage supper" are those who have conquered through faithfully persevering in the midst of all their sufferings and through remaining loyal to Christ Jesus. They are those who have not worshiped the beast or its image, and those of the same kind throughout history. They are clothed in white robes coming out of the great tribulation (see 7:14)—that is, the three-and-a-half-year Jewish-Roman War—in particular, Rome's destruction of Jerusalem (see 11:1–3; 12:5–6; 13:5). We will find out in chapter 21 that this bride of the Lamb is, in fact, the new Jerusalem coming down from above. The new Jerusalem has replaced old Jerusalem, just as the new covenant has replaced the old covenant (cf. Matt. 9:14–17; 21:33–44).[47]

This "marriage supper of the Lamb" symbolizes the flawless, mutual fellowship and enjoyment of the bride with her Husband. This supper is not a one-time event, but rather the endless joy of the church in her Lord and her Lord in His bride (cf. Song 2:4; 4:1–5:1). Jonathan Edwards wrote that since we are permanently creatures and Jesus is permanently Creator, our understanding of Him will eternally increase, and, with it our joy in Him will increase exponentially forever![48] This is one of the many reasons why heaven is so amazingly beyond what we can currently fathom. May we delight ourselves in our great God and Savior now, in white-hot anticipation of what will be in eternity!

The angel announces to John that all these words are true. Why? God Himself is Truth ,and in Him there is no lie (see 1 John 1:5; 2:27).

Verse 10a: "Then I fell down at his feet to worship him, but he said to me, 'You must not do that! I am a fellow servant with you and your brothers who hold to the testimony of Jesus. Worship God.'" In response

---

47 Wilson, *When the Man Comes Around*, Kindle Location 2348.
48 See Jonathan Edwards, *Works of Jonathan Edwards, Vol. IV, Sect. VII*, Christian Classics Ethereal Library, https://www.ccel.org/ccel/edwards/works1.iv.iv.vii.html.

to the sheer beauty of the angel's message concerning the marriage supper of the Lamb, the apostle cannot help but fall down at the messenger's feet in worship. In direct contrast to Jesus's reaction to Thomas after His resurrection (John 20:26–29), the heavenly messenger immediately rebukes John for his act of idolatry. The angel identifies himself as belonging to the same category as John—that is, they are both creatures. For this reason, he is urged to worship God instead, who alone is the true Creator.

This is an exceedingly important distinction to maintain in our thinking. The blurring of this line has resulted in many, many theological deviations. At the conservative end of the spectrum, some varieties of evangelicalism have so emphasized Yahweh's relational attributes that He has become to them little more than an overgrown version of their favorite uncle. At the deeply heretical end of the spectrum, Latter-day Saints hold a view that completely conflates the two categories such that the god of our planet is merely an exalted man and, upon attaining our own exaltation, we too can become the gods of our own planets someday. As James White puts it, "Theology matters!"[49] That is to say, theology has consequences in how people live their everyday lives. Therefore, it is absolutely vital that we take the time to strive to understand who Yahweh is and how He works in the world according to how He has chosen to reveal Himself in His Word, not only in the broad strokes, but also in the details.

Verse 10b: "For the testimony of Jesus is the spirit of prophecy." In reflection on what just happened, John gives the reason for the angel's rebuke—namely, that they both testify of Jesus, which is akin to prophecy. Deuteronomy 18:15–22 makes it clear that a prophet's testimony must invariably be true since he speaks on behalf of Yahweh who is Himself Truth. Since the heavenly messenger is like John in being a testifier of the Truth, and not the Truth Himself, giving him worship would be utterly blasphemous.

---

49   Dr. James White serves as director of Alpha & Omega Ministries, which has a micro-blog entitled, "Theology Matters." See https://www.aomin.org/aoblog/theology-matters.

The Eighth Vision (19:11–21)

Verses 11–21 present the way in which history progresses until it finally reaches its zenith in the wedding of the Lamb and His bride, the new Jerusalem. Elsewhere we learn that the new Jerusalem from above is identified as the true Israel of God—that is, those having the same faith in the Messiah as their spiritual father, Abraham.[1]

THE KING'S CONQUEST

Chapter 19, verse 11: "Then I saw heaven opened, and behold, a white horse! The one sitting on it is called Faithful and True, and in righteousness he judges and makes war." This brings us back to the rider on the white horse mentioned in 6:1–2. This image symbolizes how Jesus Christ the Righteous is conquering the whole world. While this certainly does take place through the spread of His gospel, the focus here seems to be on the other manner in which He does this—that is, through providentially eliminating His enemies. In 6:2, John saw the rider coming out "conquering, and to conquer." Similarly here, "in righteousness he judges and makes war." Both express the sentiment of Psalm 2:8–9, Psalm 110:1–7, and 1 Corinthians 15:24–26. According to the apostle Peter in his sermon on the Day of Pentecost, the Messiah has already sat down on David's throne and has begun to rule over all the nations (Acts 2:32–36). Thus, the following verses describe how Jesus is progressively putting all His enemies under

---

[1] See Gal. 3:7, 3:29; 4:26; 6:16.

His feet through providentially subduing His foes, whether they be human or ideological, until "he has established justice in the earth" (Isa. 42:4) and "the earth shall be full of the knowledge of [Yahweh] as the waters cover the sea" (Isa. 11:9).

Verses 12–13: "His eyes are like a flame of fire, and on his head are many diadems, and he has a name written that no one knows but himself. He is clothed in a robe dipped in blood, and the name by which he is called is The Word of God." The phrase "his eyes are like a flame of fire" harkens back to when John first saw the Son of Man in chapter 1. This symbolizes His utterly pure nature, and thus His intense need to remove all that is impure from His most holy presence. The words "on his head are many diadems" harken back to John's vision of the dragon in chapter 12 and the beast of the sea in chapter 13. In direct contrast to both Satan and Rome, Jesus has real and ultimate authority that lasts forever and supersedes all others. Furthermore, we are informed that "he has a name written that no one knows but himself," which brings the mind back to the white stone promised to those who conquer.[2] Where the name on the white stone is "Mount Zion, the new Jerusalem," and is known only to the elect, Jesus bears the name "the Lamb," which He alone knows since He alone is the conquering Lamb who was slain (see 5:5–6). Indeed, "his works were finished from the foundation of the world" (Heb. 4:3)!

This conquering Rider is said to be "clothed in a robe dipped in blood." Wilmshurst brings out the similarities between Isaiah 63:1–6 and this passage, which is an important observation.[3] The focus in that prophetic passage is Yahweh bringing judgment on those coming forth from Edom. He does so as a strong man pressing out grapes in a winepress so that the blood of His enemies flows out and splatters upon His legs and garments. In the same way, the Lord Jesus progressively accomplishes the destruction of His enemies throughout history, including Jerusalem—the divorce of apostate Israel is, after all, what the scroll in chapter 5 is all about. This also is an allusion back to Psalm 110:5–7, which shows that the Messiah King will "shatter kings on the day of his wrath ... filling [the nations] with corpses" and then drinking the fresh blood of those slain in the road (cf. Ps.

---

2   See notes at 2:17.

3   See Wilmshurst, *Revelation: The Final Word*, Kindle Location 2792. While there's disagreement with Wilmshurst on the point of when these things transpire historically, the substance of his cross-canonical connection is noteworthy.

2:12), symbolizing His utter victory over them. With both of these Old Testament passages in mind, the blood on Jesus's robe is the blood of His enemies as they are justly slain.[4]

Finally, the text explains that "the name by which he is called is The Word of God." This links the Son of Man as presented here in the Apocalypse back to the Word made flesh first presented in John's Gospel (John 1:1–18). Truly, the same Holy Spirit who moved the apostle to write of Jesus as the Word now works through him to picture our Lord as such in this much different context! How incredibly consistent is our God!

Verse 14: "And the armies of heaven, arrayed in fine linen, white and pure, were following him on white horses." While this image could be derived from 2 Corinthians 2:14–17, it is much more likely that these heavenly armies, while those truly saved and belonging to Christ, are spectators of His conquering rather than participants. Wilson points out that their garments stand in direct contrast to those of their King—His are drenched in the blood of His enemies, while theirs are "white and pure."[5] These saints are those of 14:4 "who follow the Lamb wherever he goes," including into all-out war against His foes. Truly, Messiah's bride is not always active in the war—sometimes she is present to cheer Him on as He delivers her and conquers His enemies, as is the case here. This is one way in which Jesus is reigning from heaven over all the nations and putting all His enemies under His feet to the praise of His most glorious name!

How encouraging must these words have been to those suffering saints within the seven Asian churches who were seeking with all their might to be faithful to the Lamb! What a deep comfort is this image for all Christ's saints seeking to persevere through various and sundry tribulations for His name's sake down through the centuries. As the biblically derived cultural moorings of the West, which have given us the many civil liberties we have enjoyed these last centuries, collapse around us at Mach 10, how will we fare in the face of persecution? Will we keep our eyes fixed on Christ, the conquering King? Will we continue to believe His promise that "he must reign until he has put all his enemies under his feet" (1 Cor. 15:25), and thus, "seek first the kingdom of God and his righteousness" (Matt. 6:33), despite what our eyes may be witnessing in our present situation? Will we

---

4 See Ps. 2:12; Ps.110:6–7; Isa. 63:1–6; Isa. 65:11–16.
5 Wilson, *When the Man Comes Around*, Kindle Location 2404.

continue to trust in His holy rule in the earth according to His command, or will we succumb to pressures from without, even tyrannical government, as well as pressures from within the church? Will we be content with a severely anemic version of Christ's authority in every arena of society, such as is currently plaguing the modern evangelical landscape? Truly, King Jesus will be victorious as He conquers, whether through our faithfulness or in spite of our unfaithfulness. So let us be faithful sons of the kingdom, cheering on our great God and King with the eyes of faith!

Verse 15: "From his mouth comes a sharp sword with which to strike down the nations, and he will rule them with a rod of iron. He will tread the winepress of the fury of the wrath of God the Almighty." The opening words of this verse, "From his mouth comes a sharp sword," harken back to 1:16 where John sees the Son of Man and "from his mouth came a sharp two-edged sword." This symbolizes that when the Messiah speaks, His words are piercing and effect exactly the purpose for which they're meant.

The phrase "to strike down the nations, and he will rule them with a rod of iron" is a slightly modified quotation from Psalm 2:9, which describes how Yahweh responds to the nations' rebellion by setting His Anointed King to rule over them (see also Isa. 11:3–5).[6] Psalm 2:9 says, "You shall break them [the nations] with a rod of iron and dash them in pieces like a potter's vessel." This sentiment is repeated and expanded upon in Psalm 110:1–2: "[Yahweh] says to my Lord: 'Sit at my right hand, until I make your enemies your footstool.' [Yahweh] sends forth from Zion your mighty scepter. Rule in the midst of your enemies!" It continues to be expressed in verses 5–7 after the accomplishment of this utter victory is made known in the high priestly work of the Messiah. Furthermore, in their prayer, the Jerusalem believers specifically quote Psalm 2:1–2 in connection with their Lord's crucifixion (Acts 4:25–26). This demonstrates that, just like in Psalm 2, these saints expected Yahweh's response to be swift and terrible judgment upon those truly responsible for His death—namely, apostate Israel (see Acts 2:23). In addition, we know that Messiah is currently fulfilling these things from His Father's right hand on high because Paul and John interpret Psalm 2:7, "You are my Son; today I have begotten you," as speaking to His resurrection from the dead (Acts 13:33). This means that the Son has *already* asked for the all nations to be His treasured possession and is currently in the process of taking them all for Himself, which,

---

6   See Beale and McDonough, "Revelation," 1143–1144.

according to the psalmist, necessarily involves "ruling them with a rod of iron." This is precisely what's happening here in this vision of the Apocalypse. In the broader context, this means that Jesus is putting His enemies under His feet not only through the spread of His gospel, but also through providentially orchestrating their temporal defeat. It is in the latter case that Jesus is here devoutly carrying out His Messianic mission of putting an end to rebellion everywhere until the whole world is loyal to Him and His righteous rule alone! Hallelujah!

In addition, the text utilizes the words "he will tread the winepress of the fury of the wrath of God the Almighty," which echo Psalm 110:5. In that final stanza of the psalm, the Holy Spirit speaks to the Father about the Son's faithfulness in putting His enemies under His feet: "The Lord is at Your right hand; he will shatter kings on the day of his wrath" (Ps. 110:5). It is at this juncture in chapter 19 that the language assigned to apostate Israel in judgment is repeated. We are reminded of 14:9–10, where the angel warned, "If anyone worships the beast and its image and receives a mark on his forehead or on his hand, he also will *drink the wine of God's wrath*, poured full strength into the cup of his anger . . . ." Similarly, at 16:19, the apostle John comments that "God remembered Babylon the great, to make her *drain the cup of the wine of the fury of his wrath*" (author's emphasis). Thus, with the repetition of language, the Apocalypse continues to be held together as one unified whole, tied directly to the inscripturated revelation of the Old and New Testaments given up until this point. Furthermore, the combination of language brings together a general description of Jesus's inter-adventual Messianic rule from on high and a specific expression of that kingdom-rule in history—that is, the dispossession of national Israel through the destruction of her capital city and temple.

Verse 16: "On his robe and on his thigh he has a name written, King of kings and Lord of lords." This is the very same title given to Jesus at 17:14, where it is clear He is defeating Babylon the Whore, who symbolically is Jerusalem. Here is given an indication that this passage is, at least in part, describing the Messiah's victorious slaying of apostate Israel. Jesus specifically called the destruction of Jerusalem and her temple the "days of vengeance, to fulfill all that is written" (Luke 21:22).[7]

---
7   See Wilson, *When the Man Comes Around*, Kindle Location 2401.

Truly, Messiah Jesus's holy rule extends over every leader, every ruler, and every authority on every possible level. His dominion is truly over "all peoples, nations, and languages" that they "should serve him" (Dan. 7:14). This is why He has the right to put all His enemies under His feet! The reason He has been exalted to His Father's right hand is that all the nations, indeed the whole world, will actually come to humbly bow the knee in heartfelt loyalty to Him alone, and that all His enemies will actually be defeated at the sound of His word (cf. Phil. 2:9–11). Since Jesus has already been highly exalted in His resurrection, ascension, and enthronement, these things are a current reality gradually unfolding in history until His second advent on the Last Day, at which point He will finally defeat death itself (see 1 Cor. 15:24–26). Such is the Messianic King's activity in history! Truly, His rule is not for the faint of heart!

THE OVERTHROW OF THE BEAST AND THE FALSE PROPHET

Verses 17–18: "Then I saw an angel standing in the sun, and with a loud voice he called to all the birds that fly directly overhead, 'Come, gather for the great supper of God, to eat the flesh of kings, the flesh of captains, the flesh of mighty men, the flesh of horses and their riders, and the flesh of all men, both free and slave, both small and great.'" This "great supper of God" is given in direct contrast to the "marriage supper of the Lamb" of which is spoken in verse 9.[8] The former expresses His total victory in utterly destroying those resolvedly unrepentant who remain in rebellion against Him. The latter expresses Christ's total victory in subduing the hearts of His elect bride so they happily enjoy Him forever (cf. Phil. 3:20–21).

The mention of "kings," "captains," "mighty men," and "horses and their riders" together indicates a great battle involving historical armies. Considering the context of the previous verses, particularly those of verses 15–16, these armies seem to be Jewish rebel fighters in conflict with Roman legions. History records for us that the Zealot forces in Jerusalem during the First Jewish-Roman War were led by John of Gischala and Simon bar Giora.[9] Meanwhile, the Roman military forces were under the command of

---

8 See Wilmshurst, *Revelation: The Final Word*, Kindle Location 2820 and Gill, *Exposition*, Kindle Location 361130.

9 See notes at 16:19.

Titus, son of Vespasian.¹⁰ In this way, through the military might of Rome, the Lord Jesus triumphed over unrepentant, apostate Israel. Once again we see the general and the particular interwoven throughout this visionary passage.

Verse 19: "And I saw the beast and the kings of the earth with their armies gathered to make war against him who was sitting on the horse and against his army." Though Rome and the regional rulers of Israel are at war with each other, they yet have a common enemy whom they hate most fiercely. This common enemy is the King of kings and Lord of lords, along with His saints who conquer with Him by "the sword of the Spirit, which is the word of God" (Eph. 6:17).¹¹ They make war against the Lord ultimately because they both seek to rid themselves of the Lamb and His saints. The Jews would rather have Caesar as their ultimate authority than their own Messiah (see John 19:14–16). On the other hand, the Romans hated the saints because they refused to acknowledge Caesar as the Lord over all rulers, giving their full allegiance to Messiah Jesus (see Acts 4:12; Rom. 10:9–10).

Verse 20: "And the beast was captured, and with it the false prophet who in its presence had done the signs by which he deceived those who had received the mark of the beast and those who worshiped its image. These two were thrown alive into the lake of fire that burns with sulfur." King Jesus decisively orchestrates the demise of the beast, the false prophet, and all those who have been deceived into worshipping the beast. At this point, the image of the beast shifts from the generic to the specific as it is Nero who is personally brought low by the Lord Jesus.¹² Revelation 12:5 presents an ultra-condensed history of Christ's life on earth, jumping from His incarnation to His ascension all in one stroke. In like manner, this verse provides an ultra-condensed view of Caesar Nero and his comrade, the Jewish high priest—in one moment, they are brought to their knees and in the next, they are cast headlong into the lake of fire. We can see that this collapsed history represents thousands of years, as we learn in 20:13–15 that Hades is where the unrepentant dead currently reside, and only on the Last Day will they be cast into the eternal, physical place of conscious, punitive torment. Indeed, *Gehenna* (hell), according to Jesus, is the place

---

10   See notes at 16:12.

11   See notes at 13:11 for a fuller explanation of Rome and Jerusalem's relationship.

12   See Gentry, *He Shall Have Dominion*, 433–434 on 2 Thessalonians 2:8–9.

"where their worm does not die and the fire is not quenched" (Mark 9:43–48).[13] This is the final destination of *all* the unrepentant throughout history, not merely the parties mentioned in this verse. Thus, although both Emperor Nero and High Priest Phannias ben Samuel did, in fact, enter into perdition upon being slain two thousand years ago, it will not be until the final judgment on the Last Day that they will be officially judged and "thrown alive into the lake of fire that burns with sulfur." They currently exist as disembodied spirits, being tormented in Hades along with all the unrepentant, until the day of their resurrection from the dead.[14]

Verse 21: "And the rest were slain by the sword that came from the mouth of him who was sitting on the horse, and all the birds were gorged with their flesh." "The rest [who] were slain" are those from verse 20 who were deceived by the false prophet and "had received the mark of the beast and ... worshiped its image." By this is signified Jerusalem and the rest of apostate, national Israel. They had pledged their allegiance and worship to the beast at Jesus's trial before Pontius Pilate (John 19:14–16). When King Jesus speaks judgment on Israel's capital city, His words effect precisely and decisively all the details entailed in that judgment as they unfold in history. His vengeance is so severe and sweeping that all that's left of the city is fit only for vultures and carrion birds on which to feast, just as was true at the time of Jerusalem's former downfall at the hands of the Babylonians (Jer. 19:7–8).[15]

---

13 See Reformation Study Bible notes, Revelation 19:20.
14 See notes at 20:13–15.
15 See notes at 18:2 for further comments on the same point.

The Ninth Vision (20:1–15)

CHRIST REIGNS TRIUMPHANT

Chapter 20, verse 1: "Then I saw an angel coming down from heaven, holding in his hand the key to the bottomless pit and a great chain." John has already seen a vision of an angel holding the key to the bottomless pit in 9:1. The meaning portrayed here is that this messenger has been given the authority to open this kind of cosmic prison. Where he was releasing demonic creatures from the abyss in chapter 9, here he is about to put the devil therein.

Verses 2–3a: "And he seized the dragon, that ancient serpent, who is the devil and Satan, and bound him for a thousand years, and threw him into the pit, and shut it and sealed it over him." The dragon is identified as the devil and *Satan*, which in Hebrew means "Accuser." The angel binds him with the great chain he holds, which represents a kind of powerful binding from which he has no way to release himself. The heavenly messenger imprisons Satan in the abyss, which only adds to the severity of his restrictions.

The length of his binding is symbolically one thousand years, which is the same time period the saints reign with their Messianic King (v. 4). This fits with what Jesus already taught His disciples. "But if it is by the Spirit of God that I cast out demons, then the kingdom of God has come upon you. Or how can someone enter a strong man's house and plunder his goods, unless he first binds the strong man? Then indeed he may plunder his house" (Matt. 12:28–29). John's gospel records a slight variant: "Now is the judgment of this world; now will the ruler of this world be cast out. And I, when I am lifted up from the earth, will draw all people to myself"

(John 12:31–32). This means that Satan was bound in Jesus's death and resurrection since in His humiliation He destroyed "the works of the devil" (1 John 3:8; cf. Col. 2:14–15) and in His exaltation "all authority in heaven and on earth has been given to [Him]" (Matt. 28:18; see Acts 2:32–36 and 1 Cor. 15:20–28).

Verse 3b: "so that he might not deceive the nations any longer, until the thousand years were ended. After that he must be released for a little while." This was the same reason for which he was "thrown down to the earth" at 12:9, since he "is called the devil and Satan, the deceiver of the whole world." Hendriksen observes the clear parallel between chapters 12 and 20.[1] First of all, Satan is explicitly portrayed as a dragon (12:7–9; cf. 20:2). As well, he is bound or cast out (12:8–9; cf. 20:2–3). In addition, the reason for this binding/casting out is to prevent him from deceiving the nations any longer (12:9; cf. 20:3). In both portions of the Apocalypse, this takes place at the *beginning* of the Messiah's kingdom-rule, which was given Him in His exaltation (12:10; cf. 20:4). Finally, the ones reigning with Jesus are faithful saints, both those faithful in their living testimony and those faithful in their martyrdom (12:11; cf. 20:4). Thus, chapter 12 helps us discern John's intended meaning of this most debated portion of Holy Writ.

The text continues by informing us that after the thousand years are complete, "for a little while" the devil will be released from his restraints to once again have a very short window to deceive the nations. This is almost the same wording that's utilized at 6:11 when the angel tells the martyrs to "rest a little longer" until their blood should be avenged. Once again, the theme of extreme brevity comes through, yet here it is in the context of Satan's final stand before his fall once and for all, at the close of human history. As has become clear, and will become more transparent in the following verses, this last permitted attempt at insurrection against the high crown of Jesus will take place directly prior to our Lord's corporeal second coming on the Last Day to judge all the living and the dead. The devil and his minions haven't even a slight chance!

Verse 4: "Then I saw thrones, and seated on them were those to whom the authority to judge was committed. Also I saw the souls of those who had been beheaded for the testimony of Jesus and for the word of God, and

---

1   See Hendriksen, *More Than Conquerors*, Kindle Locations 3203–3212.

those who had not worshiped the beast or its image and had not received its mark on their foreheads or their hands. They came to life and reigned with Christ for a thousand years." John the apostle tells us, "Then I saw thrones." These thrones are in heaven since all other reference to "thrones" in the Revelation, specifically in relation to the Lord and His people, are located in heaven.[2]

The apostle continues: "Seated on them were those to whom the authority to judge was committed." This seems to be a subset of the saints of whom are about to be spoken. Hendriksen understands the souls of the saints as those sitting on the thrones, but this doesn't seem to fit because the Greek word *kai* ("and," "also") joins the second group to the first—namely, the one at this junction discussed.[3] The two groups already surrounding God's throne, and in some way ruling with Him, are the four living creatures and the twenty-four elders, the latter standing as representatives for the entirety of both old and new covenant believers. Jesus specifically told His disciples that when He sat down to rule, they would also sit down with Him to make judgments (Matt. 19:28), which is what the text says here. Gill includes the notion of the twelve apostles seated on twelve thrones, but expands it out to all saints seated and reigning with Christ on the basis of Daniel 7:9.[4] Beale concurs with this cross-canonical linkage.[5] Yet this expansion seems to be contextually difficult since the "and" separates those on the thrones from the souls of the saints, as noted above. Wilson takes this to mean that the twenty-four elders are those seated on the thrones in heaven, which fits the context best.[6]

The text continues: "Also I saw the souls . . ." in reference to the second group in view. At this point, the passage shifts from the general to the specific. This group is comprised of two subgroups: those martyred for faithfulness to Jesus and those still living who refuse to worship the beast. As for the former subgroup—namely, "the souls of those who had been beheaded

---

2   See 1:4; 3:21; 4:2–10; 5:1–13; 6:16; 7:9–17; 8:3; 11:16; 12:5; 14:3; 16:17; 19:4, 5; 20:4–12; 21:3, 5; 22:1, 3. See also Hendriksen, *More Than Conquerors*, Kindle Location 3327 and Wilson, *When the Man Comes Around*, Kindle Location 2456.

3   See NA 28 at Revelation 20:4, https://www.nestle-aland.com/en/read-na28-online/text/bibeltext/lesen/stelle/76/200001/209999.

4   See Gill, *Exposition*, Kindle Location 361318.

5   See Beale and McDonough, "Revelation," 1146.

6   See Wilson, *When the Man Comes Around*, Kindle Location 2457.

for the testimony of Jesus and for the word of God," these are those who have conquered via being "faithful unto death," and so have received "the crown of life" (2:10). Indeed, they "loved not their lives even unto death" (12:11), and on their blood the whore was drunk (17:6). These are they who were slain by the beast in the streets of the great city (11:8) and were pursued into the wilderness (12:17). As for the latter subgroup, these are "the souls of . . . those who had not worshiped the beast or its image and had not received its mark on their foreheads or their hands." These have remained faithful unto Jesus as their ultimate Lord, over against Caesar (cf. Acts 4:12; Rom. 10:9). These are they whose names had been "written before the foundation of the world in the book of life of the Lamb who was slain," which is why they have refused to worship the beast or commit their lives to its service (13:8).

Together, this second group, being composed of the aforementioned two subgroups, "came to life and reigned with Christ." It was the souls of both martyred and living saints that "came to life and reigned with [Messiah]." This indicates that this resurrection is not speaking of the soul leaving the body to be with Jesus during the intermediate state, but rather the resurrection of the spiritually dead in their sins to new life in Christ. Ephesians 2:5–6 communicates this exact concept, that "even when we were dead in our trespasses, [he] made us alive together with Christ—by grace you have been saved—and raised us up with him and seated us with him in the heavenly places in Christ Jesus." The result of this regenerating work of the Holy Spirit is being seated with Jesus in heaven to rule with Him over all the nations. The apostle Paul says here that we are doing this "in Christ Jesus," which is to say that spiritual resurrection results in vital union with Christ so that where He is, there we are also seated and reigning with Him.

John assumes the doctrine of union with Christ, but do we? Many Christians in the West have very little to no understanding of this most precious aspect of our salvation. The result is that we either tend toward antinomianism on the one hand, or legalism on the other, in a highly individualistic sort of way. We need to recognize that, via the Spirit's work of regeneration in a person, that individual is not only united to his Lord in every way so that His death is truly our death to sin and His resurrection is truly our resurrection to new and eternal life, but is also united to the rest of the body of Christ so that their joys truly become our joys and their suffering truly becomes our suffering. Just as we cannot conquer and persevere through every wind of tribulation in faithfully following Jesus without first being bound to Him, so also we cannot overcome the world by our faith without first being bound to the rest of His body. There is no "me and Jesus" spirituality in the New Testament!

The text indicates the timeframe: "for a thousand years." This most likely should not be taken as a literal thousand years for several reasons. Elsewhere cross-canonically this number is used representatively.[7] In addition, elsewhere within the Apocalypse itself numbers are used symbolically or representatively.[8] Therefore, it would be most natural to find the usage here operating in like manner. Furthermore, the numerical value "1,000" is a multiple of ten (10 x 10 x 10 = 1,000), ten often being used as a number of completion, much like three and seven.[9] Thus, the thousand years represents the complete, very lengthy period of Jesus's rule over all the nations, where He gradually and successfully puts all His enemies under His feet. According to 1 Corinthians 15:24–28, at the end of this period, Jesus will put His last enemy, death, under His feet, which will be on the Last Day when He delivers His kingdom to His Father so that He will be "all in all."

With these considerations in place, we can see that 20:1–10 chronologically parallels 19:11–21 by taking a general view of the entirety of the Son of Man's reign from His first advent right up until His second. Simultaneously, these parallels have a special interest in how His rule relates to the events surrounding Jerusalem's fall in AD 70. Indeed, the presentation of the beast in chapters 13 and 17 has already provided this kind of oscillating general/specific imagery, and we find it here in chapters 19 and 20 as well. Once again, it is evident the way the Holy Spirit superintended the unity of John's letter unto the seven Asia Minor congregations. All praise be to His glorious name alone!

Verse 5a: "The rest of the dead did not come to life until the thousand years were ended." The separation of the first and second resurrections has led some theologians to take the first as the resurrection of believers and the second to be the resurrection of unbelievers—thus, the premillennial

---

[7] E.g., Deut. 5:10; Ps. 50:10; Ps. 84:10; Ps. 90:4; 2 Peter 3:8. See Wilson, *When the Man Comes Around*, Kindle Locations 2484–2489.

[8] E.g., 1:4; 7:4–8; 14:1–3; 17:11; 21:16–17; 22:2.

[9] Beale draws a connection back to Ps. 90:4, the only other usage of "1,000" relevant to this discussion, which usage is clearly figurative of the idea of completion. See Beale and McDonough, "Revelation," 1149.

view.[10] This might make sense in that the ones reigning with Jesus for one thousand years have already come to life (cf. v. 4), while here "the rest of the dead" wait until *afterward* to be resurrected. However, there are three main exegetical problems that preclude this view. Firstly, Christ's reign from David's throne began at His exaltation to the Father's right hand (see Acts 2:32–36). The nature of His kingdom-rule is redemptive and spiritual, with real efficacy in every sphere of the temporal, physical human experience rather than being primarily political and physically located on the earth. We can see this clearly in Jesus's final words to His disciples before returning to heaven—He commands us to disciple and baptize all the nations on the basis of His universal Messianic authority, and then teach them to obey Him in everything, all with the assurance that He is with us to ensure the success of this long-term, global venture (Matt. 28:18–20). He then immediately ascends on the clouds of heaven to be enthroned on David's throne at the Ancient of Days' right hand, in the place of honor (see Dan. 7:13–14). For what purpose? To gradually take the ends of the earth, which have now been given Him, as His treasured possession, subjugating them to His good and to rule from the heart outwards, and establishing His immutable standards of righteousness and justice to the ends of them (see Ps. 2:7–8; Ps. 110:1; Isa. 42:1–4). How? Through His people faithfully and boldly preaching the gospel of His kingdom-rule, tearing down every ideology that raises itself against the knowledge of God, and being His transformative salt and light in the unbelieving culture around us (see 2 Cor. 2:14–17; 2 Cor. 10:4–6; Matt. 5:13–16). Indeed, death is the *last* enemy, to be defeated through the resurrection of all the living and dead at His coming, *not* the first (1 Cor. 15:24–26)! In this way, we can clearly see the true nature of God's kingdom and its penetrating effects in the world.

Secondly, some of those reigning with Him have not yet died, yet in some sense they have already been resurrected. We have already seen this to be the spiritual resurrection, the supernatural miracle of grace known as regeneration, where the Spirit raises sinners from the deadness of their sins to new life in Christ Jesus (cf. Eph. 2:5–6).[11]

Lastly, to take the resurrection of the saints in verse 4 in the same sense as the resurrection of the unrepentant in verse 5 would contradict the clear teaching of a general bodily resurrection on the Last Day (see John

---

10 See Gill, *Exposition*, Kindle Locations 361377–361380.
11 See notes at 20:4.

5:28–29; Acts 24:15).¹² We must allow clear didactic passages to inform our understanding of somewhat ambiguous, non-didactic passages, just as we must allow later revelation to interpret what's been given before. We must strive for harmonization of the relevant passages rather than creating a situation of textual friendly fire.

Thus, the second "coming to life" in this verse refers to the bodily resurrection of the unrepentant on the Last Day, while the first "coming to life" (v. 4) refers to the regeneration of believers throughout the entire inter-adventual period, as explained above. Although Henry takes a symbolic understanding of the second resurrection, he does understand it to be in reference to the wicked, while the first resurrection in verse 4 refers to the saints.¹³

Verses 5b–6a: "This is the first resurrection. Blessed and holy is the one who shares in the first resurrection!" The antecedent of "this," in reference to "the first resurrection," is "they came to life" in verse 4. Gill recognizes that this cannot refer to the second resurrection, yet he takes this as the physical resurrection of saints at Christ's bodily return.¹⁴ This is due to his premillennial view, which, as demonstrated above, is a position that cannot withstand exegetical scrutiny. Furthermore, even though Hendriksen understands this to mean "the translation of the soul from this sinful earth to God's holy heaven" rather than the Spirit's regenerating work, he does rightly observe that the "this" here refers back to the saints in verse 4.¹⁵ We know this to be the case because the one who "shares in [this] resurrection" is "blessed and holy," which is exactly the reason for which the elect were given to the Son from all eternity—that they "should be holy and blameless before him" (Eph. 1:4).

Truly, the way believers share in the first resurrection through being regenerated by the Spirit is the same way they come to be seated "with him in the heavenly places" (Eph. 2:6)—thus, being found "in him" (cf. 1 John 3:14).¹⁶ Since Jesus is the firstfruits of the resurrection (see 1 Cor. 15:20–23) and all true believers are united to Him in death *and* resurrection, His

---

12   Wilson, *When the Man Comes Around*, Kindle Location 2478.
13   See Henry, *Commentary*, Revelation 20:1–10.
14   See Gill, *Exposition*, Kindle Location 361382.
15   See Hendriksen, *More Than Conquerors*, Kindle Location 3352.
16   See Gentry, *He Shall Have Dominion*, 457.

resurrection has become our resurrection and His new life has become our new life in Him (see Rom. 6:4–5). Thus, due to union with the Lord Jesus, even though the first resurrection refers most directly to the spiritual resurrection of the elect, it may also indirectly refer to Christ's own bodily resurrection, which guaranteed ours.[17]

Verse 6b: "Over such the second death has no power, but they will be priests of God and of Christ, and they will reign with him for a thousand years." Those who have come to life and reign with Christ for a thousand years will never experience the second death! Verse 14 explains that eternity in the lake of fire is the second death. The lake of fire is the "hell" of which Jesus warned (e.g., Matt. 5:29–30; 10:28; etc.). This is the endless, conscious torment to which the angel at 14:9–11 refers, into which the beast and the false prophet were thrown (19:20).

In a similar context, Paul teaches the same thing in Romans 8:37–39. Indeed, "we are more than conquerors through him who loved us"! What a gloriously encouraging message, both to those suffering saints to whom John writes and to us today as we face trials of sundry kinds and degrees as part of striving to faithfully follow the Lord Jesus in His narrow way! Hallelujah!

The saints are said to be "priests of God and of Christ." This, together with reigning with Him, has already been shown to be the result of their redemption in Messiah's blood at 5:10. In that context, the location of their service as priests and of their reign is "on the earth." This demonstrates that although Jesus is reigning from heaven, the scope of His Messianic rule extends to all arenas, not only in heaven, but *also* on earth (Matt. 28:18; Eph. 1:10; Col. 1:19–20). This means that wherever there is one in a position of authority—whether as a business owner/employer, choir conductor, elder-pastor, husband/father, school principal, police chief, court judge, president/prime minister or scuba-diving instructor—Jesus is the true, ultimate authority over him in his specific station and must be gladly obeyed from the heart in all things. Indeed, as Christ's priests, we are meant to instruct and lead all such authorities in thus rightly worshiping the one true and living God. As they do so faithfully, they are ruling with their King, which is their true station as being united to Him in His death and resurrection.

---

17 See Wilson, *When the Man Comes Around*, Kindle Location 2465.

Verses 7–8: "And when the thousand years are ended, Satan will be released from his prison and will come out to deceive the nations that are at the four corners of the earth, Gog and Magog, to gather them for battle; their number is like the sand of the sea." After a long, long period of the gospel progressively and successfully taking over the whole world, Satan is temporarily released from his restraints to deceive the nations one last time before his time is over.[18] This is a very short period of time, as John sees in his vision (v. 3). The deceiving of the nations spoken of here is the power to keep sinners under the power of darkness so they can neither see nor come to the light of the gospel of Christ's kingdom (cf. Matt. 12:28–29; John 12:31–32). The result of this deception is the ability to move them unto war against the Lord Jesus and His bride, the new Jerusalem, in one final uprising.[19] Those deceived in this way are here called "Gog and Magog," which image is derived from Ezekiel 38–39.[20] In that context, Gog and Magog are great enemies of Israel who come against it swiftly, but are then utterly destroyed at the hand of Yahweh. Ezekiel's vision is thus prophetic of this final Satanic effort.[21]

Those deceived are said to be "like the sand of the sea." Since this takes place as the final historic moment of Messiah putting His enemies under His feet, meaning that by this point His rule has gained a tremendous dominance in the hearts and affairs of men throughout all the nations, this saying must be taken in terms of perception (cf. 1 Cor. 15:24–26; Isa. 42:1–4). From the standpoint of those being persecuted, the attack is so direct, fierce, and wide-scale that it's as though "their number is like the sand of the sea." After centuries of global, victorious gospel advancement and infiltration into every sphere of life, the Lord now sovereignly allows this brief moment of rebellion (apostasy) to suddenly spring up again.[22] Why? In a broad sense, we may confidently say that He does so to display His infinite glory. We may also suppose, considering the overall redemptive-historical thought throughout the Apocalypse, that He is doing so in

---

18   See Henry, *Commentary*, Revelation 20:1–10.
19   See Hendriksen, *More Than Conquerors*, Kindle Location 3363.
20   See Beale and McDonough, "Revelation," 1149.
21   See Reformation Study Bible notes at Revelation 20:8; Hendriksen, *More Than Conquerors*, Kindle Location 3363; Henry, *Commentary*, Revelation 20:1–10; and Gill, *Exposition*, Kindle Location 361469.
22   See Gentry, *He Shall Have Dominion*, 552.

this case in order that His saints may be reminded of how great is His grace in contrast to how thoroughly evil is the human heart in its natural condition.[23]

Verse 9: "And they marched up over the broad plain of the earth and surrounded the camp of the saints and the beloved city, but fire came down from heaven and consumed them." The image here portrays Gog and Magog gathering together from the four corners of the earth to surround the encampment of Christ, intent upon utterly destroying it. "The camp of the saints and the beloved city" represents the forces of the church militant who have been sent out from the beloved city, the new Jerusalem, to defend it.[24] The war is entirely one-sided, as the text denotes. Though the enemy seems to be much stronger than the defending ranks of the church militant, the true King is far superior. Before the enemy has an opportunity to do any real damage, all at once Jesus delivers a single death blow, decimating their entire army! The war is over before it has even begun!

As for the fire that "came down from heaven and consumed them," theologians agree with Henry that this speaks to Jesus's second advent at the end of human history, when He comes to judge all the living and the dead.[25] This language has already been seen in several previous didactic passages, though not necessarily concerning the Last Day. For example, 2 Thessalonians 1:7–8 reads, ". . . when the Lord Jesus is revealed from heaven with his mighty angels in *flaming fire*, inflicting vengeance on those who do not know God and on those who do not obey the gospel of our Lord Jesus."[26] Second Peter 3:7 teaches, "But by the same word the heavens and earth that now exist are stored up for *fire*, being kept until the day of judgment and destruction of the ungodly." In the same text, the apostle Peter continues, "But the day of the Lord will come like a thief, and then the heavens will pass away with a roar, and the heavenly bodies will be *burned up* and dissolved, and the earth and the works that are done on it will be exposed" (2 Peter 3:10). Furthermore, Peter talks about "the coming of the day of God, because of which the heavens will be *set on fire* and dissolved, and the

---

23 See Wilson, *When the Man Comes Around*, Kindle Location 2505.

24 See Henry, *Commentary*, Revelation 20:1–10.

25 See Hendriksen, *More Than Conquerors*, Kindle Location 3399; Wilson, *When the Man Comes Around*, Kindle Location 2516; Gentry, *He Shall Have Dominion*, 459; and Henry, *Commentary*, Revelation 20:1–10.

26 Emphasis mine throughout this paragraph.

heavenly bodies will melt as they *burn*" (2 Peter 3:12). Beale notes that "the actual wording of the fiery defeat is drawn from 2 Kings 1:10–14, which describes God's deliverance of Elijah from the armies of the ungodly king Ahaziah."[27] Because of this testimony from Scripture, the author of this commentary agrees with Wilson when he says, "I don't believe there is any reason to assume the fire here is merely figurative."[28]

It must be noted that this universal cleansing with fire *does not* in any way indicate an annihilation and removal of this present created order, only to be replaced with Creation 2.0, as it were. Many have appealed to 2 Peter 3 to argue for a kind of cosmic reboot. Yet John Owen points out that in the same way the whole world was cleansed with water in Noah's day so as to remove the ungodly human order, so also the whole old-covenant order was removed with fire from the face of the earth.[29] Where the new creation was established in seed form in Christ's resurrection from the dead, the old creation was done away with in AD 70. Clearly, just as God's good world was not a throwaway at the time of Noah, neither is it meant for the burn pile now.

What then is this final cleansing with fire all about? It's about preparing the physical created order for its resurrection and glorification by removing the last of Christ's human enemies. First Corinthians 15 teaches us that in the same way Jesus had to die in order to rise again in His resurrected, glorified body, so we must die in order to rise again resurrected and glorified on the Last Day—this is what it means that He is the "firstfruits of those who have fallen asleep" (1 Cor. 15:20). But this resurrection principle extends beyond the scope of humans to that of all creation. Romans 8:18–25 explicitly makes this connection for us and it is to this principle the apostle John also points. Romans 8 is also the only text in the New Testament to directly and extensively discuss the transition of this sin-infected creation to its eternal, consummate form. As Jesus Himself declares from the throne in 21:5, "Behold, I *am* making all [present] things new," *not*, as many modern evangelicals suppose, "I *will* make all new things—[i.e., something other than this]." Therefore, we are instructed to "flee from sexual immorality" since "your body is a temple of the Holy Spirit within

---

27 Beale and McDonough, "Revelation," 1150.
28 Wilson, *When the Man Comes Around*, Kindle Location 2515.
29 "Dr. John Owen On The 'New Heavens and Earth' (2 Peter 3:13)," Eschatology.com, https://eschatology.com/owen2peter.html.

you, whom you have from God," and "so glorify God in your body" (1 Cor. 6:18–20). The basis for this teaching is that since we have become new creations via being united to the Lord Jesus in His death and resurrection, we must live as those who we now are in Christ, even in anticipation of our bodies being united to Him on the Last Day in glorification. Likewise, we are taught to take dominion of creation as image bearers through stewarding and developing it into God-glorifying culture in accordance with His Law-Word, even taking back rebellious culture through asserting Jesus's crown rights over all areas of life (Gen. 1:26–31; 9:1–7; Matt. 28:18–20). The foundation upon which this very earthy way of thinking rests is that the new creation has already broken into history with Christ's resurrection from the dead, so we must treat it as what it already is becoming, even in anticipation of what it will one day be on the Last Day. Indeed, the Messiah is just as much about rescuing all aspects of creation from the curse of sin and death as He is about delivering the sinners who insist upon turning it into wicked cultures.[30] The Bible thoroughly resists any version of Gnosticism, and so must we!

Verse 10: "and the devil who had deceived them was thrown into the lake of fire and sulfur where the beast and the false prophet were, and they will be tormented day and night forever and ever." Where the beast and false prophet had begun their eternal judgment millennia earlier,[31] now, at the end of history, their father the devil meets the same end. As per Jesus's description of the final judgment, "he will say to those on his left, 'Depart from me, you cursed, into the eternal fire prepared for the devil and his angels'" (Matt. 25:41).[32] Just as 14:9–11 describes the eternal punishment of those who worshiped the beast and its image, it is the same for the devil and his spirit servants. The parallels are many. Firstly, the nature of their punishment is the same: they "will be *tormented with fire and sulfur* in the presence of the holy angels and in the presence of the Lamb" (14:10; cf. 20:10).[33] Next, the length of their punishment is the same: "the smoke of their torment goes up *forever and ever*" (14:11; cf. 20:10). In addition, the relentlessness of their punishment is the same: "they have no rest, *day or night*" (14:11; cf. 20:10). Lastly, the source of their punishment is the same:

---

30   See Isa. 2:1–4; 9:1–7; Eph. 1:9–10; Col. 1:19–20.

31   See notes at 19:20 for a more complete explanation.

32   See Hendriksen, *More Than Conquerors*, Kindle Location 3409.

33   Emphasis mine throughout this paragraph.

"he also will drink the wine of *God's wrath*, poured full strength into the cup of his anger" (14:10; cf. 20:10). Thus, any notion of demoniacs participating as the tormentors in hell must be rejected out of hand. Truly, they will just as equally and fully experience God's just, punitive wrath forever in hell as anyone else consigned to that most terrible place!

CHRIST JUDGES THE WORLD

Verse 11a: "Then I saw a great white throne and him who was seated on it." As will become clear in the following verses, this throne is one and the same as the "judgment seat of Christ" spoken of in 2 Corinthians 5:10, and thus the one seated upon this throne is the Lord Jesus.[34] On the Last Day, when Jesus has defeated the last of all His enemies, which is death, all the resurrected living and dead ones from every generation will appear before Him at this throne to be judged with certainty and finality.

Verse 11b: "From his presence earth and sky fled away, and no place was found for them." Conservative commentators agree that this is describing the transition into the eternal state on the Last Day. Gill takes this to mean the eternal state will be entirely void of physicality.[35] Wilmshurst's view is that this symbolizes how terrifying it will be to stand in the direct presence of the Judge of all the earth.[36] Akin understands this to describe "the universe's 'uncreation.'"[37] Furthermore, Hendriksen explains, "Not the destruction or annihilation but the renovation of the universe is indicated here. It will be a dissolution of the elements with great heat (2 Pet. 3:10); a regeneration (Mt. 19:28); a restoration of all things (Acts 3:21); and a deliverance from the bondage of corruption (Rom. 8:21)."[38] The conclusion to which he comes here at verse 11 is the one that takes all previous revelation into account and best harmonizes the meaning contained therein.[39]

Verse 12: "And I saw the dead, great and small, standing before the throne, and books were opened. Then another book was opened, which is the book of life. And the dead were judged by what was written in the

---

34 See Matt. 25:31; 2 Tim. 4:1; John 12:48; Acts 17:31.
35 See Gill, *Exposition*, Kindle Location 361582.
36 See Wilmshurst, *Revelation: The Final Word*, Kindle Location 2973.
37 See Akin, *Christ-Centered Exposition: Exalting Jesus in Revelation*, Kindle Location 6557.
38 Hendriksen, *More Than Conquerors*, Kindle Location 3410.
39 See notes above at 20:9 for a fuller explanation.

books, according to what they had done." This is the final judgment on the Last Day wherein all, both saved and unrepentant, will be judged. Jesus spoke of this occasion in Matthew 25:31–46, which describes Him judging both the sheep and the goats according to their works—that is, the fruit their life produces in demonstrating whether they truly belong to God or not. As well, 2 Corinthians 5:10 teaches there will be a judgment of believers "so that each one may receive what is due for what he has done in the body, whether good or evil." In this way, this vision has both of these judgments in view simultaneously.

Here lay two sets of books: one set judging according to works and one judging according to grace. The book judging according to the electing grace of God is the book of life. This peculiar book was mentioned in chapter 13, where it spoke of "everyone whose name has not been written before the foundation of the world in the book of life of the Lamb who was slain" (13:8). The Father has decreed in eternity past the names of those included in His Son's meritorious and efficacious saving efforts, not for any good in them, nor for any foreseen faith, but simply "according to the purpose of his will, to the praise of his glorious grace" (Eph. 1:5–6). Such is the nature of grace—it is *freely* given to those who do not in any way deserve it! On the basis of this book, all true believers have been accepted into the Beloved and now will receive the fullness of their eternal inheritance (see Eph. 1:14).

On the other hand, the books judging according to the works of men, whether good or evil, are now opened. Unto the unrepentant, the opening of these books is a most terrifying experience. Why? All their intentional and unintentional lawbreaking in thought, word, and deed is laid bare before all. All their good deeds in the eyes of men, but really amounting to disobedience due to the desires and motivations of the heart, are read aloud to their utter shame. The truth of their works before an infinitely holy God (cf. Isa. 6:3) demonstrates the hardness of their hearts in rebellion against Him, as well as the justness of their sentence.

Simultaneously, unto those redeemed by the Lamb, this is a most sober occasion, yet one that emphasizes God's grace toward them. Hendriksen and Wilson agree that the book of life is for believers while the books of works are for unbelievers, but Wilmshurst also includes believers in the judgment of works—a judgment unto rewards rather than degrees of judicial, punitive condemnation.[40] There is agreement with Wilmshurst at this point—the "judgment seat of Christ" of 2 Corinthians 5 and the "great white throne" here are indeed one and the same.[41] All the sins of the saints that were repented of before death have already been forgiven, and thus are completely absent from these books. All their efforts to obey, yet with mixed motives from the heart, are testimonies to the perfect, meritorious obedience of Christ in their stead. As for these grace-produced works of obedience, they receive rewards that are then cast down at the feet of the Lamb in worship for His undeserved favor at work in their lives. Likewise, all their intentional and unintentional lawbreaking in thought, word, and deed, of which they had not yet repented prior to death, is laid bare before all. It is laid bare as a witness to the ongoing presence of sin in the lives of true believers. Even more so, they are a testimony to the grace of God in Christ, who took the punishment for these sins, too, when He was slain. Any progress in dying unto sin, and living unto righteousness is the result of God's free grace in granting these redeemed sinners a new heart and in "renewing the whole man after the image of God" as the Holy Spirit "works in them, both to will and to work for his good pleasure."[42] What a terrifically God-glorifying way for the elect to enter the eternal state! May the name of the Lord be praised forever and ever!

Verse 13: "And the sea gave up the dead who were in it, Death and Hades gave up the dead who were in them, and they were judged, each one of them, according to what they had done." Since in the very next verse "Death and Hades [are] thrown into the lake of fire," the spirits given up here are those of the wicked, not the righteous.[43] Indeed, "Death, the separation of soul and body, and Hades, the state of separation, now cease."[44] Thus, the sea giving up the dead symbolizes the bodily resurrection of the wicked on the Last Day who are judged by King Jesus unto eternal condemnation.[45] Under the piercing gaze of the Lord, even to every corner of the heart, He

---

40   See Hendriksen, *More Than Conquerors*, Kindle Location 3410; Wilson, *When the Man Comes Around*, Kindle Location 2548; Wilmshurst, *Revelation: The Final Word*, Kindle Location 2972–2991.
41   See also Reformation Study Bible notes, Revelation 20:11–15.
42   *The Baptist Catechism [1677]*, Q. 39; Ezek. 36:25–27; Phil. 2:12–13.
43   See Luke 16:19–31, where Jesus describes the spirits of the wicked "being in torment" in Hades.
44   Hendriksen, *More Than Conquerors*, Kindle Location 3422.
45   See Wilson, *When the Man Comes Around*, Kindle Location 2553.

brings a just sentence of punishment to each one, each according to the amount of spiritual light they received yet rejected (cf. Matt. 10:14–15; 11:20–24; Mark 12:38–40).[46]

Verses 14–15: "Then Death and Hades were thrown into the lake of fire. This is the second death, the lake of fire. And if anyone's name was not found written in the book of life, he was thrown into the lake of fire." All the unrepentant receive their eternal punishment by being "thrown into the lake of fire" (cf. Mark 9:43–48).[47] This is the second death, which verse 6 says "the one who shares in the first resurrection" will never experience. Here is the eternal punishment, which Jesus taught repeatedly and is a relentless, conscious torment of the spirit and body without end. This means that those in hell will only experience God in the fullness of His unrestrained wrath and fury, while tasting none of His love, mercy, and grace. What a brutally terrifying reality! Akin well puts it: "Human language is incapable of describing both the glories of heaven and the horrors of hell. Take all the images that appear in the Bible, including 'the lake of fire' (20:14–15) and 'the lake that burns with fire and sulfur' (21:8), multiply it ten billion times, and you will still not give an adequate description of those who experience the second death."[48] Those who receive this sentence are those whose "names are not found written in the book of life"—that is, the unrepentant wicked, who have died in their stiff-necked rebellion and hardness of heart, each and every one. Again Akin explains, "Language like this leaves no room for any form of universal salvation, a second chance, or annihilation of the wicked."[49] This is a most sober subject of which all must deeply contemplate.

---

46 See Akin, *Exalting Jesus in Revelation*, Kindle Location 6604 and Gill, *Exposition*, Kindle Location 361638.
47 See Reformation Study Bible notes, Revelation 20:14.
48 Akin, *Exalting Jesus in Revelation*, Kindle Location 6626.
49 Akin, *Exalting Jesus in Revelation*, Kindle Location 6643.

The Tenth Vision (21:1–22:5)

Revelation 21:1–8 presents a complex vision of the new creation. In the same way we saw in chapters 19 and 20 an oscillation between the generic and the particular, so also we see here an oscillation between the pre-consummate and consummate aspects of reality, the "now" and the "not yet." In one moment we are given a view of Christ's new creation prior to His return on the Last Day, and then suddenly we're thrust into eternity after His second coming. This complexity continues right through to the end of 22:5 and is best understood as a "both/and" reality, rather than an "either/or."

THE NEW HEAVENS AND NEW EARTH

Chapter 21, verse 1: "Then I saw a new heaven and a new earth, for the first heaven and the first earth had passed away, and the sea was no more." This picks up on the language of Isaiah 11:1–10 and 65:17–25,[1] which describe the pre-consummate new creation under the reign of the Messiah. Isaiah 11:1–10 describes the coming of Jesus, the "shoot from the stump of Jesse," and the establishment of His holy rule in the earth. Isaiah 65:17–25 describes the height of the glories of His transformative rule in history. Calvin explains, "By these metaphors he promises a remarkable change of affairs; as if God had said that he has both the inclination and the power

---

1 See Beale and McDonough, "Revelation," 1150. Although Beale identifies Isaiah 65:17–25 with the consummate new creational order, with which there is disagreement, his noting of the obvious Old Testament usage of this passage at this point is important.

not only to restore his church, but to restore it in such a manner that it shall appear to gain new life and to dwell in a new world. These are exaggerated modes of expression; but the greatness of such a blessing, which was to be manifested at the coming of Christ, could not be described in any other way. Nor does he mean only the first coming, but the whole reign, which must be extended as far as to the last coming, as we have already said in expounding other passages."[2] Calvin is not alone in this interpretation. Henry, Alexander, North, and Gentry also take this view.[3]

How do we know Isaiah 65:17–25 concerns itself with pre-consummate realities rather than those of the consummation? What textual clues lead us to this most fantastic conclusion? Verse 20 expressly speaks of childbirth, death of the elderly, and cursing of sinners, all of which exist prior to the eternal state but will be eliminated at the Lord's second coming. These things are spoken of in the context of greatly reduced infant mortality, greatly reduced premature deaths, and greatly extended life expectancy. Indeed, the text indicates that the sinner who makes it to one hundred years of age without repenting will be accursed because his case is the exception, not the rule! This is what Christ is progressively bringing about through His saints' faithful preaching of the gospel of His kingdom (see also v. 24 and Matt. 13:23, 31–33)! He must gradually bring in this new creation ,"for the earth shall be full of the knowledge of [Yahweh] as the waters cover the sea" (Isa. 11:9; see also Hab. 2:14). He must save the vast majority of men from their sins, indeed all the nations, and bring them under His righteous rule because "God did not send his Son into the world to condemn the world, but in order that the world might be saved through him" (John 3:17). As Gentry points out, the promise of the whole world coming to salvation *does not* equal "an 'each and every' salvific universalism" as some have supposed is meant by such a statement.[4] Thus, the prophet

---

2   John Calvin, *Calvin's Commentary*, https://biblehub.com/commentaries/calvin/isaiah/65.htm.

3   See Henry, *Commentary*, Isaiah 65:17–25; J. A. Alexander, *The Prophecies of Isaiah Translated and Explained*, https://archive.org/stream/propheciesofisai02alex#page/452/mode/2up; Gary North, "Why Is It God's Way to Allow the Government Control Over Health Care—Life or Death—by Taxing and Rationing?," Specific Answers, https://www.garynorth.com/public/5318.cfm; and Kenneth L. Gentry, "Two Phases of the New Creation," Postmillennial Worldview, May 17, 2019, https://postmillennialworldview.com/2019/05/17/two-phases-of-the-new-creation/#more-12248.

4   Gentry, *He Shall Have Dominion*, 528.

gives to us the new-covenant new-creational order under the kingdom-rule of Messiah.

Here in chapter 21, John is given a recapitulation of the same vision. We can see this to be true due to the near-time indicators he gives, both at the beginning and the ending of his letter to the seven churches of Asia.[5] In light of that, the contents of the letter, vision by vision, must relate directly to those first-century believers to whom he writes, including at this late juncture. Given John's usage of the two texts from Isaiah, the new creation brought in by Jesus's resurrection from the dead is indeed what's in view here.[6]

As to the words, "for the first heaven and the first earth had passed away," this is a specific reference to the cataclysmic ending to Israel as a nation in covenant with Yahweh. Riding on the coattails of Isaiah 51:16, Isaiah 65:1–16 foretells the decimation of apostate Israel in judgment, bringing an abrupt and permanent end to the entire old covenant system, which is prophetically thought of as the "old creation," the "old heavens and earth." That is what is specifically being spoken of here.[7] Furthermore, by extension, it has already been seen in 11:15 that King Jesus is currently supplanting the kingdoms of this world with His own kingdom, thus transforming the very fabric of society and culture. In the same way He did this by putting His first post-ascension enemy, apostate Israel, under His feet, He is progressively doing the same as the gospel of His kingdom conquers the hearts of men. Indeed, He is gradually transforming this current creation, being marred by sin and rebellion against God, into "the new heaven and the new earth," which is defined by true peace under His good and just rule. In the words of the author to the Hebrews, Yahweh is in the business of removing things shakeable in order to leave behind things unshakeable (Heb. 12:25–29). The new creation has finally come in the establishment of the new covenant through our Savior's death and resurrection! We can see, then, that this passage chronologically parallels 19:11–21 and 20:1–10, even including 20:11–15, as verse 4 will soon show forth. Lastly, verse 1 states, "and the sea was no more." The previous mentions of a sea at 4:6 and 15:2 symbolize the stability God's power brings in heaven, but this sea belongs to the old creation and thus serves to symbolize the opposite.

---

5   See 1:1, 3; 22:6, 10, 12, 20.
6   See John 11:21–27; 2 Cor. 5:16–20; Eph. 1:9–10; Col. 1:19–20.
7   See Wilson, *When the Man Comes Around*, Kindle Location 2578.

This sea represents violent distress and peril caused by sin and Satan's forces. Those who are united to Jesus in His death and resurrection have been made to be new creations and, while they continue to war against the presence of sin in their lives, they will never again have to deal with being under sin's dominion (cf. Rom. 6:1–14). They are progressively becoming more of who they *already are* by grace—true believers *already are* new creations, *not* old creations striving to become new creations (cf. Gal. 2:20). In this sense, the sea of sin's perils are "no more" to them (cf. Rom. 8:31–39). What an amazing reality to consider! Such are the effects of Christ's death and resurrection in the world!

Verse 2: "And I saw the holy city, new Jerusalem, coming down out of heaven from God, prepared as a bride adorned for her husband." Henry rightly interprets the "Jerusalem" at Isaiah 65:18–19 in light of Galatians 4:26, which explains, "But the Jerusalem above is free, and she is our mother."[8] As seen above, this is the Old Testament background to John's words. Thus, the language of Galatians 4:21–31 is here picked up in describing the universal body of Christ as "the Jerusalem above [who] is free" and "like Isaac, are children of promise" (Galatians 4:26, 28). This is spiritual Israel, to which physical Israel typically pointed all throughout old covenant history. The text of Galatians 4 specifically says that the "present Jerusalem" stands for national Israel as a whole (v. 25). In quoting Genesis 21:10, verse 30 exposits that national Israel, along with the old covenant to which it was in bondage, must be cast out since she cannot inherit with spiritual Israel under the new covenant. This "casting out" historically took place when the "present Jerusalem" was destroyed with fire at the hands of the Romans as part of the First Jewish-Roman War.

Understanding Paul's message at Galatians 4 not only assists us in properly grasping Isaiah 65, and thus Revelation 21, but also other Old Testament passages like Genesis 16–17. Entire ministries and missionary strategies have been built upon the notion that since Ishmael was Isaac's brother, since Arabs are physical descendants of Ishmael, and since we are spiritual descendants of Abraham by faith, therefore Muslims and Christians are in fact spiritual cousins.[9] Thus, the line of reasoning goes, just as Jews had an underdeveloped understanding of the one true God prior

---

8 See Henry, *Commentary*, Isaiah 65:17–25.

9 E.g., Don McCurry, *Healing the Broken Family of Abraham: New Life for Muslims*, and the ministry No Cousins Left.

to Christ's incarnation, so also this is true of Muslims. Yet this view completely ignores the way the parallels get fleshed out in reality and the way the Bible itself interprets the relationship between Isaac and Ishmael. On the first, the parallel properly is between the *physical* descendants of Isaac (i.e., ethnic Jews) and the *physical* sons of Ishmael (i.e., ethnic Arabs). The problem with even this parallel is that while it can be said that all ethnic Jews can trace their lineage back to the twelve tribes of Israel, and thus to Isaac, this cannot be said of all ethnic Arabs with regard to their Ishmaelite ancestry. Thus, at best, it can only be considered a partial parallel. On the second, Hagar is interpreted allegorically to be the old covenant system and Ishmael to be physical Israel in spiritual slavery along with her. Yet Sarah is interpreted to be the new covenant and Isaac to be in spiritual freedom along with her. The parallel and contrast is between the old covenant and new covenant, and between physical Israel and spiritual Israel. In this way, Ishmael's supposed physical descendants, and thus Islam, must be the objects of application thereunto, *not* read into the interpretation itself. Therefore, any ministry or missionary strategy to Muslims that's built upon this eisegetical view rather than upon Scripture's own inspired interpretation must be discarded as foundationally unbiblical and dishonoring to the Lord (though there may be some truly biblical elements incorporated therein). Once again, it is plain that theology really does matter!

Here at verse 2, the apostle John draws from Ephesians 5:22–33, which describes the covenant relationship between Christ and the church as the marriage union of the Bridegroom and His bride. The removal of national Israel and the old covenant has left room for new Jerusalem to enter into her eternal blessings and inheritance in Christ's new covenant. This is precisely what He promised would happen in His concluding remarks of the parable of the tenants, an indictment aimed at the leaders of apostate Israel: "Therefore I tell you, the kingdom of God will be taken away from you and given to a people producing its fruits. And the one who falls on this stone will be broken to pieces; and when it falls on anyone, it will crush him" (Matt. 21:43–44). Oh, how supremely faithful is the Lord God Almighty!

Verse 3: "And I heard a loud voice from the throne saying, 'Behold, the dwelling place of God is with man. He will dwell with them, and they will be his people, and God himself will be with them as their God.'" This loud voice proceeds from the throne, indicating it belongs to one close to the throne, likely one of the four living creatures. This voice is distinguished from that of "he who was seated on the throne" at verse 5, who clearly is Yahweh. *Skene* is the word rendered as "dwelling place," but it literally means "tabernacle." This is the noun form of the same word used at John 1:14 as a verb, *eskenosen*. This usage seems to be intentional on John's part—just as at John 1:14, Yahweh's presence is immediately with His people in the person of Jesus (cf. Isa. 7:14; Matt. 1:22–23). To emphasize this point, the living creature declares, "He will dwell with them," or more literally, "and he will tabernacle with them," as *kai skenosai met' auton* more accurately means. He underscores this point by using a variant of Yahweh's traditional covenantal promise unto His people, that they will be His people, and God Himself will be with them as their God.[10] Whereas this promise was directed exclusively to the physical descendants of Abraham within the old covenant, now it is given to all those belonging to the new covenant—that is, all those possessing like faith to Abraham from every nation under heaven. Not only does Yahweh promise to personally tabernacle in the midst of His new covenant people forever, but He also promises to do so within the safety and intimacy of covenant relationship established in Christ's blood (see Heb. 9:15)! Truly, the steadfast love of Yahweh endures forever, His faithfulness to all generations!

Verse 4: "He will wipe away every tear from their eyes, and death shall be no more, neither shall there be mourning, nor crying, nor pain anymore, for the former things have passed away." Here John continues to pick up the language of chapters 11 and 65 of Isaiah's message to national Israel, specifically the southern kingdom of Judah. However, the focus shifts for a moment to include realities belonging to the eternal state. In 11:9, Isaiah announces, "They shall not hurt or destroy in all my holy mountain; for the earth shall be full of the knowledge of [Yahweh] as the waters cover the sea." Again in 65:19, the prophet proclaims, "I will rejoice in Jerusalem and be glad in my people; no more shall be heard in it the sound of weeping and the cry of distress." Thus, in an "already/not yet" fashion, the new creation is promised to take root in the world—first, progressively throughout the inter-adventual period as Christ builds His church and advances His kingdom-rule to the ends of the earth, and then climactically as it is glorified and resurrected on the Last Day.

---

10   Gen. 17:7–8; Ex. 6:7; Lev. 26:12; Jer. 7:23; 11:14; 30:22; 31:33; Ezek. 36:28; Heb. 8:10.

A further indication that the consummation is simultaneously in view here is that the list presented includes the elimination of death, which we know from 1 Corinthians 15:26 will not take place until the Lord Jesus resurrects all the living and the dead on the Last Day. The apostle Paul teaches in quoting from Psalm 110:1, "For he must reign until he has put all his enemies under his feet. The *last* enemy to be destroyed is death" (1 Cor. 15:25–26, author's emphasis).

As noted above, this passage behaves like 19:11–21 and 20:1–10. In what way? Those two passages chronologically parallel each other with a generic depiction of the Messiah's rule spanning from His first advent until His second advent. Yet, simultaneously, they have in view the events surrounding the fall of Jerusalem in specific. In this passage in chapter 21, the vision symbolizes the advancement of the new creation in the world during Jesus's Messianic rule from David's throne. Indeed, just as His kingdom is "now" progressively overcoming the kingdoms of this world, so also His new creation is simultaneously "now" overcoming sin's corruption in all the earth—Christ's historical resurrection is truly more powerful than the effects of sin and evil in the world! Hallelujah to the King of kings! Nevertheless, this vision simultaneously represents the "not yet" consummate new creation brought about in the cosmic resurrection on the Last Day.[11] Wilson would agree with the pre-consummate meaning of this text, but not the consummate.[12] There is disagreement with Wilson's conclusion at this point as he does not seem to take "and death shall be no more" into proper consideration in his exegesis. Just as was seen in chapters 19 and 20, this is a "both/and" situation, not an "either/or." What a glorious, majestic reality is ours in the Lord Jesus!

Verse 5a: "And he who was seated on the throne said, 'Behold, I am making all things new.'" The last place Yahweh is sitting on a throne is 20:11 and is in reference to the Lord Jesus in particular. It also makes sense to understand the one speaking here to be Jesus since "making all things new" is what His Messianic reign is all about! It must be noted that Jesus is using a present, active, indicative form of the Greek verb *poieō*, rendered in English as "*I am making* all things new" (author's emphasis). This also points to a gradualistic understanding of not only this statement, but also

---

11   See Akin, *Exalting Jesus in Revelation*, Kindle Location 6769 for the current majority view of this passage.
12   See Wilson, *When the Man Comes Around*, Kindle Location 2579.

the previous four verses. Jesus is "making all [present] things new," He is *not* about to "make all new things"—[something completely different].

It has been said, "You hit what you aim at." Due to a widely pervasive eschatology of historical gospel defeat in the world, really an eschatology of escape and retreat from the public square, we have become at best what David Bahnsen calls "Great Commission utilitarians."[13] What he means by this is a fairly recent development toward viewing the workplace as an opportunity to share the gospel with coworkers. He explains that while this is a step up from the purely fundamentalist view of work as the means by which the home may survive, it still misses the mark of our calling as image bearers in God's world to take dominion—that is, to transform all of creation into culture that reflects our Creator's majesty, holiness, and sovereignty. For many evangelicals in the West, the dominion mandate has little to no bearing on how we think about each and every area of the world in which we have been placed. Why? Because we don't actually believe that Jesus is King over all kings and Lord over all lords right now, save as a nice Christian slogan for t-shirts and the like, and that His gospel will actually win the whole world unto Himself within human history. Thus, we also find ourselves rejecting any intrusion of the new creation into history, save on an individualistic, solely spiritual level. Nevertheless, in our fallen world where image bearers go out of their way to turn creation into culture that rebels against Yahweh and His law, taking the whole world for Jesus, nation by nation, necessarily involves taking dominion as redeemed image bearers within the context of Messiah's established lordship over every sphere of society, not only over every individual therein. This is what it means to be salt and light in the earth.

Thus, the Christ-following recycling-truck driver is commanded to assert His crown rights in his vocation as far as the extent of his influence and authority within the company will allow. This not only involves recognizing the role that recycling plays in loving God by stewarding and developing His creation, but it also involves love for neighbor in the way the driver treats the property of the residents and the residents themselves. It extends even to the very warp and woof of the company's internal structures, management, and how it relates to other companies and to the civil government.

---

13 David Bahnsen, "Punk Rock Kuyperianism: Christ in the Public Square," 2020 Fight Laugh Feast Conference.

Likewise, the believing choir conductor must assert the crown rights of Jesus, not only in the choice of music to be sung, but also in explaining the composer's intended meaning unto the glory of the one true and living God—this without compromise or permitting reinterpretations of the lyrics on the part of choir members. This also involves the way in which the choir sings these songs. Why? Love for neighbor demands accurately representing them. Not only this, but the choir master must seek to be an example of treating others with care and respect as fellow image bearers and encourage this God-honoring type of interaction amongst the vocalists.

In like fashion, the saint whose vocation is in politics is required to assert King Jesus's crown rights in that arena as well. He must operate on God's definitions of law and justice and the role of the state, following biblical categories and evaluating the contents of each and every bill in light of His revealed Law-Word. In obedience to the Lord, his interactions with other politicians and with the public must be characterized with care and respect toward those also made in Yahweh's image. In this way, the Lord's disciples seek to consistently aim at the target of bringing all of life under their Master's kingdom-rule. They do so knowing that those sin-enslaved individuals and families involved along the way will only truly and gladly want these things as the Spirit brings them to saving repentant faith in the Son of Man. They do so to give others a living picture of what Jesus's rule in the earth looks like, although by way of imperfect, pre-consummate efforts. Finally, they do so knowing that the supremacy of God's Son in all things is ultimately where history is headed as He progressively establishes His new creation in the earth through such faithful gospel efforts.

Verse 5b: "Also he said, 'Write this down, for these words are trustworthy and true.'" At this point, Christ Jesus invites the apostle John to put pen to paper. His words are necessarily "trustworthy and true" because they come from the lips of the one who is ontologically the Truth (see John 14:6; 18:37).

Verses 6–7, "And he said to me, 'It is done! I am the Alpha and the Omega, the beginning and the end. To the thirsty I will give from the spring of the water of life without payment. The one who conquers will have this heritage, and I will be his God and he will be my son.'" The King on the throne declares, "It is done!" What is done but the successful judging of apostate Israel, the first enemy the Messiah has put under His feet since

His exaltation? At 16:17, Yahweh's voice rushed forth from the temple proclaiming, "It is done!" in response to the defeat of the covenant-breakers. Similarly, Jesus announced, "It is finished" (John 19:30), directly before He breathed His last upon the cross.[14] This indicates the same as in chapter 5 that the judgments of the scroll, along with the defeat of all God's enemies, were accomplished in Christ's death and are now being enacted in His resurrection glory. Although Gill understands these things in a consummate-only sense, he does make the connection back to Christ's humiliation and exaltation. He comments that "what was finished on the cross, by way of impetration, is now done as to application; all are saved with an everlasting salvation."[15]

The Lord continues, "I am the Alpha and the Omega . . . ." This is a repetition of what the Lord said back in 1:8 and 17. With this title He is saying that He came before all things and will continue after all things, and therefore He is in absolute control of all things between the beginning and end of time. This is an all-inclusive declaration of sovereignty. As the Teacher taught so long ago, "The lot is cast into the lap, but its every decision is from [Yahweh]" (Prov. 16:33).

Again, the Lord Jesus refers to past revelation in description of Himself. The words "to the thirsty I will give . . ." represent what was given in John 4:7–15 when He spoke with the Samaritan woman at Jacob's well. "Jesus said to her, 'Everyone who drinks of this [temporal] water will be thirsty again, but whoever drinks of the water that I will give him will never be thirsty again. The [spiritual] water that I will give him will become in him a spring of water welling up to eternal life'" (John 4:13–14). Jesus's point is that He Himself is the only source of true life, and trying to find this life in any other source will be disastrous. He seems to be playing off Jeremiah 2:13 at this point, which says that "my people have committed two evils: they have forsaken me, the fountain of living waters, and hewed out cisterns for themselves, broken cisterns that can hold no water." Clearly, the issue is about worship since Israel has become idolatrous and is about to come under judgment. This is why the conversation Jesus had with the Samaritan woman naturally turns to a discussion about worship (John 4:19–26). Indeed, drinking from the water of life is only possible by the powerful working of the Holy Spirit (see John 7:37–39)! Thus, here at verse 6, the

---

14   See Wilson, *When the Man Comes Around*, Kindle Location 2602.
15   Gill, *Exposition*, Kindle Location 361837.

Messiah promises the same thing as at John 4:13–14 and 7:37–39, indicating that the new creation is filled with true worship, rather than idolatry and covenant unfaithfulness, as the Spirit works in the hearts and lives of His saints.

"The one who conquers" refers to those who receive these benefits, having been made a part of the new creation themselves. This harkens back to the letters to the seven congregations, as well as the other exhortations unto perseverance.[16] The result is that they do, in fact, conquer with the Lamb due to the power of His word.[17]

Verse 8: "But as for the cowardly, the faithless, the detestable, as for murderers, the sexually immoral, sorcerers, idolaters, and all liars, their portion will be in the lake that burns with fire and sulfur, which is the second death." Given here is a sampling rather than an exhaustive list.[18] These are the ones who do not receive these benefits—namely, drinking from the "spring of the water of life without payment" and having Jesus's covenant promise, "I will be his God and he will be my son." Why not? They have insisted on continuing in their rebellion against Yahweh. These are the ones whose names were not "found written in the book of life" (20:15) at the final judgment. These are they who were never resurrected from the deadness of their sins through regeneration (cf. 20:6). Thus, the vision at this point again oscillates to the consummate state. Indeed, the end of the wicked is like unto the devil, the beast, the false prophet, and all those who served them, which is eternal conscious torment, experiencing nothing but the full weight of Almighty God's wrath poured out on them continually (see 14:9–11; 20:10). As Akin puts it, "An irreversible judgment and justice is all they can expect."[19] What a terribly horrific end awaits all the wicked! May the Lord scare the hell out of unbelievers, driving them to their knees in repentance!

THE NEW JERUSALEM

Verses 9–27 portray present spiritual realities for the body of Christ from God's perspective, which will eventually be completely realized in the consummation. As the Holy Spirit works in us, we are progressively becoming

---

16 See 2:7, 11, 17, 26–28; 3:5, 12, 21; 13:10; 14:12.
17 See 17:14; 19:14; 20:4, 9.
18 See Akin, *Exalting Jesus in Revelation*, Kindle Location 6836.
19 See Akin, *Exalting Jesus in Revelation*, Kindle Location 6836.

what we already are by grace.[20] What a glorious, yet truly peculiar, reality that is ours in Christ Jesus!

Verse 9: "Then came one of the seven angels who had the seven bowls full of the seven last plagues and spoke to me, saying, 'Come, I will show you the Bride, the wife of the Lamb.'" This heavenly messenger is one of the seven John saw in the vision of chapter 16. Now that the judgments on Babylon the Whore are over, he presents the faithful "wife of the Lamb" in visionary form. Where apostate Israel, the Jerusalem from below, is presented as Babylon the Whore, the church is presented as the "holy city, new Jerusalem, coming down out of heaven from God" (vv. 2, 10; cf. Gal. 4:25–26; Heb. 12:26–29).

Verses 10–11a: "And he carried me away in the Spirit to a great, high mountain, and showed me the holy city Jerusalem coming down out of heaven from God, having the glory of God." This "great, high mountain" is the true Mount Zion spoken of in Isaiah 2:2–3 and Micah 4:1–2, which "shall be established as the highest of the mountains, and shall be lifted up above the hills." In addition, Ezekiel 40 speaks of a temple-city on a very high mountain, which also symbolizes the bride of the Lord Jesus.[21] Hebrews 12:22 picks up on this imagery in describing new-covenant people of God coming to worship Him in contrast to those under the old covenant trying to do the same. The reason the city radiates with "the glory of God" is that the Messianic King is ruling through her and she has been covenantally united to Him in His death and resurrection. Thus, John is shown the bride of the Lamb.

Verses 11–21 shift into a detailed exposition of the wife's beauty, given in architectural language. They describe how the city radiates throughout with the glory of Christ.

Verse 11b: "its radiance like a most rare jewel, like a jasper, clear as crystal." This city is extraordinarily valuable and pure, for she is defined by the infinite worth and purity of her Husband.

Verses 12–13: "It had a great, high wall, with twelve gates, and at the gates twelve angels, and on the gates the names of the twelve tribes of the sons of Israel were inscribed—on the east three gates, on the north three gates, on the south three gates, and on the west three gates." It should be

---

20   See Rom. 6:1–14; Gal. 2:20–21; Eph. 4:21–32; Col. 3:1–17.
21   See Hendriksen, *More Than Conquerors*, Kindle Location 3511.

noted that this city is a perfect square since there are three gates in each of the four walls—this is confirmed in verse 16. Here is shown forth that this city is symbolically portraying the church, and thus ought not be taken as a literal city.

On each gate is inscribed the name of one of the twelve tribes of Israel. This indicates that the city is, at least in part, made up of Old Testament saints. While living under the old-covenant system, these Jews were, at the same time, in the covenant of grace by virtue of having the same faith as their father Abraham in the promise of the coming Messiah. They are here represented by their tribal heads.

Verse 14: "And the wall of the city had twelve foundations, and on them were the twelve names of the twelve apostles of the Lamb." No house or city, no matter how grand, has twelve foundations! Here also is an indication that this is symbolism. Each foundation has the name of one of the apostles. Thus, this city is comprised not only of believing Jews from the old-covenant era, but also of saints from every tribe, language, and nation under the new covenant. These regenerate ones also have the same faith as Abraham in the incarnate, crucified, risen, and reigning Messiah. Here they are represented by their spiritual heads—namely, the apostles. This is precisely what Paul taught at Ephesians 2:19–22.[22] In this way we are reminded of the twenty-four elders presented at 4:4,[23] which again serves to unite the Revelation as a whole.

Verses 15–16: "And the one who spoke with me had a measuring rod of gold to measure the city and its gates and walls. The city lies foursquare, its length the same as its width. And he measured the city with his rod, 12,000 stadia. Its length and width and height are equal." The most important statement here is the last: "Its length and width and height are equal." The city is a perfect cube, just as was the Most Holy Place in the temple (1 Kings 6:20).[24] The Reformation Study Bible agrees: "The city is a perfect cube, the same shape as the Most Holy Place in the tabernacle and the temple. The whole city is architecturally perfect, and has become the most intimate dwelling place of God."[25]

---

22   See Gill, *Exposition*, Kindle Location 361994.
23   See notes at 4:4.
24   See Beale and McDonough, "Revelation," 1152.
25   Reformation Study Bible notes, Revelation 21:16.

The length, width, and height are all twelve thousand stadion, which is also the number of the saints sealed on the forehead from each tribe of Israel (cf. 7:4–8). This is the sum of 12 x 1,000, both twelve and one thousand having consistently been used throughout the Apocalypse to symbolize completion. Twelve thousand stadion is the equivalent of approximately 2,221 km (1,380 miles). Taken literally, in Canadian terms, the city walls would stretch from Cape Spear, Newfoundland, west almost to Sault Ste. Marie, Ontario, north near to Naujaat, Nunavut, on the northern coast of Hudson's Bay, and straight up to a point midway between earth's exosphere (outer atmosphere) and the moon. In European terms, the walls would stretch from Galway, Ireland, east almost to Vilnius, Lithuania, south to a point in the Mediterranean halfway betwixt Chania, Crete, and Tobruk, Libya, and straight up to a point midway between earth's exosphere and the moon. Taking these measurements in a strictly literal way would lead one to a truly outlandish conclusion indeed! Instead, this apocalyptic imagery is meant to communicate the sheer immensity, perfection, and completeness of the bride of Christ in all her beauty to the praise of His glorious grace.

It is truly amazing that we have free, unabated access to the Father at all times through His beloved Son! Truly, as those clothed in the pure and spotless obedience of Jesus by faith, and so included in His most radiant bride, we can say that we permanently dwell in the glorious presence of the Most High! Is this not what every Jew longed for under the old covenant, with all its ritualistic processes and representations? Is this not the reason it was so incredibly shocking when the heavy curtain separating the Most Holy Place from the rest of the temple was rent in two upon the very moment of the Messiah's death? Oh, how oft we do forget this most incredible blessing bestowed upon us in the Beloved! May we never again let this truth slip from our minds, such that it radically transforms our prayers, both in terms of our willingness to come to our most gracious Father with all our petitions and thanks, and in terms of the freeness and warmth with which we do so. May Yahweh be furthered honored for the greatness that is His!

Verse 17: "He also measured its wall, 144 cubits by human measurement, which is also an angel's measurement." The wall's thickness is 144 cubits. Again, a multiple of twelve is presented here, much like at 7:4. Where 144,000 is given at 7:4 (12 x 12 x 1,000) to represent the totality of all believers in the covenant of grace, here the number is 144 (12 x 12) and functions in the same way. Taken most naturally, this is a part of the symbolic picture of the church's totality and completeness in Christ being given to the apostle John. It also serves to provide another line of connection across the Apocalypse, demonstrating its coherence.

As to "an angel's measurement," most commentators seem to avoid this point due to its mysterious nature. Gill suggests that, just as in 13:18 with regard to the number of the beast, "this calls for wisdom" in light of the fact that it is the angel who measures the wall (vv. 15, 17).[26] This means that John expected his readership to understand its meaning with godly wisdom. Some of the first usages of "angel" in the Revelation are in chapters 2 and 3 in reference to the elder-pastors of the seven Asia Minor churches—they are meant to lead the Messiah's sheep in faithfully following Him in accordance with His Word. The angel in this passage is one of the heavenly messengers who faithfully obeyed Jesus in delivering the last plagues on Jerusalem according to His Word. Thus, not only does logic demand a symbolic meaning to this vision, but John himself points his readers to interpret it redemptive-historically—that is, according to what the Lord has already revealed concerning His bride.

Verse 18: "The wall was built of jasper, while the city was pure gold, like clear glass." The imagery of verse 11 is again presented, this time with "pure gold, like clear glass" in addition to the jasper. The bride of Christ is extraordinarily beautiful and valuable, not on her own merits or qualities, but rather on the merits and qualities of the Lord Jesus, in whom she experiences the glorious presence of God truly and personally (cf. John 1:14).

Verses 19–20: "The foundations of the wall of the city were adorned with every kind of jewel. The first was jasper, the second sapphire, the third agate, the fourth emerald, the fifth onyx, the sixth carnelian, the seventh chrysolite, the eighth beryl, the ninth topaz, the tenth chrysoprase, the eleventh jacinth, the twelfth amethyst." This image is taken directly from the instructions for the high priest's breastplate found in Exodus 28:15–21.[27] "The list also corresponds roughly to the twelve precious stones of Aaron's breastplate (Ex. 28:15–21). The prerogatives once reserved for the high priest now belong to the entire city."[28] Where the twelve precious stones

---

26   See Gill, *Exposition*, Kindle Location 362022.
27   See Beale and McDonough, "Revelation," 1152.
28   Reformation Study Bible notes, Revelation 21:19.

were engraved, each with one of the names of the twelve tribes of Israel, here they correspond with the twelve apostles, one on each foundation. Not only has the new Jerusalem replaced Babylon (old Jerusalem) as Yahweh's wife, but now under the new covenant she has fulfilled the role of service the high priest once played under the old covenant. Where the high priest was permitted into God's glorious presence only once a year on behalf of the people, now each and every believer has permanent access to His presence in Jesus by His Spirit (see John 1:14; 16:7–15; Eph. 1:13–14). Indeed, where the high priest once had authority to make judgments in the congregation, now each and every believer has that privilege when bringing true testimony before the local church elders, together as two or three true witnesses (see Matt. 18:18–20). In addition, where the high priest knew Yahweh, yet had to teach his brothers within the nation of Israel to know and love Him, there is no need for brothers to do so under the new covenant because "they shall all know me, from the least of them to the greatest," each and every one (Heb. 8:11).

Verse 21: "And the twelve gates were twelve pearls, each of the gates made of a single pearl, and the street of the city was pure gold, like transparent glass." Taken literally, if each gate were three-fourths the height of the wall, they would have a height of approximately 1,666 km (1,035 miles). As Wilson points out, it would take one gigantic oyster to produce a pearl like that![29] Just as is the case in verses 11 and 18, this is a symbolic description of the incomparable beauty of Christ's wife, adorned in His own righteousness and here resulting in righteous deeds done out of loyal love for Him. Oh, what a picture of pure, unadulterated grace!

So often we miss the way in which the Lord Himself views us as His redeemed bride. As a result, we fail to strive to be who we already are by grace. This expresses itself in a plethora of ways. For example, we tend to orient our congregational worship toward what pleases people in the pews rather than toward what pleases the Lord as He defines in His Word. This is particularly evident in the way many assemblies handle the music aspect of public worship. Why? We want to be attractive to man when in fact, we are already infinitely beautiful to our King. On this principle, we are free from the fickle, subjective opinions of others to fully and joyfully worship the Lord God according to His immutable,

---

29 Wilson, *When the Man Comes Around*, Kindle Location 2632.

objective terms. What grace the Messiah has shown us that we may be who we actually are in Him!

Turning now to verses 22–27, many commentators agree that these verses are derived in large part from Isaiah 60:1–22.[30] Upon a close comparison of the two, it is evident that Yahweh's glory is in the midst of His people (Isa. 60:2; cf. Rev. 21:23). In addition, the nations come to the light (Isa. 60:3, 5, 11; cf. Rev. 21:24, 26). Also, it can be seen that the city's gates are never shut (Isa. 60:11; cf. Rev. 21:25). Furthermore, Yahweh Himself is the continuous light of the city (Isa. 60:19–20; Rev. 21:23, 25). Thus, Isaiah 60 is established as the Old Testament background to this final portion of the new Jerusalem vision shown unto John the apostle on the Isle of Patmos.

Verse 22: "And I saw no temple in the city, for its temple is the Lord God the Almighty and the Lamb." This is true since Jesus fulfilled the old-covenant temple by becoming, in His incarnation, the only meeting place between God and man. This is a well-established New Testament teaching. Matthew 1:22–23 declares, quoting from Isaiah 7:14, "'Behold, the virgin shall conceive and bear a son, and they shall call his name *Immanuel*' (which means, *God with us*)."[31] Matthew 28:20 also gives Jesus's proclamation: "And behold, *I am with you always*, to the end of the age." The apostle John explains, "And the Word became flesh and *dwelt* [lit. "tabernacled" or "templed"] *among us*, and we have seen his glory, glory as of the only Son from the Father, full of grace and truth" (John 1:14). He further records, "Jesus answered them, '*Destroy this temple*, and in three days I will raise it up.' . . . He was speaking about the *temple of his body*" (John 2:18–22). Not only this, but he also gives witness to his Master's words unto the Samaritan lady at John 4:21–23: "Woman, believe me, the hour is coming when neither on this mountain *nor in Jerusalem* will you worship the Father. . . . But the hour is coming, *and is now here*, when the true worshipers will worship the Father in spirit and truth." Thus, what John sees in his vision is nothing new. Yet at the same time, the language here seems to be a lot more directly intimate, as if the people of God are now *physically* in His presence. Once

---

30 See Reformation Study Bible notes, Revelation 21:23, 24, 25; Gill, *Exposition*, Kindle Locations 362130, 362152; Wilson, *When the Man Comes Around*, Kindle Locations 2691–2708; Hendriksen, *More Than Conquerors*, Kindle Location 3537; Beale and McDonough, "Revelation," 1153.

31 Emphasis mine throughout this paragraph.

again, the vision oscillates from pre-consummate realities to those of the consummate state, which will only come about on the Last Day.

Verse 23: "And the city has no need of sun or moon to shine on it, for the glory of God gives it light, and its lamp is the Lamb." This verse is a regiving of verse 11, yet now focusing entirely on how the bride is defined through and through by the glorious presence of Yahweh through being united to her Lord in every way. At this point in the vision, this includes union with Him via bodily resurrection, which took place on the Last Day, just as He was first resurrected from the dead.

Verse 24: "By its light will the nations walk, and the kings of the earth will bring their glory into it." John gives his apocalyptic version of Isaiah 2:1–5 and Micah 4:1–5 to show the end result thereof.[32] The meaning here is that Jesus will in fact have all the nations as His heritage and the ends of the earth His possession, within history! Indeed, the "kings of the earth" who once "set themselves . . . against [Yahweh] and against his Anointed" have now come to "kiss the Son" and "take refuge in him" (Ps. 2:1–12). This means that since Jesus has already been given "all authority in heaven and on earth," the Great Commission will actually be accomplished within human history. Truly, all the nations will be discipled, baptized in the name of the Triune God, and taught to obey all that He has commanded throughout the Scriptures (Matt. 28:18–20)! What John sees here is the sheer immensity of the innumerable multitude who comprise all the nations of the earth, along with their fully redeemed and transformed cultural activity that make those nations what they are, together now entering into eternity. Now that Messiah has successfully brought to pass the reconciliation of *all* things in heaven and on earth (cf. Eph. 1:10; Col. 1:19–20), He now brings it to its intended completion on the Last Day, forever to the praise of His glorious grace. Such is the power of Messiah Jesus and His gospel to conquer to the ends of the earth!

The twenty-first century has seen much change at an unprecedented rate. Indeed, the neo-Marxist worldview on which major leaders around the world are operating is self-contradictory, destructive, and power-hungry. This can be a point of great encouragement since, although it does seem to be God's providence to send our generation through very trying

---

32 See Beale and McDonough, "Revelation," 1153. Beale recognizes Isaiah 60's further development of 2:1–5.

times, in the long term such an unbelieving worldview will ultimately burn itself out for lack of ability to produce a meaningful, coherent, and flourishing society. Yet the Bible's view of the gradual-but-sure triumph of the gospel over all expressions of rebellion everywhere is indeed a worldview that gives rise to such societies and cultures! Our story is truly far better than any other!

Verse 25: "and its gates will never be shut by day—and there will be no night there." The glorious presence of the Lamb will never be removed from His bride since her union with Him was covenantally established in His death and resurrection (see Rom. 6:4–5; Heb. 9:15). This is confirmed elsewhere within the context of Messiah's high priestly work, performed specifically for the elect (see John 6:37–40; 10:25–30; Rom. 8:31–39). Hallelujah! The work of our Great High Priest accomplishes all for which it was intended, even into eternity!

Verse 26: "They will bring into it the glory and the honor of the nations." This statement only serves to further reinforce the point made in verse 24. Oh, the unquenchable power of the gospel!

Verse 27: "But nothing unclean will ever enter it, nor anyone who does what is detestable or false, but only those who are written in the Lamb's book of life." These are the only ones who are included in the bride, the new covenant community. These are they who have "washed their robes and made them white in the blood of the Lamb" (7:14). These are the elect who were given unto the Son that He would make them "holy and blameless before him" by His blood (Eph. 1:4), who "came to life [by the power of the Spirit] and reigned with Christ for a thousand years" (20:4). They are indeed the only ones who are included in the new covenant, who have God's law written on their hearts, who are truly His people, who all truly know Him "from the least of them to the greatest," whose iniquities have been removed, being cast into the depths of the sea, and completely forgiven (Heb. 8:8–12). These alone are the ones ushered into the very presence of Yahweh to enjoy Him for all eternity. The immeasurable treasures of God's gracious kindness toward entirely undeserving sinners are far too grand to contain within one paragraph, let alone an entire volume! They are vaster than the vastest ocean, deeper than the deepest sea, higher than the highest mountain, and more beautiful than the most beautiful coral reef! "For from him and through him and to him all are things. To [Yahweh] be glory forever. Amen" (Rom. 11:36)!

THE NEW CREATION

Chapter 22, verses 1–2: "Then the angel showed me the river of the water of life, bright as crystal, flowing from the throne of God and of the Lamb through the middle of the street of the city; also, on either side of the river, the tree of life with its twelve kinds of fruit, yielding its fruit each month. The leaves of the tree were for the healing of the nations." This is the same as the "spring of the water of life" mentioned at 21:6, now enlarged to be a river. Hendriksen in particular makes this connection plain.[33] This image is a recapitulation of Ezekiel 47:1–12 where Ezekiel is shown a vision of water coming forth from the temple, and at every thousand cubits farther downstream it is deeper until finally it is a raging river, ending in the Dead Sea.[34] According to that vision, the living water heals the unlivable waters of the Dead Sea and expands it to fill the whole land. These healed waters produce lush vegetation around it, and "their leaves [are] for healing" (Ezek. 47:12). Revelation 22:2 directly quotes from verse 12 of Ezekiel 47, applying it to all the nations whose lives have been changed by the Lamb's rule through the powerful working of His Holy Spirit. The Reformation Study Bible notes for Revelation 22:1–2 directly connect this passage with Ezekiel 47:1–12, John 4:10–15, and John 7:37–39.[35] Here is a moment in the vision that only fits within the inter-adventual period—that is, between Christ's first and second comings.

As the kingdom of God expands and takes dominance in the world through the gospel changing the hearts and lives of the elect, so does His new creation and true worship. Where the water flows out of the temple in Ezekiel's vision, here it flows directly from the throne of God and His Lamb since They are the city's temple (see Rev. 21:22). As per Ezekiel's temple vision, the expansion of new creation and true worship in the world is gradual, exactly like the Messiah's kingdom, which is like a stone that gradually expands into a mountain that fills the whole earth (Dan. 2:35, 44–45). This is precisely what Jesus taught about the nature of His rule in the earth in Matthew 13:31–33. Zechariah 14:8–9 explicitly brings

---

33   See Hendriksen, *More Than Conquerors*, Kindle Location 3577.
34   See Beale and McDonough, "Revelation," 1154.
35   See Reformation Study Bible notes, Revelation 22:1 and 22:2. See also Wilmshurst, *Revelation: The Final Word*, Kindle Location 3099; Akin, *Exalting Jesus in Revelation*, Kindle Location 6993; Hendriksen, *More Than Conquerors*, Kindle Location 3577; Gill, *Exposition*, Kindle Location 362254; Wilson, *When the Man Comes Around*, Kindle Locations 2718–2740.

together these two themes to express the same.³⁶ As the Messiah has victory in progressively putting His enemies under His feet—that is, transforming the kingdoms of this world into the kingdom of our God (see Rev. 11:15)—His new creation takes root in the hearts and lives of the nations. This, in turn, produces a culture of true worship in the public square, expressing itself in every sphere of life. As Neuhaus well puts it, "Culture is the root of politics, and religion is the root of culture."³⁷ This will come to fruition completely and sinlessly in the consummate, resurrected new heavens and new earth on the Last Day. Until that point, there remains the curse of sin and death in creation and many temptations toward false worship for the believer. These things will once and for all be no more in the glorified new creation! Yet, as Isaiah 65:17–25 demonstrates, these truths in no way negate the progress of new creation in the earth as King Jesus victoriously brings it about within history. Most assuredly, the resurrection of the second Adam is far more powerful than the sin of the first Adam!

In speaking of the Messiah's new creation, the "tree of life" of Genesis 2:9 and 3:22 is portrayed here as producing "twelve kinds of fruit," symbolizing the fruit of the Spirit produced in every member of the covenant of grace in every generation—this includes both those regenerate saints pre-cross (under the representation of the twelve tribes of Israel) and those post-cross (under the representation of the twelve apostles) (21:12–14; see also Gal. 5:16–26). The Reformation Study Bible comments on the tree of life: "This tree represents life in its highest potency—eternal life. It is available only to those who reenter the garden through the Second Adam (3:22; Rev. 22:14)."³⁸ This passage follows the pattern of 21:1–8 in presenting a "now but not yet" understanding of the new creation order as interwoven with the kingdom.

Verse 3: "No longer will there be anything accursed, but the throne of God and of the Lamb will be in it, and his servants will worship him." This statement serves to reinforce and underscore the meaning of 21:22 through 22:5. By the phrase "no longer will there by anything accursed," the apostle indicates the focus in this section is much more on the consummate new creation, while every now and again oscillating back to the

---

36 See Beale and McDonough, "Revelation," 1153.
37 Richard John Neuhaus, *The Naked Public Square: Religion and Democracy in America*, (Grand Rapids: Eerdmans, 1984).
38 Reformation Study Bible notes, Genesis 2:9.

pre-consummate, which is the exact opposite of how the visions in chapter 21 behaved up until verse 22—in 21:1–21, the focus was on the "now," while occasionally oscillating to the "not yet." In this way, there's a shift in the text toward the eternal state, all the while maintaining direct relevance to John's first-century readership.

Verse 4: "They will see his face, and his name will be on their foreheads." The words "they will see his face" harken back to 1 John 3:2–3, where the apostle John taught, "Beloved, we are God's children now, and what we will be has not yet appeared; but we know that when he appears we shall be like him, because we shall see him as he is. And everyone who thus hopes in him purifies himself as he is pure." This is the blessed hope for all God's saints in the eternal state! Continuing, the apostle reminds his readership that "his name will be on their foreheads." This harkens back to 7:3 and 14:1, indicating that only those who truly belong to Christ Jesus, having been sealed with the promised Holy Spirit, will persevere to the end of their lives in purifying themselves by faith and will truly be like unto Him in the resurrection. These are the ones who will enjoy face-to-face fellowship with their Lord and Savior for all eternity, who will worship Him sinlessly in greater and greater degrees forever!

Verse 5: "And night will be no more. They will need no light of lamp or sun, for the Lord God will be their light, and they will reign forever and ever." This verse serves to emphasize and underscore 21:23 and 25. The words "night will be no more" indicate that Yahweh is present in such a direct, intimate, and permanent way that no spiritual darkness could possibly coexist in that new creational order. This means the resurrection is most certainly now in view. Furthermore, John says "they will reign *forever and ever*," which harkens back to Old Testament promises of the Messiah's rule lasting without end (e.g., 2 Sam. 7:16; Isa. 9:7). Thus, the elect's reign with their King extends beyond temporal history and into eternity. How truly incredible is this story of the saints conquering unto comprehensive, eternal gospel victory with their beloved King!

John's Epilogue (22:6–21)

Verses 6–21 form the conclusion to John's letter to the seven Asia Minor congregations. These are his closing remarks.

Chapter 22, verse 6: "And he said to me, 'These words are trustworthy and true. And the Lord, the God of the spirits of the prophets, has sent his angel to show his servants what must soon take place.'" The heavenly messenger once again confirms to the apostle what the Lamb has just told him in 21:5, that "these words are trustworthy and true." The repetition emphasizes both the truthfulness and the importance of what has been unveiled in these visions. It is "the God of the spirits of the prophets" who has revealed these prophecies, and they are sure to come to pass according to His eternal schedule. He then repeats the opening words of the Apocalypse, emphasizing and underscoring the veritable nearness of the events therein coming to fulfillment.

Verse 7: "And behold, I am coming soon. Blessed is the one who keeps the words of the prophecy of this book." The angel is suddenly interrupted by the voice of the Messiah announcing the sheer imminence of His coming, making the "words of the prophecy of this book" a historical reality. He reminds John's readers of the promise that they will be blessed if they "keep what is written in it, for the time is near" (1:3). His first-century audience must take these words seriously and live by them because the time is close at hand for them to come to pass! The implication is that if they fail to do so, the curses aimed at apostate Israel will also fall on them.

Verse 8a: "I, John, am the one who heard and saw these things." There can be no doubt as to the authorship of this letter since John the apostle here tells us plainly.

Verses 8b–9: "And when I heard and saw them, I fell down to worship at the feet of the angel who showed them to me, but he said to me, 'You must not do that! I am a fellow servant with you and your brothers the prophets, and with those who keep the words of this book. Worship God.'" This is the second time John is completely overtaken by the visions he sees and responds by falling in worship at the angel's feet—the first time was in response to being shown the marriage supper of the Lamb (19:10). This heavenly messenger responds to the apostle's attempted worship with the same rebuke, nearly verbatim. In both cases, the angels place themselves on the creaturely level together with John and the rest of the saints, urging him to instead worship the Creator God, whose name is forever blessed.[1] All praise and glory and honor be to *His* name alone!

Verse 10: "And he said to me, 'Do not seal up the words of the prophecy of this book, for the time is near.'" This is the exact opposite instruction given to Daniel by the angel at the close of his visions, together with the exact opposite timeframe. "But you, Daniel, shut up the words and seal the book, until the time of the end. Many shall run to and fro, and knowledge shall increase" (Dan. 12:4).[2] Daniel was meant to "shut up the words and seal the book," but here John must "*not* seal up the words of the prophecy of this book." The former prophet was to expect a lengthy period of time until the end when the book may be unsealed, but the current must "not seal up the words" given him since "the time is near."[3] Once again, the text of the Apocalypse itself emphasizes the imminency of the events contained therein in relation to John's first-century readership—namely, the seven congregations located in Asia Minor. Any futurist notion of this imminency referring to our Lord's second advent at the end of human history, which now has spanned more than two millennia, is immediately rendered inviable. This is actually good news since it means that Yahweh has indeed kept His promise to those to whom it was originally given. Consequently, we can trust Him implicitly with all the other promises He has made concerning the advancement of His Messiah's kingdom-rule in the earth! There is truly no God like Yahweh!

---

1 See Ps. 72:19; 89:52; 113:2; Dan. 2:20; Rom. 1:25; 9:5; 2 Cor. 11:31.
2 See Beale and McDonough, "Revelation," 1156.
3 See Reformation Study Bible notes, Revelation 22:10.

Verse 11: "Let the evildoer still do evil, and the filthy still be filthy, and the righteous still do right, and the holy still be holy." The effect of hearing the message of this book will either be to further harden those with hard hearts or to encourage those who already have been given new hearts.[4] What power is contained here within God's holy, immutable words!

Verses 12–13: "Behold, I am coming soon, bringing my recompense with me, to repay each one for what he has done. I am the Alpha and the Omega, the first and the last, the beginning and the end." Jesus reminds John's readers that He is right at the door ready to bring His judgments upon Israel's covenant-breakers. As "the Alpha and the Omega," no one is able to escape His judgments and legitimately argue with their justness. The message is that the wicked ought to repent before it's too late. Wilson notes, "Telling the filthy and the unjust that there is no time might stir them up to act while there is still (almost) time."[5] How utterly patient and gracious is the Lord to grant them this final opportunity!

The apostle Peter also links God's ongoing patience with sinners and their need to come to repentance (see 2 Peter 3:8–9). Although differing with Revelation 22 on the point of subject (those elected unto repentance versus those committed to the rejection of the Messiah), the emphasis on Yahweh's patience is identical. Indeed, that Yahweh would be long-suffering toward any sinner for any length of time is truly incredible! His great delight is in the genuine repentance wrought in us by His Spirit, for truly He takes "no pleasure in the death of the wicked" (Ezek. 33:11). This ought to motivate us not only to strive for piety on the personal level, but also in the family, in the congregation, and throughout society. The need for ongoing heartfelt repentance of sin and glad submission to the rule of Christ, clinging by faith exclusively to His active and passive obedience, is the only kind of piety that will transform society and culture from the bottom up and from the top down. This is the vision that defined the entire mindset of the seventeenth-century Puritans, both those in England and those who came to the shores of what is now called America. May this holy, unwavering vision for all of life under the lordship of Christ be ours as well, until the earth and heavens are filled with Yahweh's glory, according to His most sure promise (see Isa. 11:9; Hab. 2:14)!

---

4 See Ezek. 3:16–21, 27; Matt. 13:10–17; 2 Cor. 2:14–17. See also Henry, *Commentary*, Revelation 22:16–19; Reformation Study Bible notes, Revelation 22:11.

5 Wilson, *When the Man Comes Around*, Kindle Location 2792.

Verse 14: "Blessed are those who wash their robes, so that they may have the right to the tree of life and that they may enter the city by the gates." John reminds his readers of what was revealed in 7:14, that those who have come to the Messiah by faith in His perfect obedience, even unto death on their behalf, are blessed with eternal life.[6] He connects this image to entering the city gates (21:27) and eating from the tree of life (22:2). The only ones who are allowed to become a part of the bride are those who have been justified by the Lamb's blood. Likewise, the only ones enjoying true life in the covenant of grace, and thus bearing fruit in keeping with repentance, are those cleansed from their sins by the blood of the Lamb. There is no room for boasting of any kind on the part of those made right and just in God's sight—only humble gratitude.

Verse 15: "Outside are the dogs and sorcerers and the sexually immoral and murderers and idolaters, and everyone who loves and practices falsehood." Here is given a repetition of 21:8 and 27, put in juxtaposition to what was just explained in verse 14 concerning the saints. This is meant to urge the wicked to repent, while they still have time, by showing them the life they're missing, as well as the consequences of their continued rebellion against Yahweh and His Anointed King (cf. Ps. 2). Truly, inside the city is eternal blessing and safety, but outside is only the curse of death and the wrath of the Lamb (cf. 1 Peter 3:18–22).

Verse 16: "I, Jesus, have sent my angel to testify to you about these things for the churches. I am the root and the descendant of David, the bright morning star." Here Jesus speaks directly to John and tells him that He has sent His heavenly messenger for the purpose of revealing the things contained in the Apocalypse for the benefit of the seven churches in Asia. The Lord previously instructed John, at 1:11, to write specifically to these seven congregations whom he personally knows. These visions are given for *their* instruction first and foremost, concerning events they personally were facing, and would soon face, in the first century. Only in light of this may we then begin making application to ourselves in our own time, or to others in times past.

The Lord refers back to the title given Him at 5:5, "the Root of David." He is the Messianic King who sits on David's throne ruling forever, who establishes justice in the earth, even to its farthest reaches! As Isaiah 42:1–4 indicates, His means of accomplishing this is not through top-down brute

---

6   See notes at 7:14.

force, as is the way of ungodly governmental systems. Rather, "a bruised reed he will not break, and a faintly burning wick he will not quench," as He, by the power of His Holy Spirit, turns the hearts of sinners to love both Him and His righteous statutes (cf. Ezek. 36:25–27). The kingdom-rule of King Jesus advances to the ends of the earth by a grassroots reformation, which necessarily permeates all spheres of society, rather than a bloody revolution, forcing the desired societal changes to take place through the strong arm of the government. Indeed, this is what our Master meant when He answered Pilate during His trial, "My kingdom is not of this world. If my kingdom were of this world, my servants would have been fighting, that I might not be delivered over to the Jews. But my kingdom is not from the world" (John 18:36). Such is the kingdom of God!

Historically, Anabaptists have understood John 18:36 to mean that Messiah's rule is entirely heavenly and has nothing to do with things earthly, unlike the kingdom to which Pilate belonged. Therefore, there exists a thick, impenetrable wall between the private and the public, the sacred and the secular, the church and the state, and Jesus's rule has everything to do with the former and nothing to do with the latter. Indeed, according to their view, the latter is evil and must be avoided by the faithful Christian.[7] Lutherans took a less extreme perspective since they acknowledged God's governance over all things, yet still headed off in much the same direction since they derived their view in large part from medieval Roman Catholicism.[8] The modern two-kingdoms movement amongst evangelicals, most notably represented by David VanDrunen and Michael Horton of Westminster Seminary California, follows closely the historic Lutheran understanding of the doctrine while trying to make it work within a Reformed covenantal framework, especially as it concerns the Noahic covenant.[9] While historically minded Anabaptists and Lutherans are thinking in

---

7   The outworkings of this view can clearly be seen in both the Swiss Schleitheim Confession of Faith (1527) and the Dutch Dordrecht Confession of Faith (Mennonite, 1632), Ch. V, XIII-XV.

8   The outworkings of this perspective are represented in "The Augsburg Confession," in the Book of Concord, Article XVI. Of Civil Affairs.

9   See David VanDrunen, *Natural Law and the Two Kingdoms: A Study in the Development of Reformed Social Thought* (Grand Rapids: Eerdmans, 2010), and *Living in God's Two Kingdoms: A Biblical Vision for Christianity and Culture* (Wheaton: Crossway, 2010). See also "The Noahic Covenant," Reformed Forum, YouTube Video, February 18, 2020, https://www.youtube.com/watch?v=lzG7EtwbOPw, and "2 Kingdom and Kuyper Discussion," Westminster Seminary California, YouTube Video, March 2, 2016, https://www.youtube.com/watch?v=agwVVqiAr9A.

"kingdom of God" and "kingdom of this world" categories—which is not to say they see these realms as identical with the "kingdom of light" and the "domain of darkness" mentioned in Colossians 1:13–14—the modern evangelical proponents of "Two Kingdom Theology" have their own nuanced classifications. VanDrunen, the leading proponent, posits that God has two ways of ruling in His world: via the spiritual, redemptive kingdom (the church) on the one hand, and via the physical, creational/common kingdom (the public square) on the other. Joseph Boot points out that in the same way that medieval Papists transformed Greek philosophical categories of "form" and "matter" into "grace" and "nature," VanDrunen has ended up transforming "grace" and "nature" into "redemption" and "creation."[10] According to VanDrunen, these two kingdoms exist on parallel tracks that can never meet, since the redemptive realm is eternal, while the creational realm is temporal. Horton agrees: "The earthly city will never be transformed into the city of God this side of Christ's return in glory."[11] Thus, while the Christian may jump back and forth between the two throughout his life, and so operate on the basis of two differing ethics, the application is that the faithful follower of Christ must invest in the spiritual things of the redemptive kingdom since they are eternal, while letting go of the physical things of the creational kingdom since they are fleeting. This way of thinking, though cloaked in biblical language, fundamentally has more in common with the dualistic cosmology of Plato and the Gnostics than it does with biblical Christianity! While many evangelicals have imbibed this view, it is contrary to the historic Reformed and evangelical understanding of the way the kingdom of God functions in the world, as revealed in Holy Writ. Calvin, Kuyper, Knox, and the Puritans all advocated a much more holistic perspective wherein both the internal kingdom (man's conscience) and the external kingdom (all of the temporal outworkings of society, including family, church, and state) are directly under the jurisdiction of Jesus's Messiahship, being governed solely according to His Law-Word.[12] Since both of these realms start out under the dominion of sin and darkness, and persons belonging

---

10   Joe Boot, "Two Kingdoms," Ezra Institute for Contemporary Christianity, YouTube Video, July 7, 2017, https://www.youtube.com/watch?v=xokCh1jbNxI.

11   Michael Horton, "A Tale of Two Kingdoms," Ligonier, September 1, 2008, https://www.ligonier.org/learn/articles/tale-two-kingdoms.

12   See Douglas Wilson, "The Two Kingdoms That Weren't," Ezra Institute for Contemporary Christianity, YouTube Video, May 22, 2020, https://www.youtube.com/watch?v=BLKguSkgDxI.

thereto can be transferred to the dominion of truth and light by the transforming work of the Holy Spirit, it follows that both of these realms can be transferred to the same dominion by the same grace. Scripture not only teaches that it *can* happen, but it emphatically insists that it *does*, since these are the necessary effects of the Messiah's rule in history. This historically Reformed and Puritan view is throughout this commentary being represented and advocated since it is the perspective that most closely reflects Scriptural teaching on the Messiah's rule as a whole.

Why does this matter? First of all, it matters because, according to Jesus Himself, the subject of His kingdom-rule is a gospel issue. Matthew records that in fulfillment of Isaiah 9, upon the conclusion of His temptations in the wilderness, Jesus immediately "began to preach, saying, 'Repent, for the kingdom of heaven is at hand'" (Matt. 4:17). A few verses later, Matthew elaborates: "And he went throughout all Galilee, teaching in their synagogues and proclaiming the gospel *of the kingdom* and healing every disease and every affliction among the people" (Matt. 4:23, author's emphasis). Later in chapter 9, at the conclusion of a two-chapter demonstration of Jesus's Messianic authority over all spheres of life, Matthew states, "And Jesus went throughout all the cities and villages, teaching in their synagogues and proclaiming the gospel *of the kingdom* and healing every disease and every affliction" (Matt. 9:35, author's emphasis). Most evangelicals in the West today have, to one degree or another, a truncated view of the good news of Jesus—that is, a message far more concerned with a "personal salvation from sin" over against the message that the exalted Christ rules from His Father's right hand over all things everywhere, whereby He is in the process of reconciling all corners of creation to Himself. Friends, this truncated message is *not* the good news which our Lord Himself preached! While getting personal salvation by grace alone through faith alone in Christ alone right is crucial and definitional to the Christian gospel, our view of the kingdom of God is equally vital. We are not allowed to "slice and dice" the gospel message, as it were.

Secondly, getting the kingdom-rule of Christ right matters because it directly impacts how we approach very practical issues. Because many evangelicals have imbibed a VanDrunian view of the kingdom, they interpret Romans 13 to mean that unless the government directly forbids the preaching of Christ crucified and resurrected or some aspect of a "personal salvation from sin" gospel message, Christians must unquestioningly submit to and obey the state. Thus, they surmise that God must be silent on issues of healthcare and economics and freedom of speech and movement, and that worldview and faith presuppositions play little to no part in the decision-making on the part of those in power—these are issues to be resolved by "common sense" reasoning. Yet the details of God's law point us in the exact opposite direction. For example, Leviticus 19:11 requires, "You shall not steal; you shall not deal falsely; you shall not lie to one another." The Creator and Sustainer of all things will hold each and every one to this most holy standard when He judges them on the Last Day, including governing authorities.

Furthermore, there is a direct connection between how we as Christians live in the public square and the acceptability of our congregational worship in the eyes of Yahweh. In Isaiah 1:12–17, Yahweh makes it clear to His people that if He is to accept their worship and prayers once more, they must "cease to do evil, learn to do good; seek justice, correct oppression; bring justice to the fatherless, plead the widow's cause." In Isaiah's day, it was due to the lack of God's people correcting oppression in the land and pleading the widow's cause that their prayers and worship were being ignored. Also, it was this oppression from Israel's governmental leaders that would soon bring them into God's judgment in the form of the Babylonian captivity. In the same way, elder-pastors today must teach God's people, and exemplify for them, that absolutely every arena in society is sacred and rightfully belongs to King Jesus, including the civil sphere, and thus must progressively come under His lordship. As Greg Bahnsen once said, "There is no neutrality!"[13] In fact, Christians have a God-given obligation to respectfully, humbly, and courageously oppose injustice, as defined by God's law, when they see it. Why? We have been created in God's image to take dominion over His good creation, which necessarily involves caring about issues of righteousness and justice in the public square (cf. Gen. 9:5–6). Therefore, as Christ's loyal ambassadors in the world, defying tyranny—that is, enforced lawlessness—in a godly way is, in fact, obedience to Christ and love for neighbor (see Acts 5:29)! And if we refuse to assert the crown rights of King Jesus—not as violent revolutionaries, but rather as prophetic emissaries—our worship in the congregation will be in serious danger of being rejected by the one true and living God! May we strive for unwavering loyalty to Jesus as the one true King over all kings and Lord

---

13 Bahnsen, Greg L., *By This Standard: The Authority of God's Law Today*, Powder Springs, GA: American Vision, 2020, Kindle Location 34.

over all lords. May His kingdom come and His will be done in Canada, and in every other nation, as it is in heaven, just as He's promised!

At this juncture in verse 16, Jesus also refers back to 2:28 where He calls Himself the "morning star." He is the Light who has invaded the darkness in the world and is in the process of driving it all out! Through this gospel victory, true peace and justice are being established among the nations. This results in all the earth rejoicing forever! Truly, "the zeal of the LORD of hosts will do this" (Isa. 9:1–7)!

Verse 17: "The Spirit and the Bride say, 'Come.' And let the one who hears say, 'Come.' And let the one who is thirsty come; let the one who desires take the water of life without price." The call to turn to Jesus and cling to Him alone for true life is now explicit. Once again, the image of living water is repeated to communicate this (see 21:6 and 22:1–2). Jesus is the water of life that eternally satisfies the soul!

Verses 18–19: "I warn everyone who hears the words of the prophecy of this book: if anyone adds to them, God will add to him the plagues described in this book, and if anyone takes away from the words of the book of this prophecy, God will take away his share in the tree of life and in the holy city, which are described in this book." The apostle picks up on Moses's warning to the second generation of Israel, about to enter the Promised Land, and applies it to the Apocalypse.[14] At several points throughout his final sermon, Moses brought this to bear. "You shall not add to the word that I command you, nor take from it, that you may keep the commandments of [Yahweh] your God that I command you" (Deut. 4:2). As well, he warns, "Everything that I command you, you shall be careful to do. You shall not add to it or take from it" (Deut. 12:32).[15] Furthermore, Deuteronomy 27–28 explains the physical curses that Yahweh would bring if Israel was unfaithful to the covenant, which included violating this command to neither add nor subtract from it. Agur would later take this principle and apply it in Proverbs 30:6 to all of God's inscripturated will.

Where Yahweh promised temporal curses in the land for national Israel, here He promises both temporal and eternal curses for violating this warning. The temporal curse will be given to anyone who adds to the words of the Apocalypse in any way; the judgments described therein will fall on

---

14   See Reformation Study Bible notes, Revelation 22:18–19.
15   See Beale and McDonough, "Revelation," 1158.

them too! The eternal curse will be given to anyone who subtracts from the Apocalypse in any way—they will be banished from the blessings of being a part of the Messiah's bride and bearing spiritual fruit in keeping with repentance. This threat is akin to those given at Hebrews 6:1–8 and Hebrews 10:26–31. All of these are real threats given to real congregations of believers following Jesus. These warnings are meant to scare believers away from covenant unfaithfulness to the Lord Jesus and toward being very careful in being faithful to Him. In the context of the Revelation, this means fleeing the temptation to become like apostate Israel in rejecting their Messianic King in any way! In the case of apostasy, these would be falling away from their confession of belonging to the new covenant, *not* from actually being a true member of the new covenant, which was established through Christ's death with all the elect. John explains in his first epistle, "They went out from us, but they were not of us; for if they had been of us, they would have continued with us. But they went out, that it might become plain that they all are not of us" (1 John 2:19). Wilson puts it like this: "This does not mean that someone can be removed from God's roster of the elect. But it does mean removal from the covenanted and visible church, and all the blessings that pertain to it."[16] AWilson's point is true and compliments what has just been explained above.

Verse 20: "He who testifies to these things says, 'Surely I am coming soon.' Amen. Come, Lord Jesus!" John is truly excited for the Lord Jesus to fulfill His promise in coming soon to bring the judgments of the Revelation to bear on Jerusalem! Why? Because His rule over all the nations necessarily involves establishing justice and righteousness in the earth by making His enemies a footstool for His feet. Again, why? Because Jesus promises that He will come *very soon* to fulfill these things! Revelation 1:7 clearly puts this expectation forward as the main message of the Apocalypse: "Behold, he is coming with the clouds, and every eye will see him, even those who pierced him, and all tribes of the land will wail on account of him. Even so. Amen."[17] Thus, the letter as a whole comes full circle.

Verse 21: "The grace of the Lord Jesus be with all. Amen." The apostle ends his letter to the seven churches of Asia by blessing them and expressing his prayer for them all that Christ would continue to pour out His unmerited favor on each of them. Indeed, the only proper response to grace

---

16   Wilson, *When the Man Comes Around*, Kindle Location 2860.
17   See notes at 1:7.

is heartfelt thankfulness (see Col. 3:15–17). May this likewise be the reflex of our hearts, those of us who have been gifted grace upon grace through the merits of our most precious Savior! Amen!

Outline of the Entire Book

1. John's Prologue (1:1–20)
    a. Introduction (1:1–3)
    b. Salutation (1:4–8)
    c. The first vision (1:9–20)
        i. The command to write (1:9–11)
        ii. The vision of the Son of Man (1:12–20)
2. The Letters to the Congregations (2:1–3:22)
    a. To the congregation at Ephesus (2:1–7)
    b. To the congregation at Smyrna (2:8–11)
    c. To the congregation at Pergamum (2:12–17)
    d. To the congregation at Thyatira (2:18–29)
    e. To the congregation at Sardis (3:1–6)
    f. To the congregation at Philadelphia (3:7–13)
    g. To the congregation at Laodicea (3:14–22)
3. The Second Vision (4:1–5:14)
    a. The Lord enthroned on high (4:1–11)
    b. The unopened scroll (5:1–4)
    c. The Lion who is the Lamb (5:5–14)
4. The Third Vision (6:1–8:5)
    a. The first seal (6:1–2)
    b. The second seal (6:3–4)
    c. The third seal (6:5–6)
    d. The fourth seal (6:7–8)
    e. The fifth seal (6:9–11)
    f. The sixth seal (6:12–17)
    g. An interlude (7:1–17)
        i. The 144,000 of Israel (7:1–8)
        ii. The innumerable multitude (7:9–17)
    h. The seventh seal (8:1–5)

5. **The Fourth Vision (8:6–11:19)**
   a. The first trumpet (8:6–7)
   b. The second trumpet (8:8–9)
   c. The third trumpet (8:10–11)
   d. The fourth trumpet (8:12)
   e. The eagle (8:13)
   f. The fifth trumpet (9:1–12)
   g. The sixth trumpet (9:13–21)
   h. An interlude (10:1–11:14)
      i. The little scroll (10:1–11)
      ii. The two witnesses (11:1–14)
   i. The seventh trumpet (11:15–19)

6. **The Fifth Vision (12:1–14:20)**
   a. The woman and the child (12:1–6)
   b. The dragon cast down (12:7–17)
   c. The beast out of the sea (13:1–10)
   d. The beast out of the land (13:11–18)
   e. The Lamb on Mount Zion (14:1–5)
   f. Babylon's fall predicted (14:6–20)
      i. Three angels proclaim judgment (14:6–13)
      ii. The reaping the righteous (14:14–16)
      iii. The reaping of the wicked (14:17–20)

7. **The Sixth Vision (15:1–16:21)**
   a. A prelude (15:1–8)
   b. The first bowl (16:1–2)
   c. The second bowl (16:3)
   d. The third bowl (16:4–7)
   e. The fourth bowl (16:8–9)
   f. The fifth bowl (16:10–11)
   g. The sixth bowl (16:12–16)
   h. The seventh bowl (16:17–21)

8. The Seventh Vision (17:1–19:10)
    a. Babylon rides the beast (17:1–18)
        i. The whore seated on the beast (17:1–6)
        ii. The identity of the beast (17:7–14)
        iii. Vengeance on the whore announced (17:15–18)
    b. The judgment of Babylon (18:1–19:5)
        i. The desolation of the city (18:1–3)
        ii. A call to leave the city (18:4–8)
        iii. The kings mourn (18:9–10)
        iv. The merchants mourn (18:11–17)
        v. The seafarers mourn (18:17–20)
        vi. The whore is overthrown (18:21–24)
        vii. All heaven rejoices (19:1–5)
    c. The marriage supper of the Lamb (19:6–10)

9. The Eighth Vision (19:11–21)
    a. The King's conquest (19:11–17a)
    b. The overthrow of the beast and the false prophet (19:17b–21)

10. The Ninth Vision (20:1–15)
    a. Christ reigns triumphant (20:1–10)
        i. The binding of Satan (20:1–3)
        ii. The rule of Christ with His saints (20:4–6)
        iii. The overthrow of Satan (20:7–10)
    b. Christ judges the world (20:11–15)

11. The Tenth Vision (21:1–22:5)
    a. The new heavens and new earth (21:1–8)
    b. The new Jerusalem (21:9–27)
    c. The new creation (22:1–5)

12. John's Epilogue (22:6–21)

Founders Ministries exists for the recovery of the gospel and the reformation of churches.

We have been providing resources for churches since 1982 through conferences, books, The Sword & The Trowel Podcast, video documentaries, online articles found at www.founders.org, the quarterly Founders Journal, Bible studies, International church search, and the seminary level training program, the Institute of Public Theology. Founders believes that the biblical faith is inherently doctrinal, and we are therefore confessional in our convictions.

You can learn more about Founders Ministries and how to partner with us at www.founders.org.

 FoundersMin

 FoundersMin

 FoundersMinistries

 FoundersMinistries

Other Titles from Founders Press

For the Vindication of the Truth: Baptist Symbolics Volume 1
By James Renihan

> I have longed to see a critical exposition of the First London Confession of Faith in print, one that provides a detailed examination of the provenance, structure, theology, editions, and impact of this notable text. This is that!
> — Michael A. G. Haykin, Chair & Professor,
> The Southern Baptist Theological Seminary

BY WHAT STANDARD? God's World . . . God's Rules.
Edited by Jared Longshore

> I'm grateful for the courage of these men and the clarity of their voices. This is a vitally important volume, sounding all the right notes of passion, warning, instruction, and hope.
> —Phil Johnson, Executive Director,
> Grace To You

Truth & Grace Memory Books
Edited by Thomas K. Ascol

> Memorizing a good, age-appropriate catechism is as valuable for learning the Bible as memorizing multiplication tables is for learning mathematics.
> —Dr. Don Whitney, Professor,
> The Southern Baptist Theological Seminary

Dear Timothy: Letters on Pastoral Ministry
Edited by Thomas K. Ascol

> Get this book. So many experienced pastors have written in this book; it is a gold mine of wisdom for young pastors in how to preach and carry out their ministerial life.
> —Joel Beeke, President,
> Puritan Reformed Theological Seminary

The Mystery of Christ, His Covenant & His Kingdom
By Samuel Renihan

This book serves for an excellent and rich primer on covenant theology and demonstrates how it leads from the Covenant of Redemption to the final claiming and purifying of the people given by the Father to the Son.

—Tom Nettles, Retired Professor of Historical Theology,
The Southern Baptist Theological Seminary

Strong and Courageous: Following Jesus Amid the Rise of America's New Religion
By Tom Ascol and Jared Longshore

We have had quite enough of "Be Nice and Inoffensive." We are overflowing with "Be Tolerant and Sensitive." It is high time that we were admonished to "Be Strong and Courageous."

—Jim Scott Orrick, Author,
Pastor of Bullitt Lick Baptist Church

ADDITIONAL TITLES

Heirs of the Reformation: A Study in Baptist Origins
By James McGoldrick

Still Confessing: An Exposition of the Baptist Faith & Message 2000
By Daniel Scheiderer

By His Grace and For His Glory
By Tom Nettles

Getting the Garden Right
By Richard C. Barcellos

The Law and the Gospel
By Ernie Reisinger

Traditional Theology & the SBC
By Tom Ascol

Teaching Truth, Training Hearts
By Tom Nettles

*Praise Is His Gracious Choice:
Corporate Worship Expressing Biblical Truth*
By Dr. Tom Nettles

Just Thinking: about the state
By Darrell Harrison and Virgil Walker

The Transcultural Gospel
By E.D. Burns

Ancient Gospel, Brave New World
By E.D. Burns

Galatians: He Did It All
By Baruch Maoz

Missions by the Book: How Theology and Missions Walk Together
By Chad Vegas and Alex Kocman

Order these titles and more at press.founders.org

Printed in the USA
CPSIA information can be obtained
at www.ICGtesting.com
JSHW012047301123
52563JS00005B/12